THE
FIRST-TIME
INVESTOR

**The complete guide to buying,
owning and selling shares**

DEBBIE HARRISON

FINANCIAL TIMES

PRENTICE HALL

PEARSON EDUCATION LIMITED

Head Office:
Edinburgh Gate
Harlow CM20 2JE
Tel: +44 (0)1279 623623
Fax: +44 (0)1279 431059

London Office:
128 Long Acre, London WC2E 9AN
Tel: +44 (0)171 447 2000
Fax: +44 (0)171 240 5771

First published in Great Britain 1998

ISBN 0 273 63301 5

British Library Cataloguing in Publication Data
A CIP catalogue record for this book can be obtained from the British Library.

10 9 8 7 6 5 4 3

Typeset by Northern Phototypesetting Co Ltd, Bolton
Printed and bound in Great Britain by Redwood Books, Trowbridge, Wiltshire

The Publishers' policy is to use paper manufactured from sustainable forests.

About the Author

Debbie Harrison is an award winning financial author and journalist who specialises in institutional and retail investment issues. She writes regularly for the *Financial Times* and is the author of *Global Pension Strategies*, published by FT Finance, *Personal Financial Planner*, published by Financial Times Pitman Publishing and *Pension Power* published by John Wiley.

Contents

Foreword

The Millennium is upon us and not far after the 'baby boom' generation starts to retire. That generation, for whom countless flat-roofed seconadary schools were built in the late fifties and early sixties, the generation who were the authors of the teenage revolution, the first wearer of the mini skirt, fans of the Rolling Stones and the Beatles, will now provide the retirement bulge. And in so doing they bring with them a demographic change of substantial proportion. Next, the average life expectation of a baby girl born today is over 80 years and, if that is the average, think what the maximum is likely to be. So we are living longer, with an increasing proportion of our active lives being after retirement and, in addition, the proportion of the population who are of retirement age is steadily increasing whilst those of working age to support them is reducing.

Public policy is also changing, aiming to concentrate social security provision towards an essential safety net whilst encouraging individuals of all incomes to save for their own and their families' future. Saving is essential. Saving means that we have the ability to live more comfortably, buy those things which we would like to buy and not be afraid of the future.

So what has all this got to do with a first time investor?

Well, saving is too often synonymous in peoples' minds with an interest earning account at either a bank or a building society. Yet saving is much more than just that. As this book so eloquently describes, money saved by investment in stocks and shares and in equities generally (and this book describes what these terms mean) has given a much better return than cash held in the traditional account. This all shows us not just the importance of saving, but also the importance of investing some money at least in shares.

Many people are already part way there as a result of the privatisations of the 1980s and the demutualisations of the 1990s. Best estimates say that some 16 million people now hold shares and so that is one foot on the ladder. But where next? It is not as simple to get involved with shares as it is to buy a lottery ticket, though the returns are generally much better. It can be hard to know where to start and difficult to understand the strange terms that financial people use. So as a first step, read this book. It is a truly definitive and an understandable guide. As a second step, take good independent financial advice. Such advice is essential. For how to find it, what to ask for and where the snags lie again, *The First-Time Investor* is an excellent readable and comprehensible source.

Angela Knight
Chief Executive, Association of Private Client Investment Managers
and Stockbrokers

Preface

Today we are all investors. Some have a wide range of investments, including a portfolio of direct equities. Others invest in the stockmarkets through collective funds designed to provide a pension at retirement, repay the mortgage, pay for school fees, or simply to save for long-term capital projects.

Given the plight of the Welfare State, there is little doubt that the Government will encourage us to put aside even more to cover our financial needs. It may even force us to save for major expenses such as retirement and long-term care.

While few would contest the importance of self sufficiency, not everyone feels ready to proceed with confidence. Moreover, we often do not know who to turn to for help. After all, the history of fraud is littered with plausible rogues.

This book is designed to help you to help yourself. *The First-Time Investor* takes a robust, no-nonsense approach to the world of investment and reduces to the level of common sense a process where jargon and obfuscation have for too long been employed in order to justify inflated fees.

Some readers will be keen to undertake their own research before they invest. In these pages you will find everything you need to get started plus plenty of useful tips on how to improve your skills.

Others may like the idea of running their own portfolio, but, due to business and family commitments, simply do not have the time. It is a shame to waste time and money building a portfolio, only to see it struggle and fail due to hasty decisions and simple neglect. In this case you will need an adviser.

Well, the good news is that there are literally thousands of advisers out there just dying to help you run your investments. The bad news is that it is not immediately obvious which are the experts and which have just made the switch into finance following a short career in double glazing.

The First-Time Investor will show you how to identify the right type of advice for your needs and explain how to track down the best firm for your requirements.

Choose well and you can delegate the job of running your portfolio to an expert, leaving you free to do what you are good at, namely running your business and/or your family.

Whatever your investment needs, *The First-Time Investor* may not turn you into an expert, but it will certainly help you to become wise before, rather than after the event.

Debbie Harrison
June 1998

Acknowledgements

Many experts provided information and advice for this book. In particular my thanks go to Justin Urquhart-Stewart and James Bevan of Barclays Stockbrokers who gave up their valuable time to read the manuscript and who made countless recommendations. Mark Toller of Henderson Investors and Robert Brown of Cantrade Investments also provided useful information and comments which were a welcome addition to the book. In addition, several organisations helped to provide essential research material. These include the Association of Investment Trust Companies (AITC), the Association of Private Clients and Investment Managers (APCIMS), the Association of Unit Trusts and Investment Funds (AUTIF), FTSE International, the Stock Exchange and ProShare.

Introduction

If you are one of the many millions of people who invest directly or through collective funds in the stockmarket yet do not consider yourself a member of that elite group of 'private investors', this is the book for you.

Your starting point

Most of us start our investments when we join the company pension scheme which is designed to build up a fund to pay for our old age pension. Or we might take out a mortgage and start an endowment which builds up a fund to repay the debt after 20 years or more.

We tend to associate these types of investments with our employer or our building society, both of which seem a far cry from the risky and volatile stockmarkets.

This misconception is perpetuated by financial institutions, which encourage us to compartmentalise our investments rather than to create a coherent portfolio. So, we end up with a pension plan for retirement, an endowment for the mortgage repayment, life assurance funds or unit trusts for the children' s school fees, and so on.

In addition to these collective funds, you may be one of the millions of investors who own a collection of individual shares which were not chosen because of the companies' long-term profit forecasts or because you wanted to invest in utilities or financials to balance your portfolio's asset allocation. Rather, they were bought because you subscribed to a tempting privatisation issue or you are one of the six million people given shares when your building society or life insurance company demutualised.

You may also have a collection of shares bought to take advantage of the £3000 annual single company Pep allowance, while an increasing number of employees are encouraged to buy shares in their employer's company at a discount through a share option scheme.

A coherent portfolio

All of these diverse investments may serve you well, but they do not represent an efficient, balanced and properly managed portfolio. Armed with the right information and, in most cases, the right type of professional adviser, you can make your investments work a lot harder for you.

Whatever your starting point, no doubt you would like to manage your existing investments more efficiently, to learn more about the markets and companies in which you invest and, above all, to feel more confident and informed when you make future investment decisions.

Answers, not questions

This book provides in one source the answers to the most important questions for new investors:

- How do the stockmarkets work?
- What are the important characteristics of equities and bonds?
- How do I find the right investment adviser?
- How do I set appropriate investment goals?
- Which are the right savings and investment products for me?
- Which investments are tax-efficient?
- How do I select individual shares, gilts and bonds?
- Will my ethical and environmental views have an adverse effect on my portfolio?
- Should I change my portfolio to protect against a bear market?
- Which benchmarks should I use to measure performance and monitor my portfolio?

- What rights do I have as a shareholder?
- What do I do if things go wrong?

How this book can help

Section 1 explains in clear language how the UK stockmarket works. It then examines the two most important asset classes – equities and bonds – and explains what these investments can do for you. Armed with this information you will find that the financial papers and specialist publications start to make a lot more sense.

Your financial plan

The next steps, discussed in Section 2, explain how you can apply this knowledge to your own personal circumstances in order to find the right type of adviser for your needs and to determine what sorts of investments are appropriate.

This section explains that before you invest a penny you need to know the answer to two simple but crucial questions:

- What state are your finances in now?
- What are your investment goals?

You cannot answer the second question unless you have first examined your current position to determine how much capital, if any, is genuinely spare. To give yourself a financial health check, you should draw up a financial plan which sets out all your income and expenditure, and lists your current investments and liabilities.

If you find the prospect daunting it is worth consulting a financial planner (see Chapter 3 for tips on how to find an adviser) who will guide you through this process and will help you build an accurate financial profile – a family profit and loss account, if you like.

Your financial plan should cover the following aspects:

- *Protection insurance:* do you have the right level of life assurance and disability insurance to protect your family if you die or are too ill to work?

- *Emergency funds:* are your income and rainy-day savings sufficient to cover your current and future cash requirements?

- *Mortgages and pensions:* have you made proper provision for your mortgage repayment, pension and any other long-term savings requirements? These goals – and the investments you choose to meet your targets – should be incorporated into your overall investment plan.

- *Income and capital gains tax planning:* are you making the most of the Government' s annual allowances and exemptions? Could you redistribute your assets within your family to lower your tax bill?

- *Estate planning:* Have you made or updated your will? Have you considered ways to pass on your wealth using suitable inheritance tax planning methods?

Your investment goals

Once you have assessed your current financial position and tidied up any loose ends, it is time to identify your investment goals. Whether you need your investments to generate income, capital growth, or a combination of the two, your investment aims will dictate the types and proportion of each asset class (for example, equities, bonds, gilts and deposits) you should hold in your portfolio.

The place for savings and investment products

Section 3 considers the wide range of savings and investment products currently available. Some are ideal for short-term goals, others are designed for the long term and may be particularly tax efficient for some or all tax payers.

For most investors, savings products (for example, building society deposit and National Savings accounts) and collective funds (for example, unit and investment trusts, pension plans and life assurance funds) play an important part in their financial plans.

Even the very wealthy investor will use savings accounts for emergency cash and collective funds to gain access to specialist markets such as emerging markets.

Planning your portfolio

Section 4 will help you start and improve on your portfolio of directly held equities and bonds.

Here you will discover the basic asset allocation and stock selection techniques. If you have strong views on armaments or the environment, for example, there is also guidance on ethical and environmental investment. The processes involved with buying and selling as a private investor are also explained.

Interpreting economic indicators

If you choose companies which can demonstrate good long-term potential they should be able to ride out the market cycles and serve you well for many years. After all, if a company was worth investing in two weeks ago, it will still be worth holding even if the stockmarket as a whole has taken a tumble. But this does not mean you should ignore economic trends, and active investors will want to protect themselves or even improve the performance of their portfolio by keeping one step ahead of the market. Section 4 explains how to interpret the implications of market cycles – and in particular what action you could take to prepare for a bear market.

Monitoring your portfolio

Section 5 concentrates on the mechanics of running your portfolio smoothly and efficiently. You need to know how to monitor the performance of your collective funds and individual shares and how to interpret the information available to you as an existing or prospective investor.

In particular you need to know how to interpret company reports and accounts, and the statistical pages of the *Financial Times*. You also need to know what rights you have as a shareholder.

In addition, Section 5 explains how your investments will be taxed and explains how to make the most of the annual tax allowances and exemptions in order to minimise or avoid certain taxes altogether. With care, you can slash your tax bill and still pass the Inland Revenue's scrutiny with flying colours.

Finally there is a roundup of useful information about the Internet, investment clubs, regulation and making complaints. Chapter 20 lists some sources of information, and there is also a glossary to guide you through all the jargon. Terms listed in the glossary are in italic print.

Keep a clear head

Do remember, though, that however much you learn, investment is not a science, no matter how scientific you try make the process. Things can and do go wrong, simply because the stockmarkets refuse to behave in a logical way. So, arm yourself with as much useful information as you can but never fall into the trap of thinking that you have a foolproof system.

HOW THE
MARKETS WORK

Section 1

1

The stockmarkets

- A (very) brief history lesson
- Three key functions of the stockmarket

At a glance

A market is a place where buyers and sellers come together for mutual benefit and gain. The London Stock Exchange is no exception; but simply represents an important market place where on the one hand, companies can raise finance for expansion, and on the other, investors can lend spare capital and in return share in the growth of their chosen companies.

London is one of the top three stockmarkets in the world. The other two you will hear about most frequently are New York and Tokyo.

The London Stock Exchange is also the world's leading international exchange. More international companies are listed, and more international equities are traded in London, than on any other exchange.

For the history buffs, there are many books dedicated to the origins and development of the London Stock Exchange, including those available from the Exchange itself.

This Chapter covers the essential details, and helps to explain the context in which the Exchange works. Do remember that for all its fancy jargon it is, after all, just a market place.

A (VERY) BRIEF HISTORY LESSON

History teaches us that wherever there is a seller and a buyer a middle man will emerge and create a market. The Stock Exchange is no exception.

The origins of the stockmarket go back to the coffee houses of the 17th century where people who wanted to raise money met with those who wanted to invest in the original *'joint stock' companies* – the forerunners of today's *public limited companies* (plcs). Joint stock, in this context, refers to a company where partners pooled their stock, or ownership, with that of outsiders. Therefore, the company was jointly owned between the original owners and private investors.

As the volume of trade in joint stock companies grew, the number of dealers expanded. The original traders were the *brokers*, who bought and sold the shares on behalf of clients, and *jobbers*, through whom the brokers made their transactions. In 1986 jobbers were replaced by *market makers*.

The early market was a far cry from the elegant, pin-striped gentleman's club it later became. Some of the original traders were so unruly that in 1760 a group was kicked out of the *Royal Exchange*, which had largely replaced the coffee houses as a central market place.

About 150 of these financial hooligans formed a club at Jonathan's Coffee House to carry on the business of buying and selling shares. In 1773 the members voted to change the name of their meeting house to the *Stock Exchange*.

Following a tremendous boom in trade and accompanying scandals – most notably the *South Sea Bubble* (see page 163) – the members of the Stock Exchange agreed on a set of rules and tighter controls. This resulted in the 1812 *Deed of Settlement* which formed the basis of the rules for the operation of the markets today.

■ Big Bang

We now skip a century and a half and move to the 1970s, when London's pre-eminent position in international markets was under threat. In particular, in 1979 the abolition of foreign exchange controls made it easier for UK savings institutions to invest money overseas in non-UK securities. As a result, London Stock Exchange member firms were exposed to competition from overseas brokers who were also contending for UK and international company shares.

These were not the only pressures to change. In the early 1980s the government took the Exchange to court, claiming that some of the principles on which the Exchange's rules were based restricted trade. Under an out of court agreement the Exchange agreed to abolish its system of minimum commissions by the end of 1986 to encourage greater competition. This in turn was expected to bring down commission rates and the overall cost of share transactions.

Big Bang took place on 27 October 1986. The important changes were as follows:

- Ownership of member firms by an outside corporation was allowed, enabling member firms to build larger capital bases to compete with overseas competition. Many firms were bought by UK and foreign banks, and by major overseas securities firms.
- The separation of member firms into brokers and jobbers ended. All firms became broker/dealers able to operate in a dual capacity – either buying securities from, or selling them to, clients without having to go through a third party.
- Minimum scales of commission were abolished, opening the way for much greater competition on charges and services.
- Voting rights at the Exchange were transferred from individual members to member firms.
- Trading moved from the Exchange floor, where it was carried out face to face in a single hall, to separate dealing rooms, where transactions were performed using telephones and computers.
- Two computer-based systems were introduced – *SEAQ* (Stock Exchange Automated Quotations) and *SEAQ International*. These enabled investment managers to see share price information from anywhere in the UK. In 1993 *SEATS* (the Stock Exchange Alternative Trading System) was introduced for less liquid securities.

THREE KEY FUNCTIONS OF THE STOCKMARKET

The Stock Exchange has three key functions:

■ to raise capital   ■ to trade services   ■ to regulate the stockmarket.

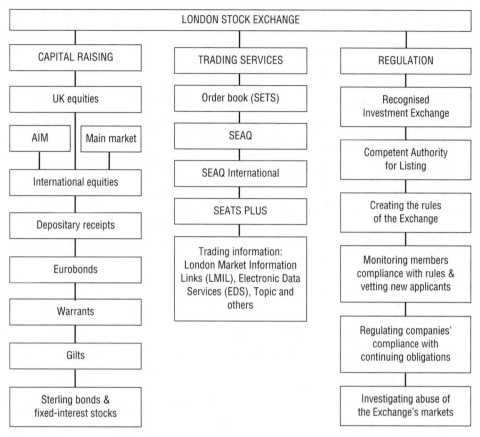

Fig 1.1   The London Stock Exchange

■ Raising capital

The Stock Exchange provides a range of markets which allow UK and international companies, governments and other entities to raise capital and to gain wide access to investors and borrowers.

How to buy and sell your shares is covered in Chapter 14 but it is worth running through the basic mechanics of the process here.

There are three main ways in which you can buy shares:

1. *The primary market for initial public offerings:* this is when a company first offers shares on the stockmarket – a process known

as a *floatation*. You may be able to buy direct (through newspaper advertisements, for example) to avoid a stockbroker's commission or, in the case of 'windfall' shares, if you are a member of a mutual building society or life assurance society, you may receive free shares in exchange for giving up your right to a share in the mutual's ownership.

2. *Further issues:* companies may need to raise more money at a later stage to fund large projects. In this case it may launch a *rights issue* where existing investors have the opportunity to subscribe for the new shares at less than the current market price.

3. *Secondary or trading market:* the most common way of investing in a company's shares is in the secondary or trading market where you buy shares through a stockbroker from existing investors who wish to sell.

So, how do companies 'come to the market' and trade their shares?

The role of the primary market

Many UK and international companies come to London to raise new capital or to have their shares more widely marketed and traded. They can raise capital via the main market (known as the *Official List*) or the *Alternative Investment Market* (AIM), which is more suitable for smaller, newer companies.

There are about 2100 UK companies on the main market, about 500 international companies, and about 300 UK companies on AIM. (See Chapter 17 for more details about listed companies and the *Financial Times* indices.)

Companies can raise capital both at the time of 'going public' and, subsequently, by issuing securities for cash. Access to equity or debt finance gives companies greater flexibility to fund expansion and development programmes or to reduce borrowings.

During a typical year, UK companies might raise over £50 billion, while a further £44 billion might be raised by government securities (gilts).

The main market (*Official List*)

Companies on the main market come from all sectors of business and range from those with a £1 million *market capitalisation* to those capitalised at £90 billion. The market capitalisation is calculated by multiplying the current share price by the number of shares in issue.

A company which applies for a listing has to supply the Stock Exchange with a great many details about its trading history, financial records, management, business prospects, information on the securities to be listed, plus the terms of any fundraising. This information is included in the company's *listing particulars* or *prospectus*. The document provides prospective investors with most of the information they need to decide whether to proceed. Clearly an independent assessment is also important.

The company must appoint a sponsor approved by the Exchange to handle its application to join. This can be a member firm, a bank, an investment manager, a firm of solicitors or accountants, among other advisers. There are about 150 approved sponsors.

Trading on the Exchange is carried out through SEAQ for UK companies, SEAQ International for international companies and SEATS Plus for smaller companies.

The companies on the main markets are divided into various categories or *sectors* so that performance can be related to the appropriate peer group. The companies are also divided into different *indices*, based on market capitalisation. Sectors and indices are discussed in Chapters 10 and 17.

The Alternative Investment Market (AIM)

AIM was launched in June 1995 and provides a market for young, usually small, but fast growing companies. Since the eligibility criteria is less stringent than for the main market, companies listed on AIM are generally considered more risky than companies on the Official List, although recently some attempts have been made to disprove this argument.

The majority of AIM companies have a market capitalisation of between £5 million and £50 million, but the range starts as low as about £3 million and rises up to in excess of £100 million

■ Trading services

The London Stock Exchange provides a secondary market for trading in more than 12 100 quoted *securities* (the generic term for UK and foreign equities, bonds, gilts and derivatives).

The Exchange provides very detailed trading and information services. In October 1997 it introduced a new Stock Exchange Trading Service (SETS) to speed up order-driven trading, initially in the FTSE 100 equities. *Order book trading* allows sales and purchases to be matched electronically rather than under the old system where quotations were sought by telephone (see page 11).

The Exchange offers markets for:

- *UK equities:* the ordinary shares issued by UK companies quoted on SEAQ or SEATS PLUS.

- *International equities:* ordinary shares issued by non-UK companies, many of which are quoted on SEAQ International.

- *UK gilts:* securities issued by the UK Government.

- *Sterling bonds:* securities issued by companies or local authorities.

- *AIM securities:* shares and fixed interest stocks of companies admitted to AIM.

- *Traditional options:* (a type of derivative, see page 21) traded on SEAQ and SEAQ International.

■ How the UK market works

Throughout the trading day, market makers display on SEAQ the following details for all the securities for which they are registered to deal:

- their *bid* (buying) price
- their *offer* (selling) price
- the *maximum transaction size* to which these prices relate.

The market makers must stick to these prices when dealing with other Exchange member firms. Prices for larger transactions are subject to negotiation. Table 1.1 shows the 20 most active UK securities in 1997.

SEAQ

The Stock Exchange Automated Quotations service (SEAQ) is a continuously updated database with market makers' bid and offer

Table 1.1 20 most active UK securities by equity turnover – 1997

Company	Security type	Business sector	Index at 31/12/97	Turnover value (£m)	Number of bargains	Shares traded (m)
British Telecommunications	Ord 25p	Telecommunications	FTSE 100	38,544.8	402,246	9,195.8
Shell Transport & Trading	Ord 25p	Oil, integrated	FTSE 100	25,194.7	186,719	4,220.0
British Petroleum	Ord 25p	Oil, integrated	FTSE 100	23,270.0	157,411	3,004.0
Glaxo Wellcome	Ord 25p	Pharmaceuticals	FTSE 100	22,832.2	179,541	1,898.6
Lloyds TSB	Ord 25p	Banks, retail	FTSE 100	20,788.2	304,771	3,344.6
HSBC	Ord 75p	Banks, retail	FTSE 100	19,658.3	123,420	1,147.1
HSBC	Ord HK$10	Banks, retail	FTSE 100	19,504.6	39,714	1,168.3
Barclays plc	Ord £1	Banks, retail	FTSE 100	19,437.0	125,785	1,555.3
National Westminster Bank	Ord £1	Banks, retail	FTSE 100	15,312.9	132,099	1,878.3
Halifax	Ord 20p	Banks, retail	FTSE 100	14,409.1	269,536	1,960.0
BAT Industries	Ord 25p	Tobacco	FTSE 100	14,371.7	122,218	2,664.3
Grand Metropolitan	Ord 25p	Alcoholic beverages	FTSE 100	13,549.6	77,900	2,428.6
Reuters	Ord 2.5p	Media	FTSE 100	11,602.7	74,244	1,718.1
Zeneca	Ord 25p	Pharmaceuticals	FTSE 100	11,297.2	95,157	598.0
SmithKline Beecham	Ord 12.5p	Pharmaceuticals	FTSE 100	11,078.3	76,570	1,118.4
Imperial Chemical Industries	Ord £1	Chemicals	FTSE 100	10,688.6	80,086	1,296.0
Abbey National	Ord 10p	Banks, retail	FTSE 100	9,991.9	235,306	1,181.6
Diageo	Ord 25p	Alcoholic beverages	FTSE 100	9,958.0	66,835	1,870.2
BTR	Ord 25p	Diversified industrials	FTSE 100	9,816.3	138,130	4,406.8
Royal & Sun Alliance Insurance	Ord 25p	Insurance	FTSE 100	9,720.3	63,426	1,928.9
Total				**331,026.5**	**2,951,114**	**48,583.2**

Source: London Stock Exchange

prices and sizes of trades. Registered market makers must maintain their prices during the mandatory quote period – 08.30 to 16.20, Monday to Friday. See Figure 1.2 for an example screen.

The information is analysed to create the SEAQ 'yellow strip' across the screen which identifies for the investor at any moment of the day, the best bid and offer prices for every SEAQ security, and also identifies up to four market makers quoting this price.

SEAQ international and SEATS Plus operate in a similar way.

Stock Exchange Electronic Trading Service

In October 1997 the 'order book' was introduced. This is known as the Stock Exchange Electronic Trading Service (SETS). SETS signals the London equity market's switch from the existing *quote-driven* system of share trading, under which buying and selling of shares is largely conducted by telephone, to an *order-matching* system. See Figure 1.3 for an example screen.

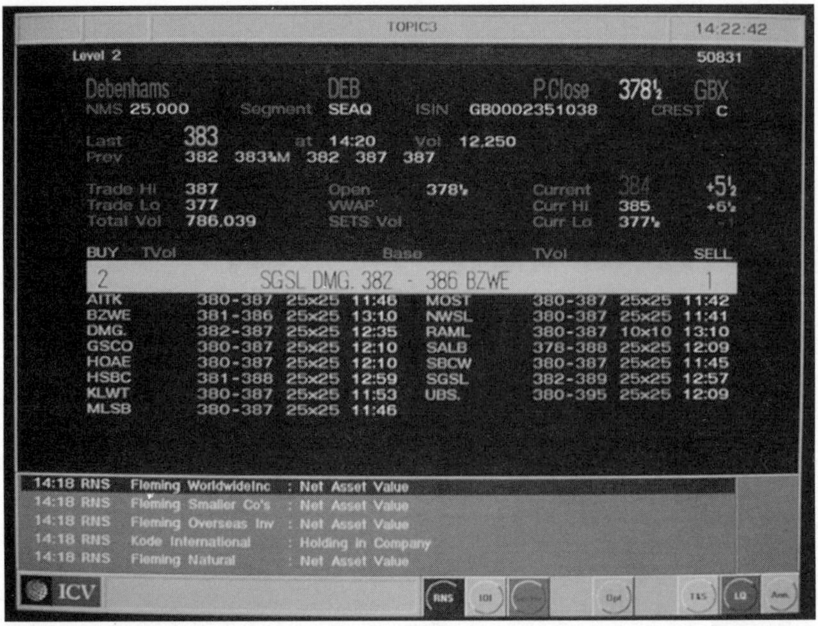

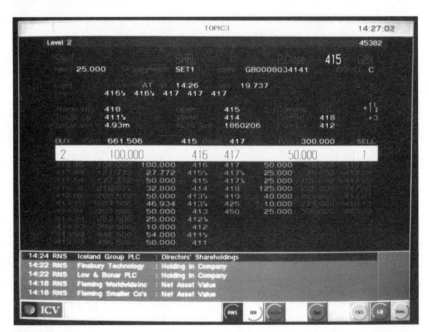

Fig 1.2 SEAQ screen
Source: London Stock Exchange

Fig 1.3 SETS screen
Source: London Stock Exchange

So, instead of market makers placing buy and sell orders by phone, now when bid and offer prices match, orders will automatically pair off. Initially SETS' order book will be limited to the FTSE 100 companies (and those which were in the index but have subsequently dropped out) because the system is designed to cope with frequently traded shares. Non-FTSE 100 company shares will continue to trade under the SEAQ system.

In theory this should improve efficiency and drive down transaction costs, because it automates the execution of trades and narrows the spread between buying and selling prices, which represents the market maker's 'turn' and adds to the investor's costs.

From the private investor's point of view, if you use an *execution-only* service (where no advice is given – see page 41) you will still telephone your stockbroker and agree a price at which you are willing to buy or sell a particular share. The broker will enter the order directly into the order book and it will be displayed anonymously to the entire market along with other orders.

In the example shown in Figure 1.3, the investor wants to sell 4000 shares immediately at the best price available. At the time the best 'buy' order is for 17 800 shares at 938 pence. The 'sell' order for 4000 shares will automatically trade against this buy order, leaving 13 800 shares at 938 pence on the order book.

As soon as the order is carried out the trade is automatically reported to the Exchange and the market is informed immediately that the trade has taken place. Only the member firms involved in the trade will discover the identity of the firm with which they have dealt.

Settlement services

After an order has been carried out, the settlement process transfers stock from seller to buyer and arranges for the exchange of money from buyer to seller.

A new electronic share dealing settlement and registration system, CREST (not an acronym), was introduced in 1997. In effect this is an electronic book entry transfer of registered stock, so its aim is to reduce the movement of paper, although investors can still keep share certificates if they wish.

■ Regulation: The Financial Services Act (1986)

The regulatory system designed to protect investors was completely overhauled with the introduction of the Financial Services Act (FSA) 1986. The Exchange had always been responsible for regulating member firms, but the Act added a new statutory dimension so that it is now illegal for anyone except those authorised or exempted under the Act to carry on investment business.

Under the Act, the Stock Exchange regulates both *capital raising* and *trading markets*. Its activities include:

- to assess the credentials of companies that apply to join the main market (the Official List)
- to monitor listed companies' compliance with the rules
- to deal with any breaches of the rules
- to supervise the conduct of the 300 member firms which deal on its markets.

If you want to find a good stockbroker, see Chapter 3, which explains how to check a firm has the right regulatory authorisation and what other key factors to consider in the selection process. Chapter 20 includes a guide to making complaints, should anything go wrong.

The point to remember about regulation is that if you ask a stockbroker to provide a discretionary service he or she should select the investments that best suit your requirements. If, at your initial meeting, you and your broker agree that a portfolio of low risk collective investments is most appropriate to your needs, and you end up with individual shares listed on AIM, then clearly you have a justified complaint. But if you deal through an execution-only stockbroker and your shares take a tumble, or if your adviser recommends a sensible spread of FTSE100 shares and the entire stockmarket crashes, then that's just bad luck.

Sources

The London Stock Exchange publishes many useful information leaflets and books. For details contact: The Public Information Department, London Stock Exchange, London EC2N 1HP. Tel: 0171 797 1372. Fax: 0171 410 6861. www.londonstockex.co.uk

Summary

- London is one of the top three stockmarkets in the world.

- Big Bang improved competition on dealing costs and introduced important technology.

- The Stock Exchange's main functions are to raise capital for companies, to trade services and to regulate the stockmarket.

- There are about 2100 UK companies on the main market – the 'Official List'.

- The Alternative Investment Market is for young, fast growing companies.

- Throughout the trading day, market makers display details of the securities for which they are registered to deal on SEAQ (Stock Exchange Automated Quotations).

- In October 1997 the Stock Exchange Electronic Trading Service (SETS) introduced 'order book' trading, which matches sales and purchases electronically for shares in the largest UK companies.

2

Equities and bonds without tears

- Securities
- The main asset classes
- Comparing equities, bonds and cash (deposits)
- Different types of institutional fund management

At a glance

Savings and investment institutions are adept at dressing up what are essentially quite straightforward assets. As a result, it is easy to fall into the trap of investing in 'products' and to end up with a growing number of plans and schemes which, when examined in more detail, represent anything but a co-ordinated, well-balanced portfolio.

This Chapter explains the characteristics of the asset classes you will come across in your quest for the best investments for your requirements. Keep this information in mind when you consider the wide range of products discussed later in Section 3. The trick is to keep a co-ordinated approach to the underlying asset allocation and only to use the tax-efficient product wrappers where they can enhance the return of your preferred investments.

To make the best of the available tax breaks, you also need to understand the basics of taxation from the family as well as the individual point of view. For example, if you have a non-working spouse, it makes sense to put income-generating assets in his or her name to make use of the annual income tax allowance.

Equally, you can often eliminate a potential capital gains tax liability by giving some of your assets to your spouse so that he or she can make use of the annual capital gains tax exemption. Taxation is discussed in Chapter 19.

SECURITIES

Investment literature uses a lot of confusing jargon. Commonly used (and misused) terms include 'securities', 'stocks' and 'shares'.

Securities is the general name for all stocks and shares. What we call shares today, originally were known as 'stocks' because they represented part ownership in the joint stock companies – the precursors to today's public limited companies or plcs (see Chapter 1). So, to some extent the terms stocks and shares are interchangeable, and we still use the terms *stock*markets and *stock*brokers.

Broadly speaking stocks are fixed interest securities and shares are the rest. The four main types of securities listed and traded on the UK Stock Exchange are:

- *UK ('domestic') equities:* ordinary shares issued by over 2000 UK companies.
- *Overseas equities:* ordinary shares issued by non-UK companies.
- *Gilts:* bonds issued by the UK Government to raise money to fund any shortfall in public expenditure.
- *Bonds:* fixed interest stocks issued by companies and local authorities, among others.

THE MAIN ASSET CLASSES

■ UK equities

If a company wants to raise finance, it has two main options: it can sell part of the ownership of the company by issuing ordinary shares (equities) or it can borrow money by issuing bonds, which are a sophisticated IOU. Shares and bonds are bought and sold on the stockmarket.

Equities are the quoted shares of companies in the UK and tend to dominate most private investors' portfolios, whether they are held directly or are pooled through collective funds such as unit and investment trusts or a pension fund.

The return achieved by UK equities, when measured over the long term, has exceeded both price and earnings inflation (see page 25).

As we discovered in Chapter 1, companies 'go public' when they are quoted on the Stock Exchange or Alternative Investment Market. In this way a company can raise the money it needs to expand by issuing shares.

A *share* or equity literally entitles the owner to a specified share in the profits of the company and, if the company is wound up, to a specified share of its assets. The owner of shares is entitled to the *dividends* – the six-monthly distribution to shareholders of part of the company's profits. The *dividend yield* on equities is the dividend paid by a company divided by that company's share price.

There is no set *redemption date* for an equity when the company is obliged to return your original investment. If, as a shareholder, you want to convert your investment into cash ('to realise its value') you must sell your shares through a stockbroker. The price will vary from day to day, so the timing of the purchase and sale of shares is critical.

■ Share classes

There are different classes of shares. Most investors buy *ordinary shares*, which give the holder the right to vote on the constitution of the company's board of directors. Since this is the most common type of share, the term 'ordinary' usually is dropped, unless it is to distinguish the shares from a different category.

Preference shares carry no voting rights but have a fixed dividend payment, so can be attractive to those seeking a regular income. These shares have 'preference' over ordinary shareholders if the company is wound up – hence the name.

There are several sub-classes of equities or equity-related investments.

Convertibles and warrants

Convertibles and warrants are special types of shares with characteristics that make them attractive in certain circumstances.

Convertibles are more akin to bonds (see page 22), in that they pay a regular income and have a fixed redemption date. However, a convertible confers the right to convert to an ordinary share or preference share at a future date. This can be an attractive proposition if the price is attractive on the convertible date.

Warrants confer a right, but not an obligation, on the holder to convert to a specific share at a predetermined price and date. The value of the warrant, which itself is traded on the stockmarket, is determined by the difference or *premium* of the share price over the conversion price of the warrant.

Derivatives

Derivatives, as the name suggests, derive their value from the price of an underlying security. This is the generic term given to futures contracts and options, both of which can be used to reduce risk in an institutional fund or, in the case of options, even in a large private portfolio.

A *futures contract* binds two parties to a sale or purchase at a specified future date. The price is fixed at the time the contract is taken out. These futures contracts can be used by institutional funds to control risk, because they allow the manager to quickly increase or reduce the fund's exposure to an existing asset class. Futures have also proved popular as a cost-cutting mechanism, particularly in index-tracking funds and other funds where there are rapid changes of large asset allocations.

Options allow you, for a down payment, to have the right, but not the obligation, to buy or sell something at an agreed price on a specific date. Some private investors use options as a type of insurance policy to protect their portfolio against a fall in the market. Options are discussed in Chapter 13.

■ Overseas equities

Overseas equities are similar in principle to UK equities, but there are differences in shareholder rights. Investment overseas provides exposure to the growth in foreign markets including younger, fast growing economies. However, these shares also expose you to currency fluctuations. This can be both good and bad, of course, but the point is that it adds an extra layer of risk.

The taxation of foreign shares can be less favourable than UK equities. In particular, some or all of the withholding tax on dividends deducted by the foreign country may not be recoverable.

As a rule of thumb, exposure to the major developed economies, for example the European Union countries, the US, and Canada, is considered beneficial, but generally is achieved through collective funds – for example investment trusts (see Chapter 6). Exposure to the emerging economies is high risk and so only suitable for those prepared to take a punt.

■ Bonds

UK bonds are issued by borrowers, for example the Government (these bonds are known as *gilt-edged securities* or just 'gilts') and companies (*corporate bonds*). Bonds are also issued by local authorities, overseas governments and overseas companies.

In return for the loan of your money, the borrower agrees to pay a fixed rate of interest (known as the *coupon*) for the agreed period, and to repay your original capital sum on a specified date, known as the maturity or *redemption date*.

UK domestic bonds are either *secured* on the company's underlying assets – for example the company's property – or *unsecured*, in which case there is no physical asset backing the bond's guarantee to pay interest and to repay the capital at maturity.

Secured bonds are known as *debentures* and unsecured bonds are known as *loan stocks*. Since the security offered by debentures is greater than for loan stocks, the former tend to pay a lower rate of interest.

The point to remember about fixed interest securities is that the investment return is determined more by the level of interest rates than the issuing company's profitability. Provided the issuer remains sufficiently secure to honour the future *coupon payments* (the regular interest) and *redemption payment* (the return of the original capital) you know exactly what your return will be, provided you hold the bond to maturity. Gilts offer the highest degree of security because they are issued by the UK Government.

Traded bonds

If you or a fund manager sells a bond before its maturity date, then the value of the future coupon and redemption payments will depend on the prevailing interest rates at the time of sale.

So, if interest rates are rising, then the value of the fixed interest security will fall. This is because for the same amount of capital invested, you could get a better return elsewhere. Conversely, if interest rates are falling, then the value of the fixed interest security will be higher because it provides a greater stream of income than you could get from alternative sources.

> Equities are considered more risky and volatile than bonds because they behave in an unpredictable way.

This volatile pattern of behaviour is more apparent with fixed interest securities that have a long period to run to maturity since they are more likely to be traded before redemption date.

To summarise, as a general rule equities are considered more risky and volatile than bonds because they behave in an unpredictable way whereas, provided the company or government backing a bond is watertight, the return on a bond held to maturity is predictable. However, it is not predictable if you decide to sell before maturity.

Eurobonds

UK companies can raise money outside the UK market by issuing 'Eurosterling' bonds – that is, bonds denominated in sterling but issued on the Eurobond market. Contrary to the name, the Euromarkets are not confined to Europe but are international markets where borrowers and lenders are matched.

The main advantage of Eurosterling bonds, from the borrower's point of view, is that they can reach a much wider range of potential lenders. However, this is not a market for private investors in the UK.

▩ Index-linked gilts

Index-linked gilts are issued by the UK Government and are guaranteed to provide interest payments (the coupon) and a redemption value which increase in line with annual inflation. For

> Cash does not refer to stacks of £20 notes stuffed under the mattress, but usually means a deposit account.

this reason they are one of the lowest risk assets for income seekers. Having said that, in practice they have not proved particularly attractive compared with other income-generating alternatives.

The return on index-linked gilts in excess of the Retail Price Index varies, but usually it is possible to buy these securities in the market place at a price which guarantees a real rate of return to the holder, assuming that the stock is held to maturity.

■ Cash

Cash does not refer to stacks of £20 notes stuffed under the mattress, but usually means a deposit account. Deposits have the advantage that the value in monetary terms is known and is certain at all times. What is unknown is the interest that will be received and by how much this will fall short of the rate of inflation.

■ Property

In investment terms, 'property' usually refers to the ownership of land and buildings that are used by a business or other organisation. The owner of the property receives income from the rent charged to the tenant and, over time, this rent is expected broadly to keep pace with inflation. The dominant factor in the value of a property is the desirability or otherwise of its location.

There are several problems with property. First, it is often sold in large blocks which cannot be easily split for investment purposes. As a result, only the larger institutional funds can afford (or are wise) to own property directly.

Second, property is a very illiquid asset and it can take several years for the right selling conditions to arise. Moreover, unless you invest via a collective fund, you cannot dispose of your investment piecemeal to make best use of your annual capital gains tax (CGT) exemption but instead could be landed with a whopping CGT bill.

COMPARING EQUITIES, BONDS AND CASH (DEPOSITS)

It is common practice to compare returns on equities with bonds, and both asset classes with cash (deposits). These returns are illustrated in Figure 2.1 which demonstrates that deposits do not keep pace with inflation. If you put your money in a deposit account it will increase with the interest earned and your original capital will be safe, but over the long term the value of its real spending power, after inflation, may fall.

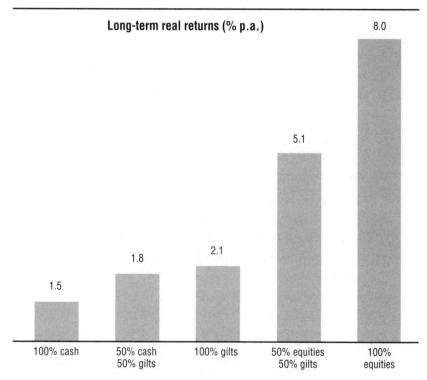

Fig 2.1 Comparison of returns on equities, gilts and cash
Source: Barclays Stockbrokers (data drawn from a base of December 1918)

Barclays Stockbrokers Equity-Gilt Study, first published in 1956, provides data and analysis of yearly returns from investments in UK equities, gilts and cash since 1918. (See the sources section at the end of the Chapter). The one overriding message from the study is that over the long term an equity investor is rewarded for taking risk. Historically, the degree of that payoff – in the form of an enhanced return – has been substantial relative to both gilts and cash. Although gilts have

25

performed relatively well in recent years compared with equities, the total returns to an equity investor have been higher.

The data for the 79 years covered by the survey indicate the inflation adjusted but before tax annual returns on the following asset mixes:

- the real return from cash would have averaged at about 1.5 per cent
- a 50:50 mix between gilts and cash would have increased this average return to 1.8 per cent
- a 100 per cent investment in gilts would have raised the real return to 2.1 per cent per annum
- 50:50 mix between gilts and equities would have produced a real return of 5.1 per cent per annum
- a 100 per cent commitment to equities would have produced 8.01 per cent.

The term used by stockbrokers to describe the higher risk/return characteristic of equities is the *equity risk premium*.
Barclays Capital Equity-Gilt Study reveals the following key facts:

- £100 invested in equities in December 1918 with all income reinvested gross was worth £884 714 in December 1997. The equivalent figures for gilts would be £10 652 and for cash £6521. When inflation is taken into account, the returns would reduce to £43 891 (equities), £528 (gilts) and £324 (cash).
- The average real return (that is, the return in excess of inflation) for equities for the entire period 1918–96 was 8 per cent a year. If tax is deducted at the basic rate, the real rate of return has been 6.8 per cent. If we allow for the taxation of dividends at the highest marginal rate, this reduces to 4.1 per cent. This is higher than the underlying growth rate of the economy.

It is important to remember that these figures do not make any allowance for the charges that would be deducted on your savings and investments. For example, if you invest directly in equities you would pay dealing costs, including stamp duty and the stockbroker's charges, while for collective funds such as unit trusts, you would have to take account of the manager's initial and annual charges.

Investors keen to keep up with the comparative movements of gilts and equities should refer to the *Financial Times* which publishes the gilt-equity yield ratio. This tracks the yield on gilts divided by the yield on shares. As a rule of thumb the normal range is between 2 and 2.5, so if it dips or soars well out of this range it may indicate that shares are very expensive or that gilts are very cheap. Market analysts use this as one of the signals to indicate that a bull (lower figure) or bear (higher figure) market is imminent. (See Chapter 13 for more details about economic cycles.)

■ Inflation

It is also important to keep in mind the relationship between inflation and returns. At the time of writing the Government's aim was to keep inflation under 2.5 per cent. This is based on a definition of retail price inflation that excludes mortgage interest payments (see Chapter 13).

> It is also important to keep in mind the relationship between inflation and returns.

Barclays' guide points out that inflation is a key determinant of investment returns. Stockmarkets may not be prepared for an inflation 'shock' (a sudden and unexpected change) but they adjust over time and provide a long-term hedge against price rises. Gilts and cash are not suitable inflation hedges.

■ Period of investment

Clearly, long-term returns on equities, gilts and cash should be viewed with some caution and certainly should not be treated as a guide to the future. While history indicates that equities should provide a better return than bonds over the medium to long term, there is an important caveat. 'Medium to long term' means a minimum of five years. If you go into the stockmarkets for shorter periods you are in danger of getting your fingers burned either because the markets take a tumble just before you want to get out or because the fixed costs associated with setting up your investment undermine the return over the short term.

■ Dividend reinvestment

This is important. Barclays' long-term fund analysis is based on £100 invested in December 1918 with all income reinvested gross at the beginning of each new calendar year. As mentioned above, for equities this figure would have grown to £884 714 by December 1997. Allowing for inflation this figure reduces to £43 891. If the income was spent and only the value of capital is measured, the return reduces to £18 442.

For most private investors, building society deposit rates are the obvious choice for holding deposits and tax has to be paid on investment income. The following tables reflect this.

Figure 2.2 shows that the value of £100 invested in December 1945, allowing for income to be reinvested net of basic rate tax, would have been £30 952 (equities), £675 (gilts) and £1089 (cash). If we allow for inflation (Figure 2.3) the figures are £1417 for equities, £31 for gilts and £50 for the building society account.

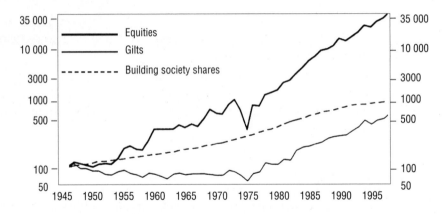

Figure 2.2 Barclays investment funds, net income reinvested nominal terms

These long-term trends can also be represented by a calculation of the annual returns broken down into their capital and income components (Table 2.1).

Barclays' conclusion is that the long-term real capital values for equities have increased by an average of 2.8 per cent per year over the entire period since 1918, or 2 per cent if we look at the post-Second World War period.

By contrast the real capital values for gilts have been falling for many years. Higher income yields provided some compensation, but

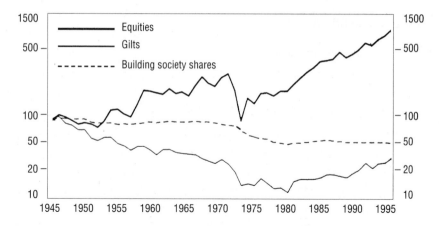

Figure 2.3 Barclays investment funds, net income reinvested real terms

investors who spent their income from gilts rather than reinvesting it would have seen a significant erosion in the real value of their wealth. Since 1990, however, the capital values for gilts have been improving slowly.

The study states: 'Dividends account for nearly two-thirds of total returns to equities over long periods of time. Gilts have been poor long-term investments but income from them has outweighed the reduction in capital values. Since 1990, however, the capital values of gilts have been improving'.

Table 2.1 Investment returns (allowing for inflation) (% p.a.)

	Equities			Gilts		
	Capital	Income	Total	Capital	Income	Total
Post-war period 1945–97	2.0	5.0	7.0	−7.3	7.6	0.3
Entire sample 1918–97	2.8	5.2	8.0	−4.2	6.3	2.1

Source: Barclays Investors

■ Stock selection

Income from equities or gilts?

Cantrade Investment provided the following succinct argument in favour of equities as a source of income, as well as capital growth (see the Sources section at the end of this Chapter).

> 'Equities represent part ownership of a business. Equity investors provide the core finance for the business and in return they receive dividends paid out of the company's profits. The remainder of the profits are retained by the company for reinvestment in its business, thus building up its assets, earning power and future dividend paying potential.
>
> The value of equities, therefore, rests on the value of the dividend flow which investors receive.
>
> If dividend payments grow over the years then, all other things being equal, the value of shares will rise too since the income stream will be more valuable and the total return (income plus capital growth) increases. Investors may buy and sell shares for short-term gain but in the final analysis equity investment is really about income.'

The interest on gilts will look attractive compared with the current income from equities but since gilt income is fixed, the flow of income from the gilt cannot rise over time in the same way as equity dividends (unless the gilt is index-linked – but here the initial income would be quite low).

> 'Eventually the cash value of the rising equity dividend will catch up and exceed the value of the fixed interest payment. Furthermore, the rising dividend flow will have pulled up the value of the shares whereas the capital value of the gilt will not have changed.
>
> This process is accelerated by inflation. By and large companies are able to absorb the costs of inflation by passing on cost increases to customers in the form of higher prices.'

This preserves the profitability of the business, whereas with fixed interest gilts your capital and income are exposed to inflation.

Stock selection refers to the process where the investment manager or private investor chooses individual securities. This topic is covered in Section 4 and in particular in Chapter 10.

At this stage, it is helpful to understand the jargon that investment managers love to use to confuse.

Don't imitate the big boys

It is rarely wise for a private investor to imitate the style of an institutional fund manager. The large pension funds, for example, are worth millions of pounds. Some run into billions. This means they can make money on minor price changes due to the sheer volume of their transactions.

Moreover, compared with a private client, institutional funds benefit from very low dealing costs and, in the case of pension and charity funds, automatic exemption from capital gains tax and most income tax. This means that what might trigger a buy or sell transaction in the institutional market often should be interpreted as a much more cautious 'hold' position by the private investor.

DIFFERENT STYLES OF INSTITUTIONAL FUND MANAGEMENT

It is also helpful to understand the tactical and strategic techniques employed by institutional managers. These may not be appropriate for your own portfolio, but will certainly be employed by those managing your collective funds.

For dedicated enthusiasts keen to employ suitable strategic investment techniques for private investors, a more advanced book on investment, such as Gillian O'Connor's *A Guide to Stockpicking* is an excellent guide (for details see page 277).

The following descriptions are intended as a broad guide only.

■ Active managers

Active investment managers aim to increase a fund's value by deviating from a specific benchmark – for example a stockmarket index. There are two basic techniques used in active stock selection.

The starting point for active managers who adopt a *bottom up* approach is the company in which the manager may invest. The manager will look at in-house and external research on the company's history and potential future prospects. This will include an examination of the strength of the balance sheet, the company's trading history, the management's business strategy and the price/earnings ratio (the market price of a share divided by the company's earnings/profits per share in its latest 12-month trading period).

From the company analysis the manager will proceed to look at the general performance and prospects for that sector (for example oil, retailers and so on) and then take into consideration national and international economic factors.

The *top down* manager works in reverse, looking first at the international and national economic factors that might affect economic growth in a country, geographic area (for example the 'Tiger' economies of south east Asia) or economic category (emerging markets, for example) and gradually work down to the individual companies.

Among private investors, the *fundamental analyst* focuses almost exclusively on individual companies and would tend to disregard the economic climate and market conditions.

The *technical analyst*, also known as a *chartist*, concentrates on historical price movements and uses these charts as a way of reading future movements in share prices.

■ Passive managers

Passive managers aim to track or replicate a benchmark. This style is also known as *index tracking*. It may sound simple but in practice this is a complex process based on emulating the performance of a particular stockmarket index by buying all, or a wide sample, of the constituent shares.

The passive manager does not consider the merits of each stock, of different sectors and economic cycles. If it is in the index then it must be represented in the fund. To date index-tracking funds have done very well compared with actively managed funds, largely because the passive manager's charges are very low in comparison with the active manager.

Passive management becomes very complex when the process tries to outstrip the index returns by deviating in a specific way. This is known as *quantitative management.*

Sources

> *Barclays Stockbrokers Investment Study* is available from Barclays Stockbrokers, Ebbgate House, 2 Swan Lane, London EC4R 3TS. Tel: 0171 956 3511. Cantrade Investments' *Compendium of Stockmarket Investment for the Private Investor,* for details contact Cantrade at 4 Chiswell Street, Finsbury Square, London EC1Y 4UP. Tel: 0171 614 8000.

Summary

- 'Securities' refers to UK equities, overseas equities, gilts and bonds.

- If a company wants to raise finance it can issue shares, which represent a share in the ownership; or bonds, which are a form of debt and behave like a sophisticated IOU.

- Shares and bonds have sub-classes which have different characteristics and can be used to achieve different investment aims.

- If you want to match or beat inflation, historically you would have had to invest in equities.

- The higher risk/return characteristic of equities is known as the equity risk premium.

- Inflation has a major impact on the real return provided by your investments.

- Equities are only suitable for the medium to long term due to their volatility and the cost of investing.

- The reinvestment of dividends increases your return substantially.

- It is important to understand but not to imitate the large institutional fund managers.

GETTING STARTED

Section 2

3

How to choose your investment adviser

- Which type of advisory service?
- Stockbroker services
- Your stockbroker's resources
- Selecting your adviser
- How to pay for your advice
- Investor protection

At a glance

In the complex world of investment it is helpful to remember that there are two major factors which affect your return. The first is *performance* – and more is said about this in Section 4. The second is the *level of charges*. This includes purchase costs, the regular charges imposed by fund management groups (for example the annual charge on unit trusts) and, if relevant, your adviser's fees.

Very experienced investors enjoy making their own decisions based on their own research. You can also get a lot of fun if you join an *investment club*, where you can exchange ideas and invest modest amounts as a group. It is cheering to note that the collective wisdom of many clubs enables them to achieve better performance than the experts. These clubs are discussed in Chapter 20.

With or without other private investors to help you, if you are a beginner, you probably need an adviser to guide you or make the investment decisions on your behalf. Even more experienced investors may not have the time to run their portfolio unaided.

This Chapter looks at the wide range of advisers authorised under the Financial Services Act. It explains the different levels of advice on offer and highlights some of the main points to consider. The contact details for all of the trade associations are set out in Chapter 20. These associations will send you either a complete directory of their members or, in some cases, a list of their members in your area.

WHICH TYPE OF ADVISORY SERVICE?

Your choice of adviser will depend to a large extent on the type of service you need and the amount you have to invest. For example, if you want an advisory service for a portfolio of shares you will go to stockbroker. If you want a unit or investment trust and you are happy to go to just one fund manager, then you can buy direct, or go to one of several thousand independent financial advisers.

The term *independent financial adviser* covers many different types and styles of firms ranging from the one-man band with limited resources and qualifications to the well-resourced professional firms of chartered accountants, actuaries and solicitors which specialise in financial services. Even here the boundaries between independence and 'tied' blur, as more and more firms launch their own range of funds.

> **TIP** Many advisers are not independent. This does not mean that they will necessarily give inferior advice, but it does mean that the range of products on which they can advise is limited.

Step one, therefore, is to know what an adviser can and cannot do. This is determined largely by the way firms are authorised and regulated.

The *Financial Services Act 1986* requires all companies involved in managing and selling investments to be authorised by one of several self-regulatory organisations. These are in the process of merging under the new 'super regulator' – the Financial Services Authority. For more details on regulation see Chapter 20.

Under the Act advisers are divided into different categories.

■ Company and appointed representatives

These advisers are not independent. *Company representatives*, as the name suggests, work for just one company. Traditionally, company representatives were only paid when they made a sale. This put them under tremendous pressure to sell the products that preferably paid the best commission rates, but in any event, to sell something.

Clearly, this does not encourage good practice, and today most companies pay representatives a basic salary which is topped up by bonuses related to sales, in a bid to distance themselves from the image of the pushy, foot in the door salesman.

Appointed representatives are companies that have a contract with a financial institution – a life assurance company, for example – under which they agree to sell exclusively one or more of that institution's products in return for an agreed level of sales commission.

Rather confusingly, the appointed representative may act independently in other non-investment related product lines. For example, a building society will conduct its own lending and borrowing business but might only sell the endowments or personal equity plans of one institution.

The main point to note about company and appointed representatives is that they are authorised only to discuss the products of the company they represent. They are not authorised under the Financial Services Act to tell you whether their products are competitive compared with what you could get elsewhere, in terms of cost and performance.

It might be convenient to buy all your financial products from one supplier but frankly it's a bit of a gamble.

■ Independent financial advisers

Independent advisers in theory should have a thorough knowledge of the whole investment and insurance market and select the most appropriate products for your requirements in terms of risk, investment aims, performance and charges.

One of the encouraging developments in financial services is the increasing emphasis placed on qualifications and training. All advisers must pass at least one basic competence test in order to deal with the public.

In addition there are several associations that require members to undertake specific training and also run some highly professional examinations. Two worth noting are the Society of Financial Advisers, a professional body set up by the Chartered Insurance Institute, and the Institute of Financial Planning.

■ The professionals

Many firms of professional advisers now offer a complete range of financial services. In addition to stockbrokers, chartered accountants and solicitors are particularly active in financial services (see Chapter 20).

STOCKBROKER SERVICES

If investment management is your primary requirement you should consider a Stock Exchange firm. These firms currently are regulated by the *Securities and Futures Association* which has a register of members who are qualified to deal with the public. For this they must have passed the Registered Representative exam and been vetted by the association. The Securities Institute runs a range of voluntary exams and it is worth looking for those who have passed the Securities Industry Diploma which covers private client investment advice.

> If investment management is your primary requirement you should consider a Stock Exchange firm.

The *Association of Private Client Investment Managers and Stockbrokers* (APCIMS) represents well over 90 per cent of private client stockbrokers as well as an increasing number of other investment managers. Members have direct access to the stockmarket for buying and selling shares. The APCIMS directory of members (see page 271) provides a brief guide to the services offered by its member firms and gives you an indication of the minimum size of portfolio accepted by the firm.

In theory there are three types of stockbroker service, although in practice the boundaries between advisory and discretionary blur, and many investors require a combination of the two. The following definitions, therefore, are intended only as a guide:

■ Dealing or 'execution-only'

This service is designed for investors who do not require advice but who need a stockbroker to buy and sell shares for them. Some stockbrokers specialise in this low cost, no frills service and offer competitive rates and a rapid service. Do remember though, with an execution-only service you will get information on prices of shares but the broker will offer no comment or opinion on the merits of your choice. So don't expect a phone call even if your broker has a hot tip.

■ Advisory

With an advisory service, usually you would make the buying and selling decisions yourself based on a combination of your own ideas and the advice of your manager.

In practice there are different types of advisory service. You may want a stockbroker to advise on the sale and purchase of your shares. Alternatively, you may want a more comprehensive service to include advice on capital gains tax and to provide regular valuations of your portfolio.

The main point to remember is that an advisory manager will not take any investment decisions without your authority, although he or she will give you an opinion. Whether you contact your broker at regular intervals or he or she phones you with tips is a matter of preference. A mixture of both is probably pragmatic.

■ Discretionary

If you want your stockbroker to make all the decisions for you then you need a discretionary or portfolio management service.

> If you want your stockbroker to make all the decisions for you then you need a discretionary or portfolio management service.

This does not mean you lose control entirely. You and your manager will have meetings to discuss your current financial circumstances, your investment aims and any ethical views you may have. Your discretionary manager will work with this plan and keep you up to date with changes in your portfolio. Your manager should send you a contract note every time a transaction takes place and regular portfolio valuations.

■ Comprehensive financial planning

In addition to investment management many stockbrokers offer a broader financial planning service. This can cover tax, pensions, mortgages, life assurance, school fees, inheritance tax, cash and deposits.

YOUR STOCKBROKER'S RESOURCES

The main factor which influences a private investor's choice of stockbroker tends to be personal recommendation, which is very useful but difficult to quantify and compare with other firms. A useful benchmark is to examine the firm's resources and the quality of the research on which your stockbroker bases the decision to buy, sell and hold.

Ask about the *internal research* carried out by the firm's *analysts*. Smaller firms of stockbrokers may not employ full-time analysts, but the larger firms are likely to have several dedicated to UK companies – the primary market for private client direct equity investment.

To supplement this research the firm probably will use the monthly *Estimate Directory*, which provides aggregate earnings and company forecasts for about 1300 UK companies covering the FTSE All-Share index and the Alternative Investment Market.

The firm may also have an analyst for each of the major international markets, but here the aim will be to identify the best collective funds (for example unit and investment trusts) rather than individual companies. In practice, stockbrokers may only advise very wealthy clients to consider investing directly in individual shares outside the UK, because this can be costly and is likely to result in a risky concentration of assets.

The second source of research is the *market makers* through which the stockbroker buys and sells shares. As a general rule the market makers do not make an explicit charge for the research they provide to stockbrokers but regard it as something of a quid pro quo in return for a firm's business. However, regulatory rules forbid any tied arrangements since the stockbroker's priority is to find the best dealing price.

The level of research provided depends on how valuable a stockbroker is regarded as a client. Market makers may provide the smaller firms of stockbrokers and financial advisers with weekly reports on companies and sectors and on unit and investment trusts. They might also provide the bigger stockbrokers with daily commentary and, for the favoured few, an on-line service which would be re-routed around the entire firm.

The value of this research is best viewed in the context of the market maker's own resources. The private client stockbroking arm of a major bank, for example, would have access to the parent company's research which could be generated by several hundred investment managers and analysts worldwide.

If you are particularly interested in the quality of the institutional research your stockbroker uses, you can check how the market makers' analysts are rated. The most detailed information is published by **Extel Business Information** (see the Sources section at the end of the Chapter). Extel's annual survey ranks the analysts of 230 firms in the UK, covering 97 sectors.

Stockbrokers tend to regard the market makers' research as raw data which must be interpreted for the private client market. As mentioned in Chapter 2, the tips that may be worth acting on for a large pension fund may be wholly inappropriate for the private investor. For example, a small movement in a share price might trigger a decision to buy or sell for a large fund where the economies of scale would make it worthwhile. For the private investor the small price change would not be worth chasing.

It is worth checking whether your stockbroker's analysts actually visit the companies they recommend. Typically a team might select 50 or 60 stocks from among the top FTSE 100 or 350 companies, looking for consistent earnings and dividend growth, a clear business aim and strategy, a reasonable allocation of cash to internal investment and a decent return to shareholders in the form of dividends.

Some stockbrokers publish a model private client portfolio (see Chapter 9). The firm would usually send this to clients every month, although it would probably be updated daily for internal purposes. Recommendations would be based on the same profit forecasts used by the institutional managers but for the private client the firm would be less likely to recommend short-term changes for potentially small profits per share.

SELECTING YOUR ADVISER

Once you have decided on the type of adviser or stockbroker service you require you need to draw up a shortlist and make the final selection.

The following checklist may help you in your search for a financial adviser or planner, as well as a stockbroker. Before you start do check with the Financial Services Authority (FSA) that the firm is authorised and registered with the appropriate regulator. Also check the adviser's level of qualifications and find out how highly these are rated by the examining body.

- How long has the firm been trading? (New firms should be investigated thoroughly.)
- What is the company's turnover?
- Who are the directors and what relevant experience do they have?
- Does the firm offer the right level of expertise for your requirements?
- How many clients does the firm have?
- What criteria does the firm use to select an investment company?
- How does it assess performance, charges and commercial strength?
- How much will the advice cost per hour, including VAT?
- If your adviser is away, who will look after your business?
- What methods does the firm have for dealing with complaints and disputes?

In a survey carried out among its readers by *Investors Chronicle* (see the Sources section at the end of the Chapter), the following features were identified as the most important in a stockbroker's service:

- efficiency in carrying out orders
- ease of contact by phone
- dealing with paperwork efficiently
- prompt settlement
- low charges
- real-time dealing
- good reputation

- friendliness, helpfulness
- in-depth market knowledge
- available outside normal working hours
- regular newsletters/ seminars
- Internet/online dealing.

Many stockbrokers use their own funds to achieve exposure to specialist markets, smaller companies and foreign investment, for example. This is not necessarily a bad thing, and the funds may well be among the best in their field (ask to see performance statistics from an independent measurer like Standard & Poor's Micropal or HSW Hindsight, for example).

However, as a general rule, you are more likely to achieve better returns if your stockbroker is free to choose from the whole range of funds available.

■ More than one stockbroker?

Some investors like to retain a good financial planner, who will keep the whole of the family's finances in order, and to use a stockbroker for the direct equity selection.

> Some investors like to retain a good financial planner, who will keep the whole of the family's finances in order, and to use a stockbroker for the direct equity selection.

This approach makes a lot of sense, but you should think carefully before you decide to split your assets and appoint two or more stockbrokers. While it can be reassuring to know that you have limited the damage if one stockbroker underperforms, there are additional costs involved, both in terms of annual fees and dealing costs. Also you could end up with duplication if the brokers decide to use some of the same shares and funds.

HOW TO PAY FOR YOUR ADVICE

Independent advisers may work on a purely commission or on a fee basis. Many will accept both. In some cases commission payments represent a fair exchange for the work undertaken. In others, particularly where you want to invest a large sum, the commission will be out of proportion to the work. Moreover, purists argue that what you should pay is a fee for the advice, not a commission for the purchase of a financial product.

Professional firms usually do not accept sales commissions and where these are paid – for example by a unit trust company – the commission is offset against your fees.

Stockbroker charges fall into two categories. First there are the commissions which are charged on the purchase or sale of securities. Usually this is a percentage of the money invested. Alternatively the firm may charge a fee once or twice a year for a continuing investment management service. Some firms use a combination of both fee and dealing commissions.

Finally, you may be able to negotiate performance-related fees. If you wish to do so, first read Chapter 17 which discusses this topic.

INVESTOR PROTECTION

Under the Financial Services Act there is an investors' compensation scheme which pays out if you lose money through an adviser's fraud or negligence. However, it won't pay out if your selected shares and funds do not perform well.

One problem with the scheme is that the maximum payout is £48 000. For many investors this is too low and therefore it is important to check your adviser has appropriate professional indemnity (PI) insurance. Typically, the firm's PI insurance should be able to pay up to £1 million per valid claim.

Sources

The Estimate Directory is published by Edinburgh Financial Publishing. Tel: 0131 538 7070. *Extel Ranking of Investment Analysts Survey*, is published by Extel, FT Information. Tel: 0171 825 8000. *Investors Chronicle Stockbroker Awards*, published 19 September 1997.

Summary

- The two main factors that affect your return are performance and the cost of your investment, including the advice.

- You can learn a great deal from other investors if you join an investment club.

- Unless you are sure of your ability to research the market thoroughly, seek independent advice.

- Consider which type of firm is suitable – for example do you need a stockbroker to advise on direct equity investment or would you be happy with one of the firms of advisers that specialise in collective investments such as unit and investment trust plans?

- Check in particular the level of qualifications held by the staff and the firm's research resources.

- Ideally pay for your advice by fees rather than commission as this removes any potential bias in the firm's recommendations.

- Check the firm's level of professional indemnity insurance.

4

Risk and your investments

- Inflation risk
- Capital risk
- The importance of spreading risk
- Your risk assessment kit
- Tax efficiency

At a glance

This Chapter explains how to identify your short-term and longer-term investment goals. Crucial to this process is a clear understanding of your attitude to that four-letter word 'risk'.

The technical definition of risk, in financial terms, is 'the standard deviation of the (arithmetic) average return'. This is very handy for statisticians, but for most private investors, its meaning is more simple: the biggest risk is the loss of your original capital.

There is no such thing as a 'safe' investment or saving scheme but some are safer than others in terms of protecting your original capital. On the other hand, they may not protect you from inflation.

The two chief dangers for private investors, therefore, are *capital loss* and *inflation*.

We mentioned in Chapter 2 the equity risk premium – that is, the payoff you may receive for taking the risk of investing in equities. Clearly, then, when you take a risk you expect a commensurate reward.

> Risk is very subjective. Like beauty, it is in the eye of the beholder.

The reward for investors is the *total return*, which is usually expressed as a percentage increase of the original investment. This may be a combination of income (or yield) plus capital growth (or rise in the market price).

In conclusion, risk is very subjective. Like beauty, it is in the eye of the beholder. To help you gauge your attitude to risk it is helpful to consider the twin evils, capital loss and inflation, mentioned above.

INFLATION RISK

Savings and investments that expose you to inflation risk usually fall into the 'safe' category. For example, we all tend to think of building society deposit accounts as risk free. But are they? If you are worried about the risk of losing your original capital, then, provided you stick to the well regulated UK building societies, you can put your money on *deposit* and your original capital will indeed be safe.

Your capital will not diminish, indeed it will grow, assuming income is reinvested. However, the growth will be modest, and in real (that is, inflation-adjusted) terms, it may even be negative, depending on the rate of inflation.

This does not mean you should ignore deposit accounts. In practice they play a very important part in providing you with an easy access home for emergency funds and for short-term savings where capital security is your primary goal (see Chapter 3). The point about access is important. You will find that in order to get a better rate of interest you may need to tie your money up for one, three or 12 months, for example, while the particular deposits may be run as postal accounts to minimise the borrower's overheads.

As a general conclusion, over the medium to long term, deposit accounts are synonymous with *capital erosion*.

Bonds, which are issued mainly by the Government (gilts) and companies (corporate bonds – see Chapter 15), can offer the prospect of higher returns than a deposit account but there is a risk that the borrower may dip into your capital in order to maintain the flow of income. Also, like deposits, conventional bonds do not offer any guaranteed protection against increases in inflation.

> When you see the statutory wealth warning that your investment can go down as well as up, take it seriously.

CAPITAL RISK

Historically, if you wanted to match or beat inflation over the long term you would have had to invest in *equities*. However, with equities, unless your fund offers a guarantee (and these can be costly – see page 173), your capital certainly is at risk. So, when you see the statutory wealth warning that your investment can go down as well as up, take it seriously.

THE IMPORTANCE OF SPREADING RISK

Risk can be managed in different ways. You can concentrate it in a single investment or spread it over a wide range. For example, if you invest all your money in a single share and it does well you will be in clover. If the company goes bust you could lose the lot.

It is wise to spread risk by investing in a range of shares either directly or through collective funds such as unit and investment trusts. Note, however, that even with collective funds the risk rating varies considerably. At one end of the spectrum are the higher risk specialist funds which tend to be small and managed on an aggressive basis. At the other, more comfortable end, are the large UK or international equity funds which offer greater immunity to the capricious behaviour of stockmarkets. Bear in mind, though, that even the most broadly diversified funds will be hit when stockmarkets crash.

You can protect yourself further from risk if you diversify into different asset classes – for example, instead of just investing in different types of equities, you could include some bonds, gilts, deposits and, possibly, property in your portfolio. These behave in a different way from equities and therefore do not share the same vulnerabilities to certain economic cycles.

YOUR RISK ASSESSMENT KIT

Before you consider the various investment options outlined in the following chapters, you need to get acquainted with a set of benchmarks which help you judge the merits of an asset class, product or scheme and to compare it with other alternatives.

It doesn't matter if you are looking at deposit accounts, collective funds, direct equity and bond investments or high risk investments such as enterprise investment schemes, which invest in the shares of unquoted trading companies. In each and every case the benchmarks will help you judge whether this is right for you.

The benchmarks will also help you to focus on the important fundamentals as opposed to the bells and whistles which are used so successfully in marketing literature to make products and services look more attractive, safer, tax efficient, or ethical than they really are.

These are the most important questions you should always ask:

- *Aims:* what are the stated aims and benefits of the investment? Do these fit in with your own aims and objectives?
- *Returns:* compare the potential net returns of the investment with after-tax returns on very low risk products such as 120-day notice building society deposit accounts, short-term conventional gilts and National Savings. Is the potential outperformance of your chosen investment really worth the additional risk?
- *Alternatives:* which other investments share similar characteristics? Are they simpler, cheaper, or less risky?
- *Investment period:* for how long can you genuinely afford to invest your money? Compare this with the stated investment term and then check how the charges undermine returns in the early years. Also make sure you know about any exit penalties and remember that anything described as a 'loyalty bonus' usually acts as a penalty in disguise if you don't stick out the investment for the required period.
- *Risk:* what is the risk that the investment will not achieve either its own stated aims or your own private objectives? What is the most you can lose? Is your capital and/or income stream at risk? What is the likely effect of inflation? Find out how the investment is regulated and what happens if the firm/investment manager goes bust.
- *Cost:* look at the establishment costs and ongoing charges. Watch out for high annual management charges on collective funds, particularly for long-term investments, as these will seriously undermine your return. With direct equity portfolios watch out for the high transaction charges and turnover costs associated with 'portfolio churning'.
- *Tax:* the way the fund and you, the investor, are taxed is important because it will affect your ultimate return. Check for income tax

and capital gains tax implications and consider how these might change over the investment period.

TAX EFFICIENCY

Tax is worth a further mention. Many investments covered in the next section are tax efficient for at least one, sometimes several, categories of investor. In some cases you benefit from income tax relief at your top rate. In others you may qualify for tax relief on income and dividends at the 'savings rate' of 20 per cent.

But if there is one piece of advice central to successful investing, it is this: never invest purely for the sake of obtaining tax relief. Your investments must be suited to your circumstances and must be able to stand up with or without the tax breaks. You only have to recall the hundreds of ill-advised investors who ploughed into the now infamous early business expansion schemes (BES) – and lost virtually everything – to see that this caveat makes sense.

Summary

- Whatever the investment, check whether your money is at risk from capital loss or capital erosion due to inflation.

- The total return from capital growth and income is your reward for taking a risk.

- Diversification reduces risk.

- Always use the risk assessment benchmarks provided to assess a new investment opportunity and to compare it with alternatives.

Section 3

SAVINGS
AND INVESTMENT
PRODUCTS

5

Savings schemes and income-generating products

- Your investment aims
- Easy access deposits for rainy days
- Safety at a price
- Tax status
- Choice of products
- A rising income
- Purchased life annuities

At a glance

In a good financial plan there is always a place for simple deposits to house your emergency, instant-access funds. Many investors, particularly the retired, also need other income-generating investments which guarantee to protect their original capital.

The object of the exercise, therefore, is to identify the right products for the job and accept their shortcomings. As mentioned in the previous chapter, the main demon to bedevil this category of products is inflation.

If you are still not convinced about the risk from inflation, consider this. Since the Second World War annual inflation has averaged over 6 per cent. At this rate, in retirement if your annual investment income from deposits, gilts, and bond funds is a level £10 000, its real purchasing power after just seven years will shrink to £6450.

YOUR INVESTMENT AIMS

As we discovered in the previous chapter, the term 'safe', like 'risk', is subjective and means different things to different people. It might be 'safe' to shift your pension fund into medium-dated and long-dated gilts in the run up to retirement, but it would be far from prudent to adopt the same strategy for a personal pension in your early forties when the investment period could last 25 years.

The phrase *reckless conservatism* aptly sums up the hidden risks in going for investments which appear to be safe but which in fact are wholly inappropriate and expose you unnecessarily to the very serious risk of inflation over the long term. The trick is to recognise *capital guarantees* for what they are. Use them wisely, but avoid the trap of investing too much in products which are not designed to provide long-term capital growth.

EASY ACCESS DEPOSITS FOR RAINY DAYS

All investors need an immediate access emergency fund to pay for unforeseen events such as sudden repairs on the house and car. However, this is not a role for mainstream investments such as unit and investment trusts or directly held equities. If you have to pull out of equities or an equity fund in a hurry you could lose money, particularly in the early years when your investment is 'working off' the effect of the purchase costs. Moreover, many collective funds impose an exit charge if you quit during the first few years.

The traditional home for cash is the *building society*, although many other borrowers are coming into the market, such as supermarket chains and life assurance companies. Go for the best rates but avoid the common mistake of keeping too large a reserve when part of your money could be earning a potentially better return elsewhere.

The size of your emergency fund should be determined by your monthly expenditure, your liabilities and the level of 'padding' you feel is appropriate for your lifestyle and peace of mind.

As a very rough guide it is worth keeping three times your monthly outgoings in an account which has one week's notice. Accounts offering a higher rate of interest with, say, three months' notice, can be used for known future capital expenditure – for example a new car, a holiday or school fees.

If you manage your cash flow carefully then you can feed money from your other investments to your higher interest rate account well in advance of the dates these more substantial bills fall due. Do keep a regular check on your longer-term deposits as rates change frequently.

> **As a very rough guide it is worth keeping three times your monthly outgoings in an account which has one week's notice.**

Probably the best source of up-to-date information on savings products is *Moneyfacts*,* a leading provider of mortgage and savings data. Its monthly guide covers savings accounts, children's accounts, cheque accounts, credit cards, store cards, bonds, gilts, mortgages, National Savings, and loans. *Moneyfacts* also publishes a separate monthly guide to life assurance and pension funds.

In addition, you can find useful information on the best rates for a variety of savings accounts in the personal finance pages of the weekend newspapers. Most papers publish useful summaries of best buys for different types of products and accounts.

SAFETY AT A PRICE

Fixed income products are something of a gamble. The risk here is that you lock in for, say, five years, to what looks like an attractive guaranteed interest rate, only to find that a few months later interest rates rise and your fixed rate now looks uncompetitively low. What's more, you can't get out without incurring a penalty.

Of course, the reverse is also true. You could lock in before rates plummet and will be very pleased you did what turned out to be the right thing. However, before you take a punt on interest rates, remember that most experts consistently make errors in their predictions so this apparently rock-solid product can have a nasty sting in the tail.

TIP For most people *inflation-proofing* is an essential element in their income-generating portfolio of investments, even if inflation remains comparatively low.

The purchasing power of £100 would be just £64 after 15 years of inflation at 3 per cent and £48 if the inflation rate is 5 per cent.

So, the hidden cost of income guarantees is a reduction in the *real purchasing power* of your capital. As a rule, guaranteed income products exclude the prospect of capital growth. Moreover, with some products part of your capital could be used to bolster income if returns are lower than expected. Exposure to this type of investment should be limited.

> If investing for income growth is a better way of describing your requirements, then you should include *some* equity investments within your portfolio.

If investing for *income growth* is a better way of describing your requirements, then you should include *some* equity investments within your portfolio. Chapter 9 outlines the *asset allocation of income, growth and balanced portfolios* and you will see that even in the income model there is a substantial UK equity component.

Clearly, equities expose you to the risk of capital loss, but provided you aim for diversity and avoid the exotic, your main concern will be fluctuations in income rather than the fear of losing everything. Section 4 of this book is devoted to sensible asset allocation and share selection.

TAX STATUS

Tax status is a crucial factor in your choice of savings products. For example, the income from National Savings (NS) Pensioners' Bonds is paid gross, but the income from insurance company-guaranteed bonds in effect is paid net of basic rate tax because this is deducted within the fund and you cannot reclaim it if you are a non-taxpayer.

In theory this should make the NS bonds a clear winner for non-taxpayers, but the slightly higher income available on the insurance bonds can offset this tax advantage. Depending on rates at the time, non-taxpayers should consider both products.

CHOICE OF PRODUCTS

The following brief guide outlines the choice of income-paying savings and investments.

■ National Savings

National Savings offers a wide range of accounts and bonds designed for every age and tax status. *Income bonds*, for example, have a three-month notice period for withdrawals and the bonds must be held for a minimum period of one year. If you don't give the required notice, you lose 90 days' interest. For savers looking for capital growth there is also a *Capital bond* which offers a fixed return.

NS Savings Certificates can be either fixed rate or index linked and both run for five years. The maximum investment per person is £10 000 per issue. At the time of writing there were two issues (one index linked, one fixed rate). This gives a maximum of £20 000 per person, £40 000 per couple. You can double this to £80 000 if each spouse holds the maximum in trust for the other spouse. All returns are tax free.

NS Pensioner bonds can be bought by anyone over age 60 and offer a monthly tax-free income guaranteed for five years. One of the attractions of NS products is that you can buy them through the Post Office and there are no charges. Bear in mind though that NS changes its interest rates less frequently than building societies so you should always compare rates before committing yourself.

For details of the complete range of NS products ask at your local Post Office or use the contact details provided at the end of this Chapter. Remember, NS does not pay commission to advisers – which may explain why many commission-based advisers fail to recommend these worthy products!

■ Tax-exempt special savings accounts (Tessa)

These five-year savings accounts are due to disappear in 1999 when they are absorbed into the new Individual Savings Accounts (ISAs – see Chapter 7), although existing accounts will be allowed to complete their five-year course. After this you would have to transfer your Tessa into the new ISA if you want to retain the tax-free status. The overall maximum limit for ISAs is £50 000.

Remember that Tessas are not specifically designed to generate income, but it is possible to make partial withdrawals of the interest and retain the tax-exempt status. Most Tessas pay a variable interest rate, although a few societies offer a fixed rate for either one year at a time or for the full five years. Unfortunately, switching between Tessas is rarely worthwhile due to the transfer charges or the loss of interest penalties imposed by providers.

The total maximum over five years is £9000, divided as follows: up to £3000 in year one, and £1800 in years two to five (but only up to £600 in year five if you paid maximum contributions in years one to four). If you prefer you can make regular savings of up to £150 per month.

Currently, if your first account has matured, provided you act within six months of the maturity date, you can transfer the capital (up to a maximum of £9000) to a new account and enjoy a further five years tax-free growth. If the transfer is for less than £9000, you can make additional contributions to your new Tessa to bring it up to the £9000 maximum.

■ Gilts and bonds

For more details on gilts and bonds, see Chapters 2 and 15. Bonds are like an IOU. You lend the money and in return the borrower (companies in the case of corporate bonds and the Government in the case of gilts) promises to repay the loan in full at a fixed date in the future.

With conventional gilts and bonds the borrower pays interest, known as the *coupon*, twice a year at a fixed rate. As a general rule, the longer the term, the higher the rate – but also the greater the potential drop in the real value of your capital by the time you get it back.

From April 1998, all gilts pay interest gross. Previously this was only possible if you bought through the *National Savings Stock Register* (NSSR). The NSSR still remains a particularly convenient way to make purchases and it is also the cheapest method. The main drawback for active investors is that NSSR applications must be made by post, so you will not know in advance what the buying price will be.

Both gilts and qualifying bonds (not convertibles and preference shares) are free of capital gains tax on any profits because the 'return' is classed as income.

For details on how to assess the income from gilts and bonds, see Chapter 15.

■ Guaranteed income bonds

Guaranteed income bonds (GIBs) are offered by many insurance companies – usually for a period of one to five years. The longer you are prepared to commit your money the higher the income.

Do note the point mentioned above on taxation. Interest on GIBs is paid net of basic rate tax and this is not reclaimable even by non-taxpayers. However, since these bonds generally pay slightly higher rates of income than the tax-free NS products it is worth considering both options.

The minimum investment in GIBs is usually about £5000 but some companies offer higher rates if you invest £20 000 or even £50 000. Income is paid monthly, but if you can manage with annual payments you can secure a slightly higher rate.

Two other options that guarantee to return your original capital are *National Savings premium bonds* and *guaranteed equity bonds*. However, both are unsuitable for income seekers. In the case of premium bonds, no income is paid and you have to rely on the probabilities of winning on a fairly regular basis in order to earn the equivalent of interest on your investment.

> Many investors, particularly pensioners, need to squeeze as much income as possible from their savings, yet at the same time are reluctant to take any risks with the capital.

Guaranteed equity bonds use derivatives to guarantee a percentage of stockmarket growth. A few of these funds offer to pay an income but only when the relevant index has achieved a specific return. For more details on guaranteed funds, see Chapter 13.

A RISING INCOME

Many investors, particularly pensioners, need to squeeze as much income as possible from their savings, yet at the same time are reluctant to take any risks with the capital.

The problem with this objective is that inflation eats into the real value of both capital and income. This is why most advisers recommend that income seekers should have at least some equity-based investments in their portfolios.

But if you genuinely believe you cannot afford the risk of ordinary shares it is worth considering a halfway house – that is, investments which offer some capital protection and a rising income. This category of investments includes index-linked gilts, corporate index-linked debentures, escalator bonds, the stepped preference shares of split capital investment trusts and the corporate bond personal equity plan (although see comments on the demise of Peps in Chapter 7).

■ Index-linked gilts

These bonds are issued by the Government and guarantee to increase in line with the retail price index (RPI) both the six-monthly interest payments and the 'nominal' or original capital investment which is returned to you on the redemption date.

Since the starting RPI figure used is eight months before the date of issue, the final value of the investment can be calculated precisely seven months before redemption (RPI figures are published one month in arrears).

Don't forget that the guarantees offered by gilts or corporate bonds only apply if you hold the bonds to maturity. Like conventional gilts (see Chapters 5 and 15), the index-linked variety are traded actively, so the price and real value of the income generated can fluctuate significantly between the issue and redemption dates.

Investors seeking absolute guarantees from their income-yielding portfolios may be tempted to put all their money in gilts. In this case you might be better off with a balance between conventional gilts, which offer a comparatively high fixed income but no index linking of the capital value, and index-linked gilts, which offer a low initial income but protect both the income and capital from rising inflation.

■ Corporate index-linked debentures

These bonds work in a similar way to index-linked gilts, paying interest twice a year which, along with the original capital investment, is linked to the RPI. The main benefit of the corporate version is that the coupon or interest rate is higher than for gilts. This is to compensate for the slightly higher risk in lending to companies rather than the Government.

There are not many index-linked corporate bonds around and so advisers recommend that most investors should stick to gilts due to the poor liquidity (difficult of buying and, in particular, of selling) in the corporate market.

■ Escalator bonds

These bonds, available from certain building societies, share some of the characteristics of gilts in that the account pays a pre-determined rate of interest for the first year and then increases that rate by a fixed amount for subsequent years. This type of investment could play a small part in your portfolio but the interest rates are unlikely to be sufficiently attractive to make it significantly better than gilts.

■ Stepped preference shares of split capital trusts

Investment trusts are discussed in Chapter 6. 'Stepped prefs' (in the jargon) offer an income which is guaranteed to rise each year at a fixed rate, and a fixed redemption price for the shares when the investment trust is wound up. Each trust offers a different yield and annual increase, depending on the nature of the underlying assets.

The factors to consider here are the risk profile of the trust's underlying assets, the current dividend yield, and the gross redemption yield – that is, the total return expressed as an annual percentage, assuming the share is bought at the present price and held to maturity.

The best source of information on all types of investment trusts is the *Association of Investment Trust Companies* (AITC), which publishes useful fact sheets and a Monthly Information Service, which provides a breakdown of all the member trusts and performance statistics. (For contact details, see page 273).

PURCHASED LIFE ANNUITIES

Annuities, sold by insurance companies, guarantee to pay a regular income for life in return for a lump sum investment. The annuity 'rate' – or the level of regular income you secure in return for your lump sum – will depend on several important factors including your life expectancy and interest rates.

Women tend to live longer than men so usually receive a lower income in return for the same level of investment. If you are in ill health you may be able to get a better rate if the insurance company assumes that your life expectancy is less than the average for your age. This is known as an ill health or 'impaired life' annuity.

The main point to remember with annuities is that unless you pay extra for a capital guarantee, once you hand over your money it is gone for good, even if you die the following day. Annuity rates are affected by interest rates and fluctuate considerably so do seek expert advice over the timing of the purchase and the choice of annuity company.

Sources

Moneyfacts is published monthly by Moneyfacts Publications. Annual subscription £48.50. Telephone 01692 500765. For a complimentary copy telephone 01692 500677 or write to Moneyfacts Publications, North Walsham, Norfolk NR28 0BD.

National Savings products are available from post offices but NS also has a sales information help line: 0645 645000. Current interest rates are given in a recorded message on the following numbers: South: London 0171 605 9483/9484; North: Blackpool 01253 723714; Scotland: Glasgow 0141 632 2766.

Summary

- The description 'safe' can lead you up the garden path if you fail to keep a clear focus on the specific risks you are trying to minimise or avoid altogether. A low or zero exposure to one risk – capital protection, for example – goes hand in hand with exposure to another risk, in this case inflation.

- Watch out for 'reckless conservatism' – the temptation to put your money into certain investments which appear to be safe but fail to protect you from the ravages of inflation over the long term.

- Check the hidden cost of income guarantees. You may face a reduction in the real purchasing power of your capital.

- Keep about three times your monthly outgoings in a deposit account which has one week's notice.

- Accounts offering a higher rate of interest with, say, three months' notice, can be used for known future capital expenditure – for example a new car or a holiday.

- For the longer term, consider National Savings, gilts (conventional and index linked), bonds, Tessas and guaranteed income bonds, among others.

6

Collective funds for equity investment

- Daunting choice
- The selection process
- Collective equity funds
- Unit trusts
- Investment trusts
- The difference between investment and unit trusts
- Unit trusts v insurance company bonds
- Mortgage endowments
- Offshore funds
- Open-ended investment companies

At a glance

As a very rough guide, investors with less than £100 000 to invest usually are advised to choose a range of collective funds rather than invest directly in equities. This is partly because you need a decent spread of equities to diversify and reduce risk, and partly because the cost of buying and selling would be uneconomic for a smaller portfolio.

In practice many investors hold individual shares because they belong to an employee share option scheme at work, or they received free shares when their building society or life assurance company demutualised.

Equally, investors with a large portfolio will often use collective funds to gain exposure to more specialist areas – for example smaller companies and overseas markets.

For most people, the biggest long-term investments are earmarked for some specific purpose – for example, to repay your mortgage, to pay school fees and to provide an income in retirement. However, it is important not to compartmentalise these investments but to include them in the overall portfolio planning.

This Chapter looks at the main choices of collective funds.

DAUNTING CHOICE

Ironically, one of the main problems you are likely to encounter with collective funds is the sheer number available. Some of these will qualify for certain tax-efficient wrappers such as pension plans and schemes, personal equity plans (Peps) and the Individual savings accounts (ISAs) which will replace Peps and Tessas in 1999.

> **Tax-efficient vehicles do not offer a magical solution to investment performance. What they do offer is a shelter from income tax, capital gains tax, or both.**

Tax-efficient vehicles do not offer a magical solution to investment performance. What they do offer is a shelter from income tax, capital gains tax, or both. If you run your own pension plan or Pep then you can invest in most asset classes and the returns will be enhanced due to the tax breaks.

The important point here is to set your investment goals first and only then to decide which types of assets are best held in the different tax-efficient plans.

THE SELECTION PROCESS

When it comes to selecting a good fund, there is plenty of advice on what not to do and very little on positive selection criteria, so what follows is to some extent subjective. No doubt over the years you will develop your own pet theories.

The financial press and several firms of consultants produce annual surveys which highlight the best and worst in the various categories of funds. You must take great care when you examine past performance statistics because these can be very misleading.

What the surveys do offer is some ideas on how to screen funds, so it is well worth checking out the methodology used in the most authoritative examples. A good all-rounder is the annual personal pension survey on unit-linked managed funds from consultant Bacon & Woodrow.* Unit-linked funds are similar to unit trusts in that you buy units in the collective fund and the price of those units rises and falls in line with the value of the underlying assets.

Interestingly, one of the chief findings of the 1997/98 Bacon &

Woodrow (B&W) survey was that institutional fund managers, which run the big company pension schemes, generally offer much better performance than the life assurance companies, which operate mainly in the retail sector.

According to B&W, there are three good reasons for this:

■ Few policyholders or their advisers know how to monitor performance properly, so retail managers are under less pressure and are scrutinised less rigorously than institutional managers.

■ The funds have poorly-defined, unmeasurable objectives, so there are no clear benchmarks against which performance can be judged.

■ The investment processes – asset allocation and stock selection – are weak.

■ The use of past performance statistics

B&W argues that past performance statistics are a useful aid to gauge future performance, provided you bear in mind the following important caveats:

■ they must be coupled with a clear understanding of how past performance was achieved;

■ they must be combined with an assessment of the current investment style of the management team; and

■ the individuals responsible for past performance must still be in place.

B&W looked at the investment return over five years of 249 unit-linked managed funds. (Managed funds are mainly a mixture of equities, gilts, bonds and cash. Some also include property.)

The risks taken to achieve these returns were also considered. This is important because a manager might be taking very high risks in order to achieve a good return, but the investor might not appreciate that the fund is potentially very volatile and could just as easily plummet if the risks do not pay off.

The survey excluded the following:

■ Funds with a below average performance.

■ Funds under £20 million ('insufficient scope for diversification').

■ Funds closed to new business.

- Funds which are not available through independent advisers (although private investors should not rule out the direct sales operations – some of them are very good).

- Funds which are not available on nil-commission terms. (B&W believes in fee-based advice and argues that plans which pay high sales commissions to advisers can be inflexible and may penalise investors who want to stop regular payments or retire early.)

Successful companies had to demonstrate to B&W that they had a clear, measurable investment objective which was set and met by the management team. They also had to demonstrate their capacity to take on new business and maintain the current quality of service.

Only 36 funds available through 27 companies cleared all the performance screens. These were then subjected to 'reduction in premium' analysis to show what percentage of each investment you pay to the company disappears in charges. B&W's favourites were then selected from the group of top performers which could offer modest charges.

No methodology is foolproof but this type of clear analysis is about as good as it gets.

COLLECTIVE EQUITY FUNDS

Two of the most popular types of collective funds in the UK, unit and investment trusts, plus a comparative newcomer, the open-ended investment company (OEIC), share many features in common and offer a similar broad investment scope. Experts believe that over the next few years OEICs may become as popular as unit trusts as more managers switch to the new vehicle.

Your choice will depend on the finer details.

UNIT TRUSTS

A unit trust is a collection of shares and/or bonds with a specific investment aim. The trust can, for example, aim to produce an income by investing in high-yielding UK equities and/or corporate bonds. Or it could aim to generate capital growth by investing in new or expanding industries or, more riskily, in emerging markets.

Unit trusts sold to the public are authorised by the chief financial services regulator, the Financial Services Authority. You may hear about another type – 'unauthorised' unit trusts, which are used as internal funds by financial institutions and are not marketed to the public. Unit trusts are 'open ended', which means they may create or cancel units on a daily basis depending on demand.

Investors purchase units in the fund, and the value of these units fluctuates directly in line with the value of the underlying assets. In this respect a unit trust functions in a similar way to other collective funds – insurance company bonds, for example – although the tax treatment for these two types of fund is quite different (see page 77).

■ Unit trust pricing

Currently unit trusts can be priced for dealing on a 'forward' or 'historic' basis. Where the fund deals on a forward basis orders are taken from investors and the price of units is determined by the next valuation. All larger trusts have a valuation point each day, often at noon. Many groups still deal on an historic price basis. This means they buy and sell using the price agreed at the last valuation point.

■ Investment scope of unit trusts

Unit trusts can invest in 'transferable securities' (securities which can be bought and sold on the open market) listed on any market that meets the criteria set out in the European Union's Undertakings for Collective Investment in Transferable Securities (UCITS) directive.

Basically, managers are free to decide which markets are suitable for their funds but they must ensure the markets operate regularly, are open to the public and offer the appropriate levels of liquidity.

Most funds invest mainly or wholly in equities, although the number of *corporate bond* funds, which invest in corporate bonds, preference shares and convertibles, among other assets, is growing rapidly. There are also *gilt funds*. Some advisers reckon it is comparatively easy and cheaper to select the right types of gilts for your circumstances direct from National Savings Stock Register (NSSR). The main drawback with the NSSR is that you have to deal by post and there are limits on the maximum size of transactions.

Some Peps, based on unit trusts, offer *capital guarantees* or guarantee to provide part of the rise in a stockmarket index and protect you from the falls. The guarantee is 'insured' through the use of certain types of *derivatives* – financial instruments which can be used to protect a fund's exposure to market fluctuations.

Always remember that guarantees carry a cost – in this case the price of the derivatives – which will be passed on to the investor through increased management charges – and the loss of the dividends. Some advisers argue that you might be better off gaining full exposure to an index through one of the *low-cost index tracking unit trusts* and limiting your exposure to risk by investing part of your capital in gilts or National Savings Certificates, for example.

To date the guaranteed fund market has been dominated by insurance companies with their popular guaranteed bonds. (See page 90 for more details about guaranteed funds.)

INVESTMENT TRUSTS

An investment trust is not a trust as such, but is a British company, listed on the UK Stock Exchange, which invests in the shares of other quoted and unquoted companies in the UK and overseas. It may also invest in fixed-interest securities, cash or other assets.

As *public companies*, investment trusts are subject to company law and Stock Exchange regulation. The prices of most investment trusts are published daily in the *Financial Times*.

Investment trusts are controlled by boards of directors who are appointed by, and answerable to, their shareholders. The board presents annual accounts to its shareholders.

THE DIFFERENCE BETWEEN INVESTMENT AND UNIT TRUSTS

Investment trusts are different from unit trusts in several important ways and offer the active investor additional opportunities. However, these opportunities also make investment trusts potentially more volatile than unit trusts.

Investment trust companies have a fixed number of shares so, unlike unit trusts, 'units' cannot be created and cancelled to meet increased and reduced demand. As with any quoted company, the shares are only available when other investors are trying to sell.

This means there are two factors that affect investment trust share prices. The first is the performance of the underlying assets in which the company invests. This factor also affects the price of units in a unit trust.

However, where unit trust prices directly reflect the *net asset value* (the market price of securities held in the fund), investment trust share prices may not. This leads to the second factor, which is that the market forces (supply and demand) to which investment trust shares are subject may make the shares worth more or less than the underlying value of the company's assets. If the share price is lower than the value of the underlying assets the difference is known as the *discount*. If it is higher the difference is known as the *premium*.

Investment trusts can borrow money to invest – an activity known as *gearing*. This adds extra flexibility, and if the shares purchased with the borrowed money do well the company and its shareholders will benefit. Conversely, a poor return on the shares will reduce the profitability of the company.

Split capital investment trusts can have several types of shares, but generally offer two principal categories: one has a right to all the income and the other has a right to the capital growth. There are several other types of share, each offering different features. An example is *stepped preference shares* which offer dividends, which rise at a predetermined rate, and a fixed redemption value, which is paid when the trust is wound up.

Investment trust warrants also offer the active investor the right to subscribe to new shares at a certain price, on a certain date. Typically, an investment trust might have one warrant for every five ordinary shares. It is important to check how many warrants are in circulation because if the investors holding these instruments decide to exercise their right, this will effectively dilute existing ordinary shareholders' rights because the net asset value is divided by a greater number of shares.

■ Taxation and charges

In terms of taxation, the unit and investment trust route is very similar. Where these investments are held outside of a Pep (or, from April 1999, outside an Individual Savings Account – see page 83) the capital gains tax liability falls on the investor, who can offset it against the annual CGT exemption (£6800 in 1998/99).

Dividends are paid net of lower-rate tax. This can be reclaimed by non-taxpayers but there would be a potential additional 20 per cent liability for higher-rate payers. Where funds are qualifying, both types of trust may be held in a Pep (or in future in an ISA) in which case gains are tax free and income virtually tax free.

Remember, though, that the advantage of a capital gains tax shelter can become a disadvantage if the fund makes a capital loss because this loss cannot be offset against any gains made during a tax year in excess of the CGT exemption (see page 263).

Charges on investment trusts are generally lower than on unit trusts, with the exception of some index trackers. However, tracker funds usually are confined to the UK stockmarket and therefore do not offer such broad diversification as the larger and older international investment trusts.

In conclusion, unit trusts, with the exception of the index trackers, are generally considered slightly more expensive than investment trusts but where the investment aims are similar, unit trusts are less sensitive to market movements.

UNIT TRUSTS V INSURANCE COMPANY BONDS

Like unit trusts, a lump-sum premium in an insurance company bond buys units which directly reflect the net asset value of the fund's underlying investments. The charges for the two types of collective funds are similar.

However, the tax treatment is quite different. Insurance company bonds pay tax broadly equivalent to the lower rate on income and capital gains. The income tax cannot be reclaimed so, generally, these bonds are not considered suitable for non-taxpayers. Moreover, the capital gains tax paid by the fund cannot be offset against an individual's exemption. Advisers tend to regard this feature as a serious drawback.

MORTGAGE ENDOWMENTS

Endowments used to be the most common way of saving to repay the debt at the end of an interest-only mortgage term. An integral part of the endowment is the life assurance you need to cover the debt if you die.

In recent years endowments have decreased in popularity, partly because their original tax efficiency has all but disappeared (it used to be possible to get tax relief on contributions) and partly because their charging structure can make them very inflexible.

Moreover, the retail investment market offers many funds run by the top institutional managers, which often provide superior performance compared with the life assurance companies. Early endowments used to offer certain capital guarantees but the newer funds do not.

OFFSHORE FUNDS

There is a huge range of offshore funds run out of the Channel Islands, the Isle of Man, the Dublin International Financial Centre and Luxembourg. (There are other offshore centres but those mentioned are of most relevance to the UK market.)

The appeal of offshore funds for UK residents will depend on the tax jurisdiction of the fund and the way the fund itself is taxed (in particular, whether it distributes its income or rolls it up in the fund). It will also depend on your own tax position as an investor. For non-UK residents offshore vehicles can be very attractive but their merits are questionable for UK residents. Either way, expert advice is essential.

> For non-UK residents offshore vehicles can be very attractive but their merits are questionable for UK residents.

Additional points to consider with offshore funds include the charges, which usually are much higher than UK funds, and the regulation. It the fund is based outside of the UK, do check very carefully what protection you have if the company collapses or the fund manager runs off with your money.

TIP As a general rule for a UK resident investing in UK securities, unit and investment trusts and OEICs are likely to prove more cost effective and simpler than offshore funds.

In addition to the offshore unit trusts and their foreign equivalents, there are two main types of offshore insurance bond – distribution bonds, which pay a regular 'income' and non-distribution bonds, which roll up gross.

Investors who may gain by going offshore include UK and foreign expatriates who are non-resident for UK tax purposes and who can benefit from gross roll up non-distribution bonds if they do not pay tax in the country where they live. Higher rate taxpayers may also benefit from the gross roll up but you do have to pay tax when you bring the money back into the UK, although of course you may have switched to the lower tax bracket if you have retired by the time the non-distribution bond matures.

It is worth noting that the Government frowns on the use of offshore funds and trusts to avoid or minimise your tax liability, and in the March 1998 budget, tightened up the rules and closed several loopholes.

OPEN-ENDED INVESTMENT COMPANIES

Unit trusts are a UK product and have several features – in particular the bid/offer spread pricing system – which is regarded as unnecessarily complicated.

Open-ended investment companies (OEICs, pronounced 'oiks') have a corporate structure and combine characteristics of both unit and investment trusts. For example they can have different classes of share, which offer different features. In this respect they offer some of the flexibility of split capital investment trusts which allow investors to take maximum income at the expense of capital growth, and those seeking growth to take maximum growth at the expense of income.

OEICs do not have a different selling and buying price (known as the bid/offer spread). Instead they have just one mid-market price – literally the mid-point between the bid/offer spread – at which investors both buy and sell.

It may not be easy to compare the performance of OEICs with unit trusts. This is because some of the charges for an OEIC, as with an investment trust, are deducted from within the company, whereas with a unit trust the charges are separate from the trust itself.

As with qualifying unit trusts, qualifying OEICs can be held in a Pep and in the new ISA.

Sources

Personal Pension Unit Linked Survey 1997, Bacon & Woodrow, St. Olaf House, London Bridge City, London SE1 2PE. Tel: 0171 357 7171. Fax: 0171 716 7411. The survey costs £550 (discount for bulk purchases).

Summary

- Set your investment goals before you consider in which tax-efficient vehicle you should place certain assets.

- Past performance statistics are an imperfect guide to the future but can help if you follow the methodology used by the professional consultants' surveys.

- Check that the management group which achieved the performance is still in place and has a clearly defined, measurable investment objective for the fund in which you are interested.

- The structure of investment trusts offers greater investment opportunities but at the same time greater potential risk than unit trusts.

- For most investors, unit and investment trusts are more tax-efficient than insurance company bonds.

- Open-ended investment companies are said to combine the best features of unit and investment trusts but are too new to have proved their mettle.

- Unless there is a very good reason, UK residents will find onshore funds cheaper and simpler than their offshore equivalents.

7

Medium-term to long-term tax-efficient investments

- Personal equity plans
- Individual Savings Accounts
- Pensions
- Other tax-efficient but very risky investments

At a glance

This Chapter considers the two most important tax-efficient investments namely *personal equity plans* (Peps) and *pensions*. Peps (and tax-exempt special savings accounts (Tessas) – see page 62) will be replaced in April 1999 by *Individual Savings Accounts* so we also look at the new product's rules and how to transfer from a Pep to an ISA.

We also consider briefly several very high-risk investments, including *Enterprise Investment Schemes* (EIS), *Venture Capital Trusts* (VCTs) and *Enterprise Zone Trusts* (EZTs).

All of these investments carry the ultimate wealth warning: things can go wrong, very, *very* wrong and you could lose the lot. In the case of EZTs and Lloyd's of London, you can even end up having to pay out in losses more than the original capital you invested.

PERSONAL EQUITY PLANS

The annual investment limit for Peps is £6000 per annum for a general plan and a further £3000 for a single company plan. Peps will be replaced by ISAs in April 1999.

About £6 billion is invested in 1.7 million Peps each year. Most of this money goes into unit trust general Peps. The demise of the Pep and the arrival of the ISA (see page 84) is likely to cause the biggest shake-up in retail investment products for many years.

As explained in the previous chapter, a Pep is not an investment in its own right, but is simply a tax-efficient wrapper or basket in which you hold your portfolio to shield it from income tax and capital gains tax. Anyone who is over age 18 and is resident in the UK can take out a Pep. If you are a taxpayer and you want to invest in shares, corporate bonds or collective funds then investing through a Pep could improve your returns.

There are hundreds of different plans available from around 400 Pep managers but the market is dominated by the high street banks and building societies, the major unit trust groups and some of the big retail companies – Virgin and Marks & Spencer, for example. Some insurance companies and retail stockbroking groups also are significant players.

For the general plan, you can invest directly in equities and bonds or through unit trusts, investment trusts and the new open-ended investment companies OEICS. You can only invest in one general Pep a year but if you opt for a 'self-select' plan you can use this to hold a range of qualifying investments, so you are not restricted to the funds of just one management group.

■ Transfer to ISA

Most advisers reckon it is worth taking advantage of the Pep rules while you can, before they are replaced by the less generous ISA rules in April 1999. The maximum annual investment in an ISA is limited to £5000 per person.

For the less experienced investor who wants to build up a good core portfolio for growth, income or both, this can be achieved with UK equities held either through an index-tracking fund or an actively managed equity fund. Investors specifically seeking income should also consider a corporate bond Pep (see above and Chapter 6).

Funds held in Peps will be able to retain existing tax reliefs indefinitely and will not count towards the ISA annual limit.

INDIVIDUAL SAVINGS ACCOUNTS

ISAs will become available for the first time in April 1999 when they will replace personal equity plans and tax exempt special savings accounts.

Under the proposed rules the ISAs offer tax-free growth and income and should be used as a long-term savings vehicle into which you can put a wide range of investments.

> **ISAs will become available for the first time in April 1999 when they will replace personal equity plans and tax exempt special savings accounts.**

The big attraction of the ISA is its flexibility. You have immediate access to your money at all times (although the ISA manager or the managers of the underlying investments may still charge exit penalties). You can use the emerging fund for any purpose.

Here are the proposed rules:

- Investment limit £5000 per annum maximum (£7000 in 1999/2000).

- You can invest in deposits (£3000 maximum in 1999/2000 and £1000 maximum thereafter), up to £1000 in life assurance funds, the rest in equities, including collective funds.

- The fund is exempt from income tax and capital gains tax and there will be a 10 per cent tax credit paid on dividends from UK equities for the first five years of the scheme.

- Withdrawals can be made at any time without loss of tax relief (however providers may impose their own exit penalties).

- ISAs must be run by managers approved by the Inland Revenue.

- Investors can only have one ISA a year, although you can choose different managers for different tax years.

■ ISAs from previous tax years can be switched to a new manager. This has to be for the whole fund, though, not just part.

For the equity component there is a wide range of options including ordinary shares, fixed interest and convertible preference shares, corporate bonds (with at least five years to maturity), unit and investment trusts, and OEICS.

PENSIONS

Like Peps, there is nothing magic about a pension plan. It is a long-term investment with some attractive tax breaks and some pretty restrictive rules on how and when you take your benefits.

There are three main sources of pensions: the state, company schemes and private plans.

Since the beginning of the post-Second World War Welfare State, successive governments have tinkered with the state pension and over the past decade it has been cut dramatically. The current Government is committed to introducing a 'stakeholder' pension (possibly compulsory for those not in a company scheme). At the same time, the earnings-related element of the state pension (Serps) is likely to be cut back, while the basic old age pension will remain and a Government guaranteed top up will be paid to those who cannot save for a private pension.

■ Company schemes

Company schemes are tax efficient. Your contributions are paid free of basic and higher rate tax, while the pension fund grows largely free of income tax and capital gains tax. A substantial chunk of the final benefits can be taken as tax-free cash at retirement while the pension itself, whether drawn from a company scheme or from a life office in the form of an annuity, is subject to your top rate of income tax.

There are two main types of occupational schemes: 'final salary', also known as 'defined benefit', and 'money purchase', also known as 'defined contribution'. With a final salary scheme the employer bears the investment risk and backs the pension guarantees. With a money purchase scheme the investment risk falls fairly and squarely on your shoulders as the scheme member and there are no guarantees of the level of income your fund will generate in retirement. (No brownie points for guessing why employers are keen to switch from the former to the latter.)

> **TIP** If you are not in a company scheme you need to provide for yourself. The main option for employees who do not have access to a company scheme and for the self-employed, is a personal pension.

■ Personal pensions

Personal pensions are as tax-efficient as company schemes. Rather like Peps and the new ISA they act as a tax-efficient wrapper or basket in which you can shelter assets from income tax and CGT. They are run by life assurance companies, banks, building societies unit and investment trusts, friendly societies and some of the big retailers such as Virgin and Marks & Spencer.

Personal pensions do two jobs. First, you and your employer between you can contribute up to 17.5 – 40 per cent of your annual earnings, depending on age. These contributions build up a fund which, at retirement, is used to buy an annuity from a life assurance company. An annuity provides a regular guaranteed (but taxable) income for life.

Second, personal pensions can be used to contract out of Serps. In return for giving up your right to this element of the state pension, you receive from the Department of Social Security a rebate of National Insurance (NI) contributions which is sent to the personal pension plan manager of your choice.

In the past personal pensions were widely mis-sold to employees who would have been better off in their company scheme. New rules should prevent further problems (hopefully!).

However, the important point to bear in mind is that there is absolutely nothing wrong with the concept of personal pensions. All the problems have been a result of greedy salesmen taking huge commissions, and greedy providers imposing punitive, inflexible charges. With care you can avoid both.

How to get best value

In Chapter 6 we explained the methodology a professional consultant uses to select the best personal pension funds (see page 71). With the help of a good independent financial adviser you should be able to narrow down your choice of pension companies by considering the following factors:

■ the financial strength of the provider (it is important to be confident your pension company can survive. This very competitive market is in the throes of merger mania.)

■ the performance track record, with the emphasis on consistency over the long term and stability of staff

■ the level of charges deducted throughout the investment period

■ the flexibility of the contract, for example there should be no penalties for reducing and stopping contributions, transferring the fund and early retirement.

The annual contribution limits are as given in Table 7.1.
You can run more than one top-up personal pension plan provided total contributions fall within these limits – but do consider the impact of start-up charges. However, you can only have one appropriate plan for each tax year.

Table 7.1 Contribution rates for personal pensions

Age	% net relevant earnings*
Up to 35	17.5 per cent
36–45	20 per cent
46–50	25 per cent
51–55	30 per cent
56–60	35 per cent
61-74	40 per cent

* All personal pension contributions (but not the emerging pension itself) are subject to the earnings cap which limits the amount of salary that can be used for pension purposes to £87 600 for the 1998/99 tax year.

Don't forget – employers can contribute to an individual employee's plan, although there is no legal requirement for them to do so.

High earners

High earners with personal pensions are restricted by the 'earnings cap', introduced in the 1989 budget, which limits the amount of salary that can be taken into consideration for contributions.

For the 1998/99 tax year the cap is £87 600 which means that the maximum contribution for an employee aged 36–45 is 20 per cent of the cap – £17 520. In practice it is hard to see how this would act as a restriction for younger people who tend to be financially stretched by family commitments and mortgage repayments. Older employees, however, often pay higher contributions if they have made little provision earlier in life.

Making extra large contributions

A special provision exists for employees and the self-employed who have unused tax relief in previous years. Under the Inland Revenue's 'carry back' and 'carry forward' rules it is possible to mop up unused relief for up to seven previous tax years. This is a complex exercise and should be discussed with your accountant or a pensions adviser with tax expertise.

Life assurance

It is also possible to use up to 5 per cent of the contribution limit to pay for life assurance, which effectively gives you tax relief on the premiums. Life assurance rates vary considerably so do shop around. If your pension provider's terms are expensive it might be cheaper to buy it elsewhere.

Retirement annuities

Many people still have a retirement annuity plan – the predecessor to the personal pension. After July 1988 sales of these contracts stopped but existing policyholders can continue to contribute to existing plans, although to make life more complicated, the contribution limits are different and the earnings cap does not apply.

Investment choice

There are several investment options to consider – unit linked, unit trust, investment trust, conventional with profits, 'unitised' with profits and guaranteed funds. Before you get bogged down with the different options, remember that the main consideration is the underlying asset mix.

As a very broad guide, advisers suggest that younger people should invest virtually 100 per cent in equities because this offers the best long-term growth prospects. As you get older and closer to retirement you need to switch gradually into safer assets such as bonds and gilts and by the time you are within a few years of retirement you should probably be entirely in cash (deposits) and gilts.

Having said that, if you intend to transfer to an 'income drawdown' or 'phased retirement' plan at retirement, which allows you to keep your fund fully invested, you may prefer to maintain a high exposure to equities. These comparatively new retirement investment options are complex, so do seek expert advice.

Unit trusts, investment trusts, unit linked and guaranteed funds are described in Chapter 6, so it only remains here to discuss the funds peculiar to life assurance companies.

Companies make much of their often huge fund range but in practice most people go for the managed fund which invests in a range of the provider's other main funds and in this way offers a balanced spread of investments. Some companies offer investment links to top institutional managers. This is a very useful feature but make sure the charges do not outweigh the potentially higher returns.

Until recently, with profits funds formed the backbone of the individual pensions market because they provided a reasonable degree of security together with good potential for long-term capital growth.

The mystical path to understanding the with profits concept is littered with actuarial jargon. The with profits fund (which in fact is the fund of the life office itself) invests mainly in UK and international equities, gilts and fixed interest securities and property. Your fund builds up when the company pays 'bonuses' each year and at the end of the investment period. Once added, these bonuses cannot be taken away – rather like interest on a deposit account

These days most life assurance companies sell unitised with profits plans, which are supposed to occupy the middle ground between the conventional with profits structure and unit linked funds. One advantage of this is that investors with unit linked plans can more easily switch into the lower risk unitised with profits fund – a common strategy in the run up to retirement when you want to consolidate gains and reduce risk.

Unfortunately unitised plans are, if anything, even more complicated than their conventional predecessors and basically offer fewer guarantees. In particular, unitisation heralded the arrival of the controversial 'market value adjuster' (MVA). These adjusters are used as a safety net for life offices in the event of a mass exodus of clients following a drop in the markets. Effectively the MVA allows a company to reduce the value of units whenever it likes and by however much it wants.

■ Guaranteed equity funds

If you want exposure to equities but can't handle the white knuckle ride of the stockmarkets, you might consider one of the relatively new 'guaranteed' funds which limit your exposure to falls in the stockmarket and provide a percentage of the gains.

Guaranteed equity funds are strange beasts and in fact rarely invest in equities but instead hold mainly cash and gilts. The fund manager buys *derivatives* to guarantee a certain rise in the index and to limit the percentage of any fall in prices.

Of course the guarantee does not come free. In effect what you lose is the equivalent of the stockmarket dividend yield. When you consider the fact that over a ten-year period the yield on the FTSE 100 index accounts for roughly half of the total return, its loss seems a high price to pay.

However, experts argue that you could be compensated for the loss of yield by the fact that the fund limits your exposure to any falls in the index, so you gain from potentially greater capital growth than unprotected investors. This is particularly relevant in volatile market conditions.

Charges are higher than for most of the other funds mentioned here – largely because of the cost of the derivatives which provide the guarantee. (Guaranteed funds are also discussed on page 75.)

■ Self-invested personal pensions

Self-invested personal pensions (SIPPs) follow the same basic rules as standard personal pensions but they also allow you to exercise much greater control over your investments.

Like self-select Peps, the appeal of the Sipp lies in the product's ability to 'unbundle' the two key features of modern pension plans, namely the administration and the investment.

What generally happens is that the administration is carried out by a specialist life office and you either tackle the investment yourself or appoint an investment manager (a stockbroker, for example) to run the portfolio for you. If you are unhappy with the performance you can change the manager without having to upset the underlying administration arrangements.

SIPPs can also be used by partnerships. Schedule D taxpayers are excluded from the company-sponsored small self-administered schemes but they can use a SIPP with virtually the same effect and, if they pool their contributions and funds, they can achieve beneficial economies of scale.

The choice of investments is very wide and includes equities, gilts, bonds (UK and those quoted on a recognised overseas exchange), unit trusts, investment trusts, OEICs, insurance company managed funds, deposit accounts and commercial property.

A SIPP fund cannot purchase a firm's existing business premises from the partnership but it can buy new offices into which the partnership can move, provided the property is leased back on a commercial basis. You can also use your SIPP fund to borrow on the strength of its assets to help with property purchase. However, the SIPP cannot lend part of the pension fund back to you, the investor.

■ Group personal pensions

Group personal pensions are becoming very popular, particularly among companies that do not want the expense and administrative hassles of a final salary pension scheme. The providers are the same as for individual schemes – mainly the life offices but also a few unit trust and investment trust groups.

More recently some of the heavyweight institutional fund managers have moved into this market – a welcome development, particularly where they bring with them a first-rate performance track record.

> **Group personal pensions are becoming very popular, particularly among companies that do not want the expense and administrative hassles of a final salary pension scheme.**

If your employer offers a group personal pension check the amount your employer is prepared to pay on your behalf and whether there are any penalties if you reduce or stop your own contributions when you change jobs.

At their most basic, group personal pensions are no more than a collection of individual plans. However, the more sophisticated schemes, usually negotiated by a consultant, make full use of the potential for economies of scale to reduce administration and investment charges. More generous plans feature employer contributions, death benefits and disability benefits.

Ideally your employer will arrange the group personal pension on a 'nil commission' basis. This means that the commission costs are stripped out and your employer's adviser is paid a fee. The main advantage of this system is a clear, flexible charging structure – you can see exactly what you are paying and if you change the amount of contribution or stop paying altogether there is no penalty. With any luck your employer may cover the charges and not pass them on to scheme members.

Annuities

If your pension is designed to buy an annuity at retirement to provide your regular income, it is important to select your annuity provider (the life assurance companies) with great care. Specialist independent advice is essential because once you have made your choice you are stuck with it for the rest of your life. The annuity 'rate' or regular income will depend on the size of your fund, your life expectancy and interest rates.

It is possible to delay the annuity purchase through an 'income drawdown' arrangement. Here you keep your fund fully invested and draw an income broadly in line with what an annuity would have paid. By age 75 at the latest you must convert your fund to an annuity. Income drawdown and a similar arrangement known as 'phased retirement' are only suitable for those with large funds (over £250 000) who can tolerate stockmarket risks in retirement. Do seek expert advice.

OTHER TAX-EFFICIENT BUT VERY RISKY INVESTMENTS

There are a handful of investments which fall into the very high risk category. As such they may offer substantial tax breaks and potentially high returns but they should only be considered by those with a large capital sum to invest and then only after seeking expert advice.

It is essential to make a full assessment of the products' commercial viability. To do this you must judge each arrangement 'naked' – that is, without the tax breaks. The best way to do this is to use the benchmarks outlined in Chapter 4 which allow you to compare the aims, the alternative products that may meet some of these criteria, the investment period, the primary risks and any other noteworthy features.

Understandably, given the speculative nature of the investments, the financial services regulators do not allow companies to advertise potential rates of return. When you do discuss this with a particular company make sure you consider all the major factors that can affect the final outcome. Look at how the rates are calculated and remember that the most basic criterion for any investment is how easily you can get your money out at the end. With EISs, VCTs and EZTs there are no guaranteed exits.

Take EZTs, for example. If the building in which you invest remains unlet you may have to put in more money to cover the cost of insurance, security and marketing to prospective tenants. VCTs are considered less risky because they are a type of collective investment and pooling should dilute the risk somewhat. They are also quoted on the stockmarket but, when you come to sell, the share price may be a lot less than the underlying net asset value.

The best source of advice on these schemes is likely to be a large firm of accountants which has a financial services department. In addition there are a few specialist firms of advisers.

Your adviser should have a clear approach to judging the merits of these schemes and in particular should have met the management team and analysed its track record. You also need an adviser who can accurately assess the launch and running costs, which tend to be high with these types of investments compared with mainstream products. What you want to know is whether the costs are justified and whether they undermine the total return and the tax breaks on offer.

■ Enterprise Investment Schemes

An EIS aims to make a large capital gain from speculative equity investment in a single, small unquoted company. This is very much a 'hands-on' investment if you want to become involved in the running of the business but is attractive only to wealthy investors who have income to shelter and capital gains to roll over. The investment period is a minimum of five years.

The maximum investment in an EIS is £150 000 a year. Income tax relief is generally equal to 20 per cent of the amount invested (but reliefs may be restricted where there is insufficient income tax capacity). In addition, your investment qualifies for capital gains tax (CGT) reinvestment relief and you benefit from CGT exemption on gains made (excluding the reinvested gain). A loss on the disposal of the EIS investment can be offset against tax.

Don't forget – if you take the plunge you could lose the lot. You could also lose the tax reliefs if either you or the company in which you invest breach the rules.

■ Venture capital trusts

VCTs aim to make capital gains from a portfolio of speculative equity investments in smaller unquoted companies. (In other words, VCTs allow you to participate in EIS-type investments on a collective basis and hence to spread risk.)

Again this is attractive only to wealthy investors who have income to shelter and capital gains to roll over.

Your investment is committed for a minimum period of five years if you want the full tax advantages. The maximum investment is £100 000 a year. Your investment also qualifies for capital gains tax reinvestment relief. Income tax relief is generally equal to 20 per cent of the amount invested. In addition there is an income tax exemption for dividends and a CGT exemption for gains (excluding reinvested gains).

As with the EIS, in the worst possible scenario you could lose your total investment. You could also lose the tax reliefs if either you or the company in which you invest breach the rules.

VCTs are quoted on the stock exchange so in theory there is an exit route, but the market is very illiquid with only about a dozen schemes available. Unlike EIS, there is no hands-on involvement so you are totally reliant on the expertise of the trust manager. There could be a discount to net asset value where the value of the underlying asset could be worth more than the share price.

■ Enterprise Zone Trusts

The aim of this scheme is to make an equity investment in property, where the purchase cost is subsidised by tax relief. As such this is attractive to high income tax payers only as an income tax shelter – there is no CGT exemption or roll over provision. A more precise description of an EZT is an enterprise zone property unit trust – so this is a collective investment where you own a part share of a property.

With an EZT you qualify for full tax relief on investment in buildings but not land. You may also benefit from tax relief on interest on borrowings made to fund the investment. The relief is offset against rents.

So what are the risks? Once again these are substantial. For example you could suffer a partial loss of your investment through property depreciation. Moreover, if the property remains unlet after five years, investors may have to put in more money. As you would expect, the market is very illiquid – at the time of writing there were only about a dozen schemes available.

Advisers warn that investors must be prepared to stay with the scheme for 25 years so clearly this is for the very long-term investor. In fact you can sell after seven years but the practical minimum is 10 to 15 years. Bear in mind there is a loss of tax relief if you sell early.

Summary

- Peps are due to disappear in 1999 and will be replaced with individual savings accounts (ISAs) which allow you to hold deposits, collective funds and direct equities tax free.

- You can transfer existing Peps and Tessas into an ISA.

- ISAs have an annual investment limit of £5000, but existing Pep portfolios can retain their tax reliefs.

- In most cases it is in your interests to join the company pension scheme to take advantage of the employer's contributions, and the valuable death and disability benefits.

- If there is no company scheme invest in a personal pension and try to get your employer to contribute as well.

- Independent financial advice is essential (see Chapter 3). Check the performance, charges and flexibility of the personal pension as well as the company's financial strength.

- Enterprise zone trusts, enterprise investment schemes and venture capital trusts are only suitable for very wealthy investors prepared to take a high level of risk.

8

Employee share option schemes

- The different options
- Save as you earn
- Company share option schemes
- Unapproved schemes

At a glance

Share option schemes are enjoying a period of considerable growth. This is good news because more and more employees are likely to be offered the chance to buy their company's shares at a discount.

If you don't want to include individual shares in your portfolio, it is still worth joining in most cases because you should be able to sell the shares and make a profit.

This Chapter explains how these schemes work and considers how valuable and appropriate shares in your employer's company can be.

THE DIFFERENT OPTIONS

There are several ways in which your employer can offer you the opportunity to buy shares in the company at lower than market value.

You may be able to avoid income tax on what is effectively a benefit in kind (the difference between the reduced and the market price is a type of payment from your employer) if the offer is part of an Inland Revenue approved share option scheme.

In addition, you may be able to hold the shares in a Pep or, possibly, in the new ISA (see Chapter 7) provided the scheme is open to all employees.

The important point to remember about these schemes is that the 'option' is a right to buy, not an obligation.

There are two main types of scheme approved for special tax treatment by the Inland Revenue – *Save As You Earn* (SAYE) and *company share option schemes* (also known by their previous name, executive schemes).

SAVE AS YOU EARN

SAYE schemes allow you to save between £5 and £250 per month for either three or five years, after which you receive a tax-free bonus. You can leave your money in for a further two years and qualify for an extra bonus. At the end of your chosen savings period you can buy the shares at a 20 per cent discount to the market price when you started saving. The option to buy is valid for a maximum of six months after the contract matures.

This type of scheme is almost always well worth joining, provided the effective rate of interest provided by the bonuses on your savings is appealing.

If direct investment is not for you but the share price is attractive, you can exercise your option and sell immediately afterwards, pocketing any profits, usually with no tax to pay. Between one-third and one-half of employees do just that. In some cases the company even provides subsidised dealing facilities.

The most attractive feature of the SAYE scheme is that the option price of the shares can be fixed as low as 80 per cent of the market value at the date the option is granted – that is, when you start the contract.

There is no annual interest as such but the scheme details should set out the equivalent rate by calculating what the value of the bonuses you receive at the end of your contract are worth when spread over the entire savings period. It is important to assess this figure carefully because if you decide not to buy the shares, this will be the rate of interest your savings will have earned over the period.

The tax-free bonus is worth the value of 18 months' contributions for the seven year contract, nine months' for the five year contract and three months' for the three year contract. The equivalent tax-free annual interest rate is 5.87, 5.53 and 5.26 per cent respectively.

From time to time the Government may change the bonus allocation, but once you take out a contract it is set for the full period. This means the contract behaves like any other fixed-interest product so your gamble is that the bonus will prove competitive in relation to prevailing interest rates over the savings term. Employees who pull out early, for example because they leave the company before the option date, are penalised.

■ What will your contract be worth?

If you do want to buy, what will your contract be worth? Assume you have saved £10 000 including the bonuses. The company will calculate the number of shares your fund would have bought at the discounted rate set at the time the option was granted.

So, if the original share price was £1 and your option was to purchase at 80 pence, then you would have an option to buy 12 500 shares with your contract. If the current price of the shares is well above the option price you will have bought cheaply and made a profit. If the share price has dropped to below the option price clearly there is no point in buying.

Where the company share option scheme is open to all employees (so this does not include the schemes offered only to executives and directors), you can transfer the shares to a Pep. Provided you transfer within 90 days, you do not have to sell and repurchase the shares, so you save on dealing costs and, possibly, capital gains tax.

However, it may not always be in your best interests to do so. If, like most investors, you do not use up your annual CGT exemption (£6800 for 1998/99), the main attraction of the Pep is the shelter from income tax. A simple comparison between the Pep annual management charge and the saving you would make by not paying tax on the company's gross dividend yield provides a good indication of whether it is more cost effective to buy the shares through the sponsored Pep or direct.

TIP As a general rule the FTSE 100 companies maintain a sustainable dividend policy.

Provided the future prospects for the company do not alter substantially, the result generally is a fairly stable yield. There are exceptions where the yield is very high, which indicates changes afoot in corporate structure or perhaps a radical change in dividend policy.

> **Don't forget that Peps will be absorbed into the new ISAs in 1999, so any arrangements you make now should be revised at that time.**

Clearly, the higher the yield, the greater the tax saving. Where the yield is 5 per cent, a 40 per cent taxpayer would save 2 per cent of its value, less the annual management charge, which typically is 0.5 per cent for single company Peps. But with dividends of around 2 per cent, the tax saving achieved by using the Pep wrapper is minimal or non-existent.

Finally, don't forget that Peps will be absorbed into the new ISAs in 1999, so any arrangements you make now should be revised at that time (see page 84).

COMPANY SHARE OPTION SCHEMES

The other type of Inland Revenue approved option arrangement is the company share option schemes (also known as executive schemes because they tend to be open only to executives and directors). These are not linked to savings plans.

Under the plan you do not pay income tax on the grant of an option or on any increase in market value in the period before you exercise the option. You can purchase the shares between three and ten years after the option was granted.

Following a rule change in 1995 the shares cannot be offered at a discount (previously the discount could be up to 15 per cent) and there is a limit of £30 000 on the value of all the shares held under option by any one employee.

Some advisers believe that an executive option is always worth taking up. An option never obliges you to buy the shares and, unlike SAYE, an executive option does not even involve a savings commitment.

UNAPPROVED SCHEMES

Some companies run 'unapproved' executive share option schemes. These do not offer the tax advantages of company share option plans but in theory there is no limit to the size of the option.

However, options granted from 27 November 1996 will, on exercise, be subject to income tax under the Pay As You Earn (PAYE) system. This leads to difficulties if the employee's income tax charge is so large that it exceeds his or her salary and the company is unable to deduct it from monthly pay.

Sources

For further details of employee share schemes contact your local Inland Revenue office for leaflets on the subject. These may also be available in bank and building society branches.

A useful guide to employee share ownership is published by ProShare. Contact ProShare, Library Chambers, 13–14 Basinghall Street, London EC2V 5BQ.

Summary

- As a general rule, share option schemes represent good value.

- If you don't want to keep the shares you can usually sell at a profit. Some companies provide special dealing facilities for employees.

- Save As You Earn schemes are linked to a regular savings plan. Company share option plans are not.

- You can transfer the proceeds of a Save As You Earn or share option scheme into a single company Pep, provided the scheme is open to all employees and is not just for one section of the workforce (executives, for example). You must complete the transfer within 90 days of the scheme maturing.

- A good way to check whether it is worth buying shares through a single company plan is to compare the Pep annual management charge and the saving you would make by not paying tax on the company's gross dividend yield. As a general rule you should use your single company plan for high yielding shares.

HOW TO SELECT AND BUY INDIVIDUAL EQUITIES AND BONDS

9

The importance of asset allocation

- What is your starting point?
- Reweighting your portfolio
- Collective funds for overseas exposure
- Achieving the right asset allocation
- Model portfolios for the FTSE/APCIMS private investor indices
- Market cycles
- Stockbroker model portfolios

At a glance

This Chapter explains how to reduce risk through diversification using direct equity investment, bonds and gilts, and a range of collective funds.

Your starting point is an asset allocation plan. The large institutional pension funds refer to this important exercise as an asset/liability study. This is a helpful description because it focuses on your liabilities *first*.

In the case of a pension fund the liabilities are the income it requires to pay the pensions and the capital it needs in fairly liquid form to draw on to pay the expected tax-free lump sums of members on retirement and also the unexpected death benefits when a member dies.

For a private investor the 'liabilities' can cover a wide range of objectives. For example, your children's school fees fall due each term and represent a known cost which must be paid on specific dates in the future.

Another liability is the mortgage repayment. If you have an interest only loan, typically you might need to save over a 25-year term at which point you need a large lump sum to repay the outstanding debt.

The same is true of pension plans, which usually build up a fund to buy an annuity in retirement. In return for your lump sum payment, the life assurance company guarantees to pay you a regular income for life.

Alternatively, if you decide to keep your fund fully invested in retirement (see page 92 for details on income drawdown) your objective is to provide a regular stream of monthly income, while keeping most of your fund invested in the stockmarkets.

In addition to these obvious liabilities you may have several other aims which require different periods of investment – for example, an expensive holiday abroad, a new car, or a temporary income while you or your spouse stops work in order to raise a family.

You can see from these examples that while your overall objective may be capital growth, you also need to manage the liquidity of your capital in order to pay off the big debts on time, and the cash flow in order to meet more regular income needs, where relevant. If this exercise is particularly complicated in your circumstances then a good financial planner or stockbroker should be able to help you draw up a plan and review it on a regular basis.

This Chapter is largely devoted to asset allocation, which means deciding on the right type of investments before actually selecting individual shares, bonds and funds.

In the following chapters we take a closer look at share picking and how market cycles affect market sectors and individual companies.

WHAT IS YOUR STARTING POINT?

Your portfolio should reflect your current financial position (and that of your family), your current and future investment objectives, and your tax status. It may also reflect your ethical views which might prevent you from investing in a range of companies with whose business goals or methods you disagree (see Chapter 12).

> **TIP** Make sure you have a clear perception of your tolerance to risk. Whether you use an adviser or deal direct, this is critical.

Don't settle for a vague sentiment, but consider each investment in turn in the context of your overall asset allocation, and use the risk analysis guide on page 52 to determine which investments are appropriate for you and which ones you should avoid.

■ Dealing with risk

The problem with risk is that usually there is a wide grey margin between the worst that could possibly happen and the likelihood of this actually taking place. For example, in theory, if you invest in equities you could lose the lot if the company goes bust. As a shareholder you are last in the line of creditors so it is quite likely that

> **To what extent are you prepared to trade off higher risk against higher potential expectations – and conversely, higher potential losses?**

you would get little or nothing back if there are insufficient assets to go round.

So, how likely is it that a company will go bust? Clearly this depends to some extent on the companies you select and the state of the economy. But in practice the risk is a lot more tangible than you might think. In a stockbroker's survey,[1] 45 per cent of the private investor participants had seen one of their equity investments go into receivership.

Your task, then, is to quantify the level of risk and decide whether you feel comfortable with it. In other words, to what extent are you prepared to trade off higher risk against higher potential expectations – and conversely, higher potential losses?

This does not alter the case for equities, it just means you have to choose with care. In its *Compendium of Stockmarket Investment for the Private Investor*, stockbroker Cantrade Investments commented:

> 'Despite the low inflation environment of recent years, it is probably not safe to build investment policy on the assumption that inflation has been beaten for good. Noting that even an inflation rate of 3 per cent halves the value of money in just over 20 years, it seems advisable to continue to place the emphasis on equities. The gap between gilt and equity returns is likely to be much narrower than in the past but should still favour equities by a significant margin.
>
> At the same time the private investor will generally find it advisable to maintain a higher weighting in defensive assets than the institutional investor.'

Cantrade's suggested weighting in defensive assets is 30 per cent of the portfolio in fixed interest, index linked gilts, foreign bonds and cash. A further 50 per cent is held in UK equities and 20 per cent in overseas equities.

However, do bear in mind that any model portfolio is aimed at the mythical average investor. Clearly, each individual needs a private benchmark which reflects his or her own requirements, both short term and over the longer term. For example, some investors may avoid foreign bonds due to the currency risk, while others will regard them as an important diversification into overseas markets.

Diversification is not such a big issue within the conventional gilt market because all gilts are issued by the same source, namely the Government. This does not mean that gilts are free from volatility. The nominal coupon and redemption date are known but the real value or price during a gilt's lifecycle are not known.

If you are interested in corporate bonds because they pay a slightly higher income than gilts it is important to diversify in a similar way to an equity portfolio. 'It is rare for a company to fail to the extent of its equity capital but not its loan capital. Therefore in practice the prior charge of a loan stock provides little protection and a loan stock is best viewed as equity risk,' Cantrade warned.

REWEIGHTING YOUR PORTFOLIO

If you take your existing portfolio to a stockbroker, be prepared to allow your broker to sell some of your existing shares if he or she believes they are inappropriate for your investment aims or that they represent too large a proportion of your portfolio and therefore create a concentration of risk.

> Timing is critical to successful investments and in practice it could take six to 12 months to construct or rebalance your portfolio.

Consider, for example, the type of portfolio you may have if you responded to privatisation offers, received free 'windfall' shares from a building society or life assurance company, and you applied for cheap shares through your employer's share option scheme.

Your portfolio may have done very well in the past but it will not have a good spread of shares in the main All-Share sectors. Instead it is likely to consist of privatisation issues (utilities), windfalls (financials) and whatever category your employer happens to fall into. In this case your portfolio could lack representation in important sectors like foods, pharmaceuticals and retailers, among others.

It is also important to remember that if you intend to invest a large sum – for example an inheritance, or the proceeds from a pension or endowment plan – there is no need to complete the process in a matter of days. In practice this could be a very unwise approach.

Timing is critical to successful investments and in practice it could take six to 12 months to construct or rebalance your portfolio. During this period, keep any uninvested capital in an easy access account and be sure to shop around for the best rates.

Your stockbroker will also have to consider your tax position – particularly the capital gains tax implications of selling large chunks of shares. If you have not been making use of your annual capital gains tax exemption (£6800 for the 1998/99 tax year), then your larger holdings could well carry a hefty CGT liability. This could be reduced if you realise your gains or losses at the end of the tax year, although this was made more difficult in the March 1998 budget (see Chapter 19 on tax).

Tax may become more complicated if you are retired or close to retirement. In addition to your income tax and CGT concerns, you should give careful thought to inheritance tax (IHT) planning.

COLLECTIVE FUNDS FOR OVERSEAS EXPOSURE

Don't be surprised if you end up with a large chunk of your money invested in collective funds, even if you have a substantial sum to play with. It makes sense to adopt this route if you want to gain exposure to certain markets – smaller UK companies and overseas markets, for example. It can be risky or impractical to invest in one or two smaller companies (there are over 550 in the SmallCap index) – unless, of course, you really are convinced of a company's merits.

> Don't be surprised if you end up with a large chunk of your money invested in collective funds

Overseas markets can be more expensive to enter and individual share prices too large. In this respect the UK is quite unusual in having a relatively low price per individual share (this characteristic is maintained by companies that split shares when they become unwieldy).

Swiss companies, for example, commonly have a share price of £5000 each, so if you have £100 000 to invest overseas it is not sensible to have, say, two shares in one Swiss company. Rather, you should have £10 000 in units in a collective Swiss blue chip fund if you are keen on Switzerland – or possibly £20 000 in a European blue chip fund, which would invest in a selection of leading European companies.

In Chapters 6 and 7, we discussed the important issues to consider when you choose a collective fund. One point to bear in mind if you use a stockbroker is that some firms only offer their own funds, while others select from the entire range. This is a tricky one and there are no hard and fast rules. In theory, if your stockbroker has a good reputation for fund management, and in particular where it has a large institutional manager as its parent company, the firm's funds should be among the better performers. However, few managers can boast a top quartile (top 25 per cent) performance for all their funds so in general you might expect a better return if the choice of funds is not restricted.

ACHIEVING THE RIGHT ASSET ALLOCATION

To give you an idea of how the experts approach the task of asset allocation for private investors, it is helpful to look at two very different sources. First, the private investor indices constructed by FTSE International in conjunction with the Association of Private Client Stockbrokers and Managers (APCIMS). The indices are also discussed in Chapter 17, which offers some tips on monitoring the performance of your portfolio.

Second, we consider how a firm of stockbrokers constructs its model portfolios.

Third, we recap on the income from equities v gilts issue.

MODEL PORTFOLIOS FOR THE FTSE/APCIMS PRIVATE INVESTOR INDICES

Although each investor's objectives will be different, for the sake of simplicity, the three models we consider here are for income, growth and balanced portfolios.

FTSE International, which manages and develops worldwide equity and bond indices, recently formed a joint venture with APCIMS, the private client stockbroker organisation, to launch three indices which allow investment managers and individuals to monitor their portfolios more accurately. The asset allocation of each model portfolio is based on research from a wide range of private client fund managers and stockbrokers.

The weightings are amended on a regular basis, so the figures in Table 9.1 will not necessarily be up to date, but nevertheless they serve to highlight the different strategies used to achieve the three most common investment goals.

■ Private investor indices' asset allocation

Table 9.1 Private Investor Indices' asset allocation

Asset class	Growth %	Balanced %	Income %
UK equities	60	55	50
International equities	30	20	5
Bonds and cash	10	25	45

Source: FTSE International/APCIMS

As you can see from Table 9.1, the difference in the UK equity weighting is not as great as you might expect, but the individual shares would be selected with different priorities in mind. Growth would be achieved by taking a slightly more aggressive approach, and while you would expect a fair number of blue chips, there would also be some small and medium-sized companies to boost growth prospects.

■ The income seeker

By contrast, for the income seeker the income portfolio would focus on higher yielding shares. Some investors might have a preference for the larger companies (for example the FTSE 100 companies) which tend to have a more steady track record on dividends payments than some smaller companies.

The point to bear in mind here is that size and risk do not go hand in hand, but represent two different decisions for income seekers. Some smaller, higher-risk companies can provide a high yield but might not be appropriate for a retired income seeker.

However, many retired investors are looking not just for short-term income but for income over ten to 20 years. Over this period the bond and cash element would provide a stable guaranteed income but equities are needed to provide an element of capital growth to maintain the real value of the portfolio.

Don't assume, though, that just because you are growing older you should switch part of your portfolio out of equities and into gilts, bonds and cash. Many investors who retire early cannot or do not want to draw their pension immediately – either because it will not be paid until the employer's official pension age of 65 or because the pension would be substantially reduced. In this case you might be looking for an immediate and high income from your portfolio rather than long-term income and growth.

■ International equities

International equities play an important part in the growth portfolio. This would provide exposure to foreign markets with good growth prospects. Of course, the level of risk would depend on where you invested. There is a big difference between, say, the European Union or North American countries, and the Japan/Pacific region or the emerging markets of South America, Africa, and Central and Eastern Europe, for example.

Bear in mind that foreign investment also exposes you to currency fluctuations and, in some countries, exchange control problems. Political instability and hyper-inflation may also be features of emerging economies.

■ Bonds and cash

Finally, the weighting of bonds and cash is probably the clearest indication of the portfolio's aim. In this case the income portfolio has almost half its assets in this class, while the growth portfolio has only 10 per cent. A younger investor with a robust attitude to risk might not even bother with this amount but go wholly for UK and foreign equities.

■ UK equities

For most investors, whether looking for income, growth or a balance of the two, at least half of the portfolio will be invested in UK shares. Although there is a tendency to regard the FTSE 100 companies as somehow 'safer' than medium and small companies, it is not true to say that big is synonymous with secure (remember Polly Peck and Maxwell?).

A common strategy is to invest directly in FTSE 100 companies because these are well diversified and often have overseas interests. Exposure to the FTSE 250 (the 250 largest companies by market capitalisation after the top 100) and in particular to the SmallCap (the remaining 550 or so shares in the All-Share) can be achieved through collective funds, or direct, depending on your attitude to risk and confidence in your ability to research less well-known companies adequately.

The FTSE All-Share, which covers about 98 per cent of the companies that are listed on the London Stock Exchange, has 36 sectors. Some include a large number of companies representing a broad spectrum of industry – Engineering and Retailers, for example. Others are designed to categorise just a few important companies in a very specific market. Gas distribution, for example, has only three companies but this includes the enormous British Gas plc.

■ Overseas equities

Since 1979, when UK exchange controls were abolished, the average pension fund has increased its weighting from 5 per cent to 25 per cent in overseas equities. Private investors have also demonstrated a keen interest in overseas stocks and have been rewarded with generally good returns (see Table 9.2).

As mentioned above, in practice, for many investors, the need for diversification argues against direct overseas equity investment except where the portfolio is very large. Specialist unit and investment trusts represent a cheaper entry and a good way to gain exposure to these important markets without undue risk of over-specialisation.

Having said that, if you are interested in certain sectors – say, car manufacturing – the choice of UK shares is very limited and you may wish to buy US shares, for example, to obtain the level of exposure you desire.

Some stockbrokers believe that investing overseas is very important from the point of view of diversification. In other words, the benefits lie with reducing risk rather than increasing return. However, with the increasing globalisation of UK companies the degree of diversification overseas need not be as high as in the past.

Tables 9.2, 9.3 and 9.4 show how investing in overseas equities helps to spread risk and improve returns.

Table 9.2 World equity returns 1970–97 (nominal terms, % per annum)

Country	Local return	Exchange rate change	Total return in £
UK	16.8		16.8
USA	13.3	1.4	14.9
Germany	9.4	4.1	13.8
France	14.5	1.1	15.7
Netherlands	14.8	3.6	18.9
Japan	10.0	5.3	15.8

Source: Barclays Stockbrokers

Table 9.3 World bond returns 1970–97 (nominal terms, % per annum)

Country	Local return	Exchange rate change	Total return in £
UK	12.1		12.1
USA	8.6	1.4	10.1
Germany	7.7	4.1	12.1
France	9.5	1.1	10.7
Netherlands	8.5	3.6	12.4
Japan	7.9	5.3	13.6

Source: Barclays Stockbrokers

Table 9.4 Optimal portfolio (1979–97)

	Low risk taker	Average risk taker	Maximum risk taker
Cash	71	38	0
UK equities	7	16	56
US equities	2	7	0
German equities	3	6	9
Japanese equities	5	10	35
German bonds	12	23	0
Total portfolio	100	100	100
Portfolio return (% p.a.)	12	14	17

Source: Barclays Stockbrokers

MARKET CYCLES

As a general rule the companies in a sector share certain characteristics which make them respond in a certain way to changes in the market cycles. This is why it is important, although not essential, to build a portfolio which spans all the major sectors. This helps to spread risk and avoids your portfolio crashing in a nasty way as the economy enters or emerges from a recession. (Economic cycles, including some help with bear markets, are discussed in Chapter 13.)

> As a general rule the companies in a sector share certain characteristics which make them respond in a certain way to changes in the market cycles.

Remember, though, that many of the blue chip companies which form the FTSE 100 index have considerable exposure overseas and so are not only affected by economic cycles in the UK. As mentioned above, this is generally seen as a plus point for investors keen to spread risk.

STOCKBROKER MODEL PORTFOLIOS

Some private client stockbrokers maintain model portfolios and it is worth asking to see examples in order to gain a view of the manager's approach. In addition, a good independent guide can be found in *Investors Chronicle* which each week publishes its own model portfolios (Bearbull) to show the results of portfolios which are built for growth, income, speculative investments, and overseas investments.

Understandably, brokers may be unwilling to publish details of the specific stocks they recommend at a given time. This is partly because they guard their stock selection process from the eyes of competitors but, probably more to the point, a recommended selection of shares quickly becomes out of date as company information and economic reports flood in.

So, without revealing the names of specific stocks, the following information from Henderson Investors, gives you an idea of how the process works.

In its 'Select Portfolio Management Services', for clients with over £100 000 to invest, Henderson runs three model portfolios, again aiming for growth, a balance of growth and income, and income. (A tailored service is offered for those with about £300 000 minimum to invest.)

So, for example, if you want to pay for your children's school fees out of your portfolio, initially, assuming the children are still very young, you would be aiming for growth. Later, part of your portfolio would be adjusted so it can generate the cash required to pay the fees on the dates they fall due, without forcing you to sell your shares at the wrong time.

Where individual equities are mentioned in these model portfolios, they are selected from the FTSE 100 index and equal weighting would be given to each stock. Exposure to small and medium-sized companies for this size portfolio would usually be achieved through investment trusts. Exposure to overseas markets is achieved through a combination of equity-based unit and investment trusts.

■ Growth portfolio

Gross income yield: 2.11% (January 1998).

Suitable for: those who can afford to leave their money invested for some years.

Objective: to achieve capital appreciation over the medium to long term.

Method: Actively managing investments in UK listed equities and in investment and unit trusts covering major global markets.

Asset allocation

Cash 5%

Fixed interest (one fund) 5%

UK equities (18 individual shares) 40%

UK equities Small/Mid Cap (4 unit/investment trusts) 20%

Overseas 30% as follows:
- Europe (2 funds) 10%
- North America (1 fund) 5%
- Far East (1 fund) 5%
- Japan (1 fund) 7%
- International (1 emerging markets fund) 3%

■ Balanced portfolio

Gross income yield: 3.4% (January 1998).

Suitable for: investors seeking a balance between growth and income.

Objective: to provide an income marginally in excess of the FTSE All-Share index, with the prospect of long-term capital appreciation.

Method: investing predominantly in income-generating equities listed on the London Stock Exchange, as well as gilts and bonds when appropriate. Again, overseas investments are made through equity based unit and investment trusts.

Asset allocation

Cash 5%

Fixed interest (two gilts) 15%

UK equities (18 individual shares) 45%

UK equities Small/Mid Cap (3 funds) 15%

Overseas 20% as follows:

- Europe (2 funds) 8%
- North America (1 fund) 3%
- Far East (1 fund) 4%
- Japan (1 fund) 3%
- International (1 emerging markets fund) 2%

■ High income

Gross income yield: 5.06% (January 1998).

Suitable for: investors seeking an immediate income.

Objective: to generate a high level of income significantly in excess of the FTSE All-Share index, with the prospect of a degree of capital growth.

Method: to construct a portfolio weighted towards UK gilts and bonds, with the remainder invested in high yielding UK listed equities, unit trusts and investment trusts, selected for their longer term income and capital growth prospects. Overseas exposure is likely to be small.

Asset allocation

Cash 5%

Fixed interest (4 gilts) 45%

UK equities (12 individual shares from the FTSE 100) 30%

UK equities Small/Mid Cap (2 funds) 10%

Overseas 10% as follows:
- Europe (1 fund) 3%
- North America (1 fund) 2%
- Japan/Far East (1 fund) 5%

Sources

Details about the FTSE International/APCIMS Private Investor Indices can be found at the FTSE International web site at http://www.ftse.com, where a service called On Target will allow you to analyse the performance of the portfolios free of charge. Alternatively, the indices are reported in the *Financial Times*, other financial newspapers and publications and on a number of data vendor terminals.

For details of Barclay Capital's Equity Gilt Study, see page 33.

Henderson Investors is at 3 Finsbury Avenue, London EC2M 2PA.

Cantrade Compendium of Stockmarket Investment for the Private Investor, available from Cantrade Investment Management Ltd, 4 Chiswell Street, Finsbury Square, London EC1Y 4UP.

Summary

- Before you can decide which asset classes you should hold, you need to refer back to your aims and objectives. Then you can match assets with liabilities/goals. Institutional funds call this an asset/liability study or model.

- Your portfolio should reflect your current and expected future financial position, your tax status, any ethical views, and your tolerance to risk.

- It is not wise to build a portfolio based on the assumption that inflation has been beaten for good.

- Building a new portfolio or reweighting your existing collection of shares may take up to a year. Keep any spare cash in a deposit account during this period.

- Collective funds are commonly used to achieve exposure to overseas markets and smaller companies.

- Even an income portfolio may invest up to 50 per cent of its assets in equities.

- International equities may be held to reduce risk rather than improve returns.

10

How to select your shares

At a glance

Stock picking, we are frequently told, is an art, not a science. You can try and make it a science if you like but most professionals have given up on this one, at least in the active management market.

Passive management (index tracking) is a different kettle of fish and aims to eliminate the risk of individual stock selection. So, if your portfolio or collective fund holds a sample of different stocks or actually replicates every stock in an index (the FTSE 100 usually, but sometimes the 250 or the All-Share) over the long term, you can't lose provided your benchmark is the index itself.

Of course this does not mean your portfolio is guaranteed to rise. If the index takes a tumble, your portfolio will follow. Nevertheless, low-cost index-tracking unit trusts are very popular and worth considering (see page 77).

The fact that stock picking is an art does not mean you should abandon the pursuit of knowledge and select your shares by sticking a pin in the Companies and Markets section of the *Financial Times*. What it does mean is that you are never guaranteed success (unless you indulge in a spot of skullduggery). Nor is your stockbroker. This is why investing in shares can be very risky, particularly over the short term when the volatility of markets can temporarily depress the share price of even the best of companies.

The difference between the art of stock picking and the pin sticking exercise is information and strategy. Pin sticking is all about pure luck, stock picking is all about making informed decisions in the light of your investment aims.

Most of the discussion on equities so far has focused on their importance as an asset class. This Chapter looks at the share selection process, while Chapter 13 shows the importance of timing and the influence on share prices of market cycles. Pages 277–8 recommend some reading material and tell you what to avoid (tip sheets for one).

YOUR STARTING POINT

If you have over £100 000 to invest (some stockbrokers put the figure much higher) you could consider including direct equity investments in your portfolio. The optimum minimum number of shares depends on what you are trying to achieve.

Opinions vary greatly on this point, but as an absolute minimum you should aim to hold ten different shares. Twenty or 30 would be even better since this would help achieve a well diversified spread of risk, provided each holding was a sensible minimum size. Again, opinions also vary, but as a very rough guide you could consider a minimum holding as anything between £1000 and £5000, depending on the costs involved.

> If you have over £100 000 to invest you could consider including direct equity investments in your portfolio.

To avoid over-exposure to the risks inherent in smaller companies, some advisers recommend you put at least half of your capital destined for equities in FTSE 100 companies. An alternative is to achieve your exposure to the FTSE 100 companies through index-tracking unit trusts. On top of this you can buy a handful of carefully selected individual equities to boost your portfolio's potential growth.

INVESTMENT AIMS

Whatever your starting point it is important to have an objective and to stick to it. The more disciplined you are in this respect, the more likely you are to achieve your aims and not get sidetracked by events.

There are two important risks to consider here. First, there is the subjective risk that you might get it wrong. Second, there is a risk that you do not achieve your own private goals.

A very simplistic approach is to determine whether you are looking for growth, income or a mixture of the two. These portfolio types were discussed in Chapter 9 where models for asset allocation were examined.

You also need to devise a sensible selection process. If you ask the right questions before you buy, while there is no guarantee of success (always remembering that this is art not science), you will avoid the fads and, what may be more difficult, the shares that look genuinely attractive but are entirely inappropriate for your portfolio aims and investment timescale.

The following explanations and tips may prove useful in your search. If you already have an appropriate portfolio up and running, pay particular attention to the section on selling. It's no good selecting your shares with care if you do not have a strategy for weeding out the losers at the right time. Also see Chapter 17 for advice on how to maintain the portfolio and monitor performance.

■ Avoid frequency of trading

> **TIP** Before you start, though, it is worth pointing out one of the most obvious pitfalls for private investors, namely that the cost of frequent dealing can quickly outweigh minor gains.

The mechanics of dealing are considered in more detail in Chapter 14 but as a very rough guide you will find that the price of shares you buy will need to rise by about 4–5 per cent before you work off the sale or purchase costs.

So, a simple but nevertheless worthy tip for the largely risk-averse investors and those with comparatively small portfolios, is to trade as infrequently as possible. Of course, this does not mean you should hang on to bad shares.

Moreover, even if you buy for the medium to long term and do all your homework before investing, you need to keep an eye on your shares to make sure they still offer the same package of attractions as when you bought them. You also need to keep an eye on new offers to see if any might usurp the old favourites in your affections. Loyalty is a misplaced emotion in the private investor.

This might seem a rather mundane and pedantic way to manage your portfolio but unless you deliberately set out to be a frequent trader, it beats other systems which might rely on a percentage price drop, for example, to trigger a sell signal.

HOW SHARES ARE CATEGORISED

Shares fall into all sorts of different categories and each label tells you something important about the investment prospects. Size and type of business are the two most obvious categories.

■ Does size count?

The simple answer is, yes, and this is as good a starting point as any.

> Shares fall into all sorts of different categories and each label tells you something important about the investment prospects.

The London Stock Exchange has over 2000 listed companies and is the main securities market in the UK. It acts as a *primary market* for new issues and also as a *secondary market*. (Gilts and bonds are also listed on the Stock Exchange. See Chapter 15.)

In theory, large companies that are well diversified should be more stable than smaller companies, partly because of their sheer size and deep pockets but also because, through diversification in the UK and overseas, they should be less vulnerable to market cycles and economic factors such as a rise or fall in interest rates or a recession.

If one part of the company is affected by a fall in retail sales, for example, other parts of the group might still be thriving. In this way an investment in a blue chip company carries an inherent spread of risk, whereas a small, specialised company is much more vulnerable to economic conditions and market sentiment.

Clearly, the reverse is also true. If you pick a small growing company which doubles its turnover in one year then your shares could boom. Larger companies are less likely to experience sharp rises as well as the sharp downturns, although there are always exceptions to this rule.

In practice, of course, a large company can get into serious trouble or even go bust unexpectedly (Polly Peck and Maxwell, again). It is always a nasty shock to discover in retrospect just how well the directors can hide what should have been clear signs of impending doom.

Finally, income seekers need to decide what risks they are prepared to take. A high income generating portfolio can also be highly speculative – it does not have to be confined to larger companies.

THE FTSE INTERNATIONAL INDICES

The quickest way to assess the size of a company is by looking at the FTSE International Indices, published each day in the *Financial Times*. The indices and how to read them are discussed in more detail in Chapter 17, but it is helpful here to consider the chief characteristics of the main equity indices which are likely to contain your most popular shares.

Bear in mind though that these are theoretical characteristics. In practice markets may move in a totally unpredictable fashion so it is important to look at actual trends, not just the theory.

> **The quickest way to assess the size of a company is by looking at the FTSE International Indices.**

The FTSE Actuaries indices were developed by the *Financial Times*, the Stock Exchange and the Institute and Faculty of Actuaries. Since November 1995 the indices have been managed by a joint company, the FTSE International.

These indices are arithmetically weighted by market capitalisation so that the larger the company the greater the effect its share price movement will have on the index. 'Market capitalisation' is the stockmarket valuation of the company, which is calculated by multiplying the number of shares in issue by their market price.

■ The FTSE All-Share

This is the most comprehensive UK index and consists of just over 900 companies with a market capitalisation of above about £40 million. The All-Share is regarded as the professional investor's yardstick for the level of the UK equity market as a whole and represents about 98 per cent of UK stockmarket capitalisation. Within the All-Share, companies are allocated to 36 different categories of shares according to industrial sector. There are also eight sub-indices, including the FTSE 100 and Mid-250.

■ The FTSE 100

This index consists of the 100 largest UK companies by market capitalisation and is the standard reference point for defining Britain's 'blue chip' companies (blue chip being the highest value chip in a game of poker). The FTSE 100 companies together represent about 72 per cent of the UK stockmarket capitalisation.

Place in your portfolio: These are large companies, many of which are multinationals with substantial overseas exposure. Companies in this index tend to do better in a recession than smaller companies and their size and diversification tends to make them fairly stable investments.

Advisers usually recommend that once you have your portfolio of collective funds, this is the best place to start with direct equity investments. To further enhance your spread of risk, make sure you choose your shares from a wide range of sectors.

If you are more adventurous and want to spend your time hunting down value for money among the smaller companies in the All-Share, you could always buy units in a UK tracker fund which replicates the FTSE 100 and gain your blue chips this way (see Chapter 10), leaving you free to spend time researching smaller companies.

■ The FTSE 250

This index consists of the next 250 companies below the FTSE 100 and can include or exclude investment trusts. The Mid 250s are companies capitalised at between £150 million and £1 billion. Together, these companies represent about 16 per cent of the UK stockmarket capitalisation (including investment trusts).

Place in your portfolio: These companies may have less exposure to manufacturing in overseas markets although they may rely heavily on exports. During an economic recovery companies in this index tend to experience higher returns than the FTSE 100 but still manage to avoid exposure to the volatility experienced by some of the smaller companies in the All-Share index. A good bet, therefore, after you have built up your collection of blue chips – but do make sure you research the individual companies well before taking the plunge.

■ The FTSE SmallCap

This index does not have a fixed number of constituent companies but instead it comprises all the remaining companies in the All-Share which are too small to qualify for the top 350. Together they account for about 7 per cent of the total UK capitalisation.

Place in your portfolio: Clearly, All-Share companies which fall outside of the FTSE 350 (the FTSE 100 and Mid-250 combined) are potentially more risky and volatile than the larger companies. However, this is an area in which private investors traditionally have done well. These companies are less sought after by the professionals because very large funds cannot trade in these shares easily since the size of the deal might in itself push up or depress the share price. As a result, these companies usually are less well researched than the FTSE 350.

Certainly, if you have local knowledge of a company and you believe it has a good management team and is in an up and coming market, you could do very well. However, beginners and the risk-averse should not commit too much money to any one company because this would concentrate the risk in your portfolio.

■ Fledgling market

In total there are over 2100 companies listed on the London Stock Exchange so clearly there are many other companies in which you could invest outside of the All-Share. The Fledgling market covers all of the companies which are too small at present to be in the All-Share index but otherwise are eligible to join.

Place in your portfolio: Once you get down to this level you really have to be careful. Whatever their business, the share price of small companies can be extremely volatile. A company that specialises in one or two products is very vulnerable to price competition and a sudden reduction in demand.

Moreover, a signal from a tip sheet to buy a small company's shares could be enough to send the price through the roof, while a panic to sell on the part of very few investors can be enough to force the share price down into the doldrums.

In conclusion, intensive research and a strict ceiling on the amount you invest in any one company are essential. Also, these shares may not be very liquid so buying and, in particular, selling, can be a problem. If you plan to use a stockbroker, find one that specialises in smaller companies to save you some legwork.

■ Alternative Investment Market

AIM replaced the Unlisted Securities Market (USM) in 1995 and lists about 300 companies. It allows small and relatively new companies which are growing quickly to go public without having to go through the expensive and time-consuming full listing procedures required for a Stock Exchange main listing. Private investors should also note that AIM companies are not regulated as strictly as fully listed companies.

In due course a successful AIM company may move into the All-Share.

Place in your portfolio: These are risky companies. As with the smaller company shares listed on the Exchange but outside of the All-Share, you must be sure you have done your research well before parting with your cash. Again you should watch out for lack of liquidity with AIM companies.

■ Companies ineligible for the All-Share

Some companies are not eligible to join the All-Share or the Fledgling market. This is not usually a question of size but of some other characteristic. For example, the following are ineligible:

- foreign companies (which would also be listed on their home country stockmarket), eg Americans, Canadians and South Africans, which are listed after the AIM countries in the FT Companies and Markets section
- subsidiaries of companies already in the All-Share
- companies with less than 25 per cent of shares in 'free float' (i.e. over 75 per cent is held by the family or directors)
- companies whose shares were not traded for a minimum number of days in the previous year
- split capital investment trusts.

CLASSIFICATION BY SECTOR

The sectors used by the FTSE International categorise the All-Share group companies according to what they do. In theory this helps because the companies in a sector are likely to be affected by a similar range of economic factors. For example if we are in a dire recession people still need to eat so companies in the 'Retailers, food' sector might be a good place to find some defensive stocks, while 'Breweries, pubs and restaurants' and 'Leisure and hotels' might feel the pinch as consumers cut back on non-essential items.

However, stock picking purely by sector is not necessarily a good technique. Some sectors represent a very concentrated market whereas others – transport, for example – represents a diversified range of companies. The point to remember here is that you must consider the profile of the sector and the company itself. Just because one company is experiencing good growth does not mean that you can pick any company in the sector and be guaranteed a winner.

Where the sector classifications can help is in determining your investment position relative to the 'market'. If your aim is to beat the All-Share index, for example, you need to have a clear idea of how the index is constructed and deviate where you feel a sector is likely to perform well under the current market conditions.

SHAREHOLDER PERKS

Some shares offer certain perks – for example a discount at the company's stores or free tickets to certain events. In most cases these are no more than the free gift in the cereal box but for some sport, entertainment, or other enthusiasts the perks may well swing it. Do check, however, whether you will qualify for the perks, particularly if you use a *nominee account* (see page 182).

NEW ISSUES

Over the past decade or so new issues have been dominated by the Government's privatisation of previously public sector companies. Many new investors have done very well out of these companies which have fallen mainly into the utilities sector. British Gas, for example, was sold off the back of the famous 'Sid' campaign.

More recently several major building societies and life assurance institutions have converted from 'mutual' status, where they are owned by their members, to public limited companies owned by shareholders. Most demutualisations have been characterised by the huge *windfall* share payments, where free shares in the new company were given to existing savers and borrowers.

Both of these categories of shares have done fairly well but there are many other reasons why a company comes to the stockmarket, some of which are dealt with in Chapter 2 which explains why and how companies can raise finance to expand. For example, private owners may want to realise their capital and use it for other purposes.

When a company first comes to the market it must be accompanied by a prospectus, which provides information similar to that contained in the annual report and accounts, although usually there is more detail.

The company may go public in one of four ways:

- *Offer for sale:* where a set number of shares is offered for sale at a set price. Privatisations have generally used this route. On several occasions the price has been attractively low so that investors who secured an allocation of shares did very well. With this type of issue you can consider becoming a 'stag', that is, an investor who seeks an allocation, only to sell immediately for a quick profit.

- *A tender offer:* where the company's advisers set a minimum price but do not set the final price until all the offers are in. This makes stagging virtually impossible, and the fact that you do not know the actual purchase price at the time you seek an allocation of shares often puts off private investors.

- *Placings:* when a company offers its shares directly to financial institutions, rather than to the general public. Placings can be combined with 'intermediary offers', where up to 50 per cent of an issue placed with financial institutions can be clawed back if there are enough offers from private investors through stockbrokers.

- *Introductions:* where a company already has a number of shareholders and applies to the Stock Exchange to introduce its shares to the market.

- *Demergers:* where a company decides to hive off part of its operation into a separate company, often by offering free shares to existing shareholders. These shares are then listed separately on the Stock Exchange.

WHEN TO SELL

Deciding when to sell a share can be every bit as tricky as deciding when to buy. Again, there are no fixed rules but stockbrokers recommend that you lay down some guidelines at the outset to avoid panic reactions.

Price alone is not a good guide. It is always tempting to sell when a share price starts to fall, on the assumption that gravity is at work and what goes down must keep on going down.

> Deciding when to sell a share can be every bit as tricky as deciding when to buy.

What you want to avoid is either holding a share so long that it has outgrown its usefulness, or selling a share at the drop of a hat before you have fully investigated the information. Good shares can, over time, either turn into mediocre shares or grow so much that they knock your portfolio out of balance.

There are those who argue that if you research a company thoroughly and buy for the long term then there is no need to change your selection on a regular basis. While this is a very sensible approach for the private investor, clearly it is important to review your shares regularly and to ensure that your original assumptions still apply and that your choice of shares meets your specific requirements, particularly when your financial circumstances have changed.

Sources

Several stockbrokers publish guides to shareholder perks, including Barclays Stockbrokers (see page 33) and Henry Cooke Lumsden, Piercy House, 7–9 Copthall Avenue, London EC2B 2HY.

Summary

- Information and an investment strategy are important.

- As an absolute minimum you should aim to hold ten shares. Twenty or 30 would be even better.

- To avoid overexposure to smaller company risks, some stockbrokers advise a 50 per cent allocation to blue chips in the equity portfolio.

- The cost of frequent trading can outweigh any modest benefits in share prices.

- Each method of categorisation tells us something about a share.

- Size is important in terms of risk and diversification of business interests.

- The FTSE All-Share is the professional investor's yardstick for the UK equity market.

- SmallCap, Fledgling and AIM shares should be selected with great care as these may be under-researched and the market may not be very liquid, particularly if you want to sell.

- Classification by sector helps define a share's characteristics in terms of market cycles but stock picking by this method alone is not recommended.

- Knowing when to sell is as important as knowing when to buy.

11

How to assess a share's value

- Important information from the company
- The selection process
- How to value shares
- Key indicators in practice
- Making comparisons

At a glance

This is where you need to know your companies inside out. Each one may have particular characteristics which could make it a good addition to your portfolio or a non-starter, no matter how attractive it might be in general terms.

This Chapter provides an introduction to some of the most important considerations in stock picking. Real enthusiasts can find out a lot more by consulting specialist publications. *A Guide to Stockpicking* by Gillian O'Connor is lucid, entertaining and highly recommended (see page 277).

IMPORTANT INFORMATION FROM THE COMPANY

By law a company listed on the Stock Exchange must produce a considerable amount of documentation for its shareholders (and, of course, the regulators and accountants, among others).

Typically, this will include two sets of profit figures at six-monthly intervals. The first set in the company's financial year is known as the interim results while the second set, the final results, is produced at the company's financial year end.

These figures provide a detailed analysis of the company's trading year and its profits or losses. Chapter 16 takes a closer look at the annual report and accounts, which are available to existing and prospective shareholders.

■ The FT London Share Service

A very useful source of information is the *Financial Times'* London Share Service. In the 'Companies and Markets' section you may see a symbol after the company name. A club symbol indicates you can obtain the current annual or interim report free of charge. All you have to do is phone a 24-hour number quoting the reference number provided in that edition of the *Financial Times*.

> A very useful source of information is the *Financial Times'* London Share Service.

A character symbol indicates you can obtain a comprehensive 10–14 page report on the company including key FT stories from the past 12 months, the latest survey of City profit forecasts and investment recommendations, a five-year financial and share price performance review, balance sheet and profit and loss data, plus recent Stock Exchange announcements. The price of this excellent package of information at the time of writing was £8.45. For more details about how to read the pink pages, see Chapter 17.

THE SELECTION PROCESS

Every investor has his or her own favoured selection process, so the following tips are intended as a guide only.

Once you have made your asset allocation decisions, your first step might be to decide which types of companies are suitable for your portfolio. This involves asking yourself some specific questions, including those covered in the following section.

■ Do you have ethical/environmental views?

This topic is covered more fully in Chapter 12, but briefly, if you have strong views about the ethical or environmental habits of the companies in which you invest, you need to formulate a clear policy and screen out those companies which do not meet your standards.

A good source of information on this subject is the Ethical Investment Research Service. EIRIS maintains a database which you can use to filter an existing portfolio of directly held shares and collective funds. The service allows you to pick and choose the particular issues which concern you and to build your own screening process (full details in Chapter 13).

Be warned though. A fairly comprehensive ethical and environmental screening will eliminate over half of the FTSE 100 companies. This tends to weight ethical portfolios towards smaller companies which can provide exciting growth prospects but can also introduce extra risks.

■ Consider your income needs

Remember the earlier point about income and risk. If a company's shares generate a high income this does not mean the company is large or 'safe'. Decide whether you are looking for value (that is, inherent value which in your analysis is not represented in the share price) or potential growth. Then consider the key indicators, for example, yield, the price/earnings ratio and, where appropriate (for example with investment trusts), the discount to net asset value. These factors are discussed later in this Chapter.

■ Are you cautious or can you afford to take risks?

This will depend partly on your attitude to risk and partly on your investment time frame. Short-term investors should avoid risky companies because if the share price takes a tumble there will not be sufficient time to recoup your losses before you need the capital back. Longer-term investors can take more risks if they wish.

As a general rule of thumb, if you are very cautious and cannot afford to take big losses stockbrokers recommend you stick to the well-researched FTSE 100 shares unless you happen to know a great deal about a smaller company.

Remember, however, that stockbrokers and the big investment managers all have their UK equity teams which tend to focus on the FTSE 100 companies. These shares are popular because they can be bought and sold easily and in large quantities. The large institutions simply cannot afford to own a substantial chunk of a smaller company because this would make selling very difficult. So, the point is, you are unlikely to spot anything of interest in blue chip companies that has not already been noticed by professional analysts.

Some brokers and managers also specialise in smaller companies but generally you stand a better chance pitting your wits against the experts in this market, particularly when you have a thorough knowledge of a company.

■ Are you a very active investor or do you invest for the long term?

If, nevertheless, you are an active investor you can take advantage of sudden changes to a company's prospects or ratings, which make a share attractive for a short period.

Clearly, frequent traders should avoid churning their portfolios as the costs of frequent purchases and sales will probably outweigh the advantages offered by a comparatively cheap share price. Equally, the less active trader should still review his or her portfolio on a regular basis to make sure it is still achieving its targets and does not hold any duds.

■ Use your eyes

Not all research into companies has to involve complicated ratios. It is also possible, and in some cases makes a lot of sense, to use your own experience to back up your selection process.

This is not as difficult as it sounds. You can attend the annual general meeting, for example (see Chapter 18), or wander into as many branches of a retail company as possible. Boots, Dixons, Marks & Spencer, Safeway, Sainsbury and Tesco are all within easy reach.

Are they expanding, and if so are they attracting crowds of new shoppers as a result? Are both the quality and price of products competitive or is the checkout queue full of grumbling shoppers planning to go elsewhere in future?

First-hand knowledge of a company can be combined with information from the annual report and accounts (see Chapter 16) to build up a more accurate and detailed picture which reflects a company's prospects.

■ Directors' dealings

One way to gain knowledge is to examine the number and value of shares in a company bought and sold by the directors. By law directors have to report any transactions in their own company shares to the Stock Exchange within five days. This information in turn is published by newspapers, including the *Financial Times*, and other specialist sources.

> One way to gain knowledge is to examine the number and value of shares in a company bought and sold by the directors.

If the directors are buying in any significant quantity, in theory this indicates confidence in the company's future prospects. Of course, in practice it is not so simple, and you should be careful how you interpret the signals.

Sales are considered to be less indicative than purchases because they could just mean that the director needs some cash. However, purchases could also be used by directors as a smoke screen to give an aura of confidence when behind the scenes all is not shipshape.

In conclusion, for the private investor, directors' share dealings can be of interest but they are not a reliable basis for an investment decision. Use the information as just one useful piece of the jigsaw.

■ Balance sheets

As mentioned, the annual report and accounts provide some very detailed information about the company and its prospects. Chapter 16 shows you how to read these documents and highlights the most important information to look for.

■ Is the company fashionable?

If something looks like a fad you may be better off avoiding it altogether, even if the share price of certain companies or of a whole sector is rising. By the time the broker research and newspapers have identified a trend, you can bet your bottom dollar that the best bargains will have gone.

> If something looks like a fad you may be better off avoiding it altogether.

It is a sad but true fact that most trends are over by the time the private investors start piling in. Such is the certainty of this behavioural pattern that some professionals interpret private investor enthusiasm as a signal to get out!

■ Do you need a defensive position?

Some companies continue to plod along whether the rest of the market is dipping and soaring, while within each sector there will be companies which tend to do well at different phases in the market cycle. Whether you need to boost your holdings in companies that demonstrate certain characteristics at different stages in the economic cycle will depend on your view of the economy and on the long-awaited bear market.

If this is your concern you might also consider investing in asset classes other than equities. Gilts, bonds and cash might also be appropriate defensive weapons, particularly for older investors and income seekers, while in certain cases the use of derivatives can protect you from a sudden fall in prices. (See Chapter 13 on defensive measures.)

HOW TO VALUE SHARES

Once you have identified the shares which appeal to you and seem to fit well in your portfolio, it is time to take a closer look at the mathematics. (Alternatively, if ratios leave you cold then this is one of the best reasons going for appointing a stockbroking firm which employs its own analysts!)

There are two basic exercises here. First, you need to make a general assessment of how well or otherwise the company is doing compared with the market as a whole and second, with its peers within the appropriate sector.

Check the company's recent history. There are several online sources of information (see page 276), while the *Financial Times'* London Share Service (see page 239) provides recent news stories about the company, profit forecasts plus a five-year financial and share price performance review, among other details. Follow this information up with a thorough reading of the annual report and accounts, but do remember that this document will be out of date and should be supplemented with any recent news. The annual report is the subject of Chapter 16.

The second exercise is to consider how the market views the share price. This is a more precise activity and requires an understanding of how professionals make their calculations.

There are several important yardsticks, some of which are discussed in Chapter 16. Here we consider the *dividend yield* and the *price/earnings ratio* (or earnings multiple), which are two common yardsticks when assessing a share's value.

We also explain various other ratios employed by analysts. For some companies it is necessary to look at the *net asset value* (investment trusts and property companies, for example – see Chapter 13). *Gearing* – or the amount the company has borrowed compared with what it actually owns – is also an indicator of the company's security and an investor's sensitivity to company performance. (Gearing is known as leverage in the US.)

The following guide explains the general principles behind the ratios. Ratios or yardsticks are best employed when making comparisons between companies in the same sector.

■ The dividend yield

This is a method of examining the income from an investment based on historic information. It is the annual gross dividend as a percentage of the market price. This shows the rate of gross income a shareholder would receive on an investment at that particular share price – rather like the way you might describe the before tax interest paid on a deposit account. As with an ordinary deposit account, there is no guarantee that the dividend yield will be maintained.

Barclays Stockbrokers Investment Study (see Chapter 2) explains that a low dividend yield is associated with a high valuation for the stockmarket because it tends to be followed by low returns, whereas high dividend yields tend to be followed by high real returns, especially over the following 12 months.

The trouble is that we cannot assume the past is a guide to the future. Much will depend on the economic environment. The Barclays' study explains:

'A prolonged period of low inflation and sustained economic growth could maintain the stockmarket at levels that might appear high by past standards. ... The lesson of history is that the benchmarks for valuation can and do change.

Investment is therefore more about gauging the direction of markets and hence appreciating the new valuation norms than relying on past guidelines. Changes in the economic environment are the main determinant of changes in valuation standards. In particular, changes in the inflation rate are a major influence on the markets.'

KEY INDICATORS IN PRACTICE

Clearly, there are no hard and fast rules with dividends because they reflect the current state of the business. If the company is prone to follow the dips and peaks of market cycles (see Chapter 13), this will be reflected in the dividend payments.

Having said that, the larger companies, particularly the FTSE 100, tend to maintain fairly consistent dividend payments partly because of their size and level of profits but also because they are expected to do so and it upsets professionals and amateurs alike if they chop and change. (The pension funds, for example, rely on a stream of income to pay the pensions and other benefits guaranteed to scheme members.) This does not mean that a FTSE 100 company will never slash its dividend – it's just not common.

> **TIP** It is also important to look at the total return – that is, dividends reinvested plus capital growth. Reinvested dividends account for a substantial proportion of the total return. Over a ten-year period, reinvested dividends on the FTSE 100 index account for roughly half of the total return.

As mentioned above, analysts tend to assume that a higher dividend indicates the shares are likely to produce above average total returns over the long term, while some very successful investors only invest in high yielding shares.

However, a comparatively high dividend is always worth checking out to make sure there is nothing untoward going on behind the scenes. Look at the company's gearing (debt) to see if it is borrowing to shore up its dividend commitment. Very high dividends can be a sign that the company is in trouble.

You might also come across the term *dividend cover*. This is a stock market ratio which quantifies the amount of cash in a company's coffers. If the dividend cover is high this means the company could afford to pay out the dividend several times over from earnings per share. This indicates that profits are being retained for the business. When the cover is low it means the company had to struggle to scrape together the dividend announced and may even have subsidised it from reserves.

■ The price/earnings (p/e) ratio

This is the market price of a share divided by the company's earnings (profits) per share in its latest 12-month trading period. As a very rough guide, a high ratio means the market considers a company is likely to produce above average growth, while a low p/e ratio means the opposite.

P/e ratios are a handy benchmark to use when comparing shares of similar companies within a sector – two supermarket chains, for example. You also need to check the ratio against the average for other sectors because it could be that at a particular point in the market cycle, all shares in the sector in which you are interested might be marked down if they move in line with economic trends.

Both the dividend yield and the p/e ratio are shown in the *Financial Times* share prices pages (see Chapter 17) and in the *Investors Chronicle*'s company tables.

■ Net asset value

This is an important feature for certain types of company, particularly property companies and investment companies. Take investment trusts, for example. These are UK companies which invest in the shares of other companies. Investment trusts have a fixed number of shares which are subject to the usual market forces, so the share price does not necessarily reflect the total value of the shares the trust owns.

If the share price is lower than the value per share of the underlying assets the difference is known as the *discount*. If the share price is higher the difference is known as the *premium*. As a general rule, an investment trust share trading at a discount may represent good value.

■ Financial gearing

This is the ratio between the company's borrowings and its capitalisation – in other words, a ratio between what it owes and what it owns. As a general rule you should find out why a company is highly geared before you invest, particularly if interest rates are high, because servicing the debts could cause a considerable strain on its business and profits.

However, do consider the gearing in the context of the company's business plans. If interest rates are low, a highly geared company which is well run can make good use of its debts – for example to expand into a new and profitable market.

Another way of looking at gearing is to consider how the profits compare with the interest payments made to service the company's debt. The number of times profits can cover the interest payments is known as *interest cover*. Company analysts suggest that in very broad terms, a ratio of four times profits to interest owed is healthy. A ratio of 1:1 is definitely not.

■ The acid test

Analysts also refer to something called the *acid test* which is a ratio of the company's current assets (excluding stock) to its current liabilities. The reason stock is excluded is that if a company is in serious trouble its stock may not be worth the full market value. Sales and auctions following a liquidation usually sell at knock-down prices.

Analysts reckon that the ratio ought to be about 1:1, so that if the company did get into trouble it could meet all its liabilities (including payments to bond holders and shareholders) without having to rely on whatever the liquidator could raise by selling off its stock cheaply.

■ Asset backing

This is another way of looking at what the company would be worth if all else failed and it went bust. In practice this test is a common exercise in the analysis of a takeover bid. The aggressor and the shareholders need to know the real value of assets per share in order to calculate an attractive price for the bidding process. Clearly, the acquiring company needs to persuade the shareholders either to transfer their loyalty to the new prospective management team or simply to grab the money and run.

■ The pre-tax profit margin

This is the trading profit – before the deduction of depreciation, interest payments and tax – as a percentage of turnover. The pre-tax profit margin is considered a useful guide to the company's general performance and the management team's competence because it reveals the profits earned per pound of sales.

■ The return on capital

This is the profits before tax, divided by the shareholders' funds, and indicates the return the company is making on all the capital tied up in the business.

MAKING COMPARISONS

All of these ratios and measures must be considered in the context of a full financial picture of the company. Obviously if you rely on just one or two, you may miss something very important or get an unbalanced view of the company.

Don't fall into the trap of thinking that, just because the figures indicate a company will pay out high dividends in future or will experience capital growth, this will automatically follow. There are no guarantees. All you can achieve is an informed prediction.

> All of these ratios and measures must be considered in the context of a full financial picture of the company.

Also, remember that the real point about ratios is to spot where the market ratings are inappropriate to the company's actual prospects. Clearly, to identify this situation you would require a good deal of knowledge about the company itself and to understand why the market has got it wrong.

In conclusion, for most investors it is important to use as many sources as possible for information about markets, inflation, the economy and individual companies. However, some very successful enthusiasts adopt a very specific style. Chartists and fundamental analysts, among others, are discussed briefly in Chapter 2.

Summary

■ Examine the profit figures, both interim and final.

■ Read the annual report and accounts to assess the company's trading year and profits or losses.

■ The FT London Share Service provides a wealth of useful data for very little outlay.

■ Consider your ethical and environmental views before you buy.

■ Consider your income needs but remember that a high income does not go hand in hand with security.

■ Directors' dealings can shed light on a company's prospects but can also be used as a smokescreen.

■ There are many important yardsticks to consider, including the dividend yield and price/earnings ratio.

■ As an investor you will be interested in the total return – that is, dividends reinvested plus capital growth.

■ Financial gearing is important but do consider the figures in conjunction with the purpose to which the company puts its borrowings.

■ The acid test is a good indicator of whether the company could afford to pay bond holders and shareholders if it went bust tomorrow.

12

Ethical investment

- What is ethical?
- Define your views clearly
- Performance
- Smaller companies
- Alternative investments

At a glance

If you ask ten people what they think is ethical you will get ten different answers.

In the last Chapter we discussed the importance of maintaining a rational selection process when you build your portfolio of shares and collective funds. In this Chapter we consider how to put your ethical and environmental views into practice as an investor.

This is not necessarily easy. If you ask ten people what they think is ethical you will get ten different answers. Ethical views, by their very nature, are subjective.

WHAT IS ETHICAL?

Ethical investment is where the investor's personal views dictate the type of shares actively selected and the type of shares screened out. Environmental funds can also be regarded as ethical. Here the choice of shares will depend on a company's environmental policy in terms of pollution, ozone depletion, deforestation and waste management, among other criteria.

Whether you make your own selections or you wish to set guidelines for your stockbroker, it is essential to be able to translate your views into a clear mandate.

Bear in mind that some stockbrokers are much more sympathetic than others when it comes to ethical investment. A stockbroker who takes the matter seriously will have considerable research at his or her disposal. A cynic will probably try to dissuade you, pointing out the significant constraints on the choice of shares and how this can undermine performance.

Don't dismiss the apparently cynical approach. Remember, any strong ethical views you may have are likely to go against your stockbroker's natural instinct to make as much money as possible for you. (After all, the firm's fees usually are linked to the size of your portfolio.) If you proceed with an ethical portfolio, make sure you set an appropriate performance benchmark and do not expect it to reflect the market movements as a whole.

DEFINE YOUR VIEWS CLEARLY

The first problem you must face is to decide where to draw the line. You may, for example, feel convinced about the exclusion of tobacco and/or alcohol companies. But what about the supermarkets that sell their products? If you are opposed to gambling, do you include all the outlets that sell tickets for the National Lottery?

> If you are opposed to gambling, do you include all the outlets that sell tickets for the National Lottery?

Anti-tobacco investors would naturally exclude British American Tobacco but would they also exclude Allied Dunbar and Eagle Star, which are insurance and investment companies owned by BAT?

Some investors operate a positive screening process because they are keen on the groundbreaking research of the pharmaceutical companies in their wars against cancer and AIDS, for example. Others might exclude the same companies on the grounds that they carry out experiments on animals.

In an extreme case, even apparently innocuous products like National Savings and gilts can cause problems because they are effectively 'sold' by the Government. The same Government is responsible for the massive expenditure on armaments (and animal experiments), via public and private sector agencies and universities. You must decide whether these factors outweigh the benefits of expenditure on education, health and social security.

■ Negative or positive ethical stance?

Ethical investment can be tackled as a positive or negative process. Some of the ethical unit trusts, for example, work in a negative way by excluding certain categories of investment. The major evils tend to be arms, alcohol, tobacco, gambling, animal testing, environmental damage and the payment of exploitative wages in developing countries. But the list could extend almost indefinitely.

Some ethical investors take a more proactive approach and want to encourage companies which are working towards some desirable goal – 'green' companies involved in recycling or environmentally friendly waste disposal, for example. Beware of 'green' labels – it's the next best selling aid to 'tax-free'.

Clearly, ethical investment is a complicated subject and is not helped by the difficulty and cost of obtaining sufficient data upon which to form a view about the business of ethical companies.

■ EIRIS

A good source of information on this subject is the Ethical Investment Research Service. EIRIS maintains a database which you employ to filter an existing portfolio or to build one from scratch, using your own selection of a wide range of criteria.

EIRIS was set up in 1983 by a number of organisations including Quakers, Methodists, Oxfam and the Rowntree Trust. It monitors the screening and performance of the ethical and environmental unit trusts, so if you are interested in collective funds, this is the best place to start.

It also offers a screening process for direct equity investors. The simplest way to use EIRIS research is to request an 'acceptable list' – a list of companies which meet your ethical or environmental criteria. A 'portfolio screen' enables you to find out more about the shares you hold, while for the real enthusiast, EIRIS factsheets provide all the information on the database on the companies in question.

EIRIS researches over 1000 companies. The screening options from which you can choose include:

- alcohol
- animals (meat production and sale, leather/fur manufacture and sale)
- arms and sales to military purchasers
- community involvement
- corporate governance
- directors' pay
- environmental issues
- equal opportunities
- gambling
- greenhouse gases
- health and safety convictions
- human rights
- intensive farming
- military contracts
- newspaper production and television
- nuclear power (fuel, components and construction of plants)
- overseas interests (wages exploitation in emerging economies, deriving profits from countries with poor human rights records)
- ozone depleting chemicals

- pesticides
- political contributions
- pornography
- Third World involvement
- tropical hardwood
- tobacco
- waste disposal
- water pollution.

■ Broad brush approach

In practice many investors settle for a broad brush approach that eliminates the obvious villains but does not go into too much detail. Using the analogy above, this would exclude the tobacco companies but not the supermarkets which sell cigarettes.

This approach would also screen out the companies whose primary business is armaments but could leave you with companies with a minority interest in arms.

Probably some element of compromise is called for, but you have to decide how far you are prepared to go to identify the ethical stars and whether you are prepared to accept the resulting restriction in investment choice.

You also need to decide whether to limit your ethical investment views to your private portfolio of shares and funds or whether to take it further. For example, if you are in a company pension scheme, what influence, if any, can you have over the investment aims of the pension fund?

The chances are, this would be limited to your freedom to express your views to the trustees. Ultimately, you could decide to leave the scheme and set up your own ethical personal pension plan but this could be a very high price to pay because the company scheme is a very valuable benefit for you and your dependents.

PERFORMANCE

TIP Critics of ethical investment say that performance suffers due to the exclusion of many major FTSE 100 companies.

This could result in overexposure to certain risks and you might not be in a position to reap the rewards of a boom in certain sectors – chemicals, engineering or pharmaceuticals, for example.

Table 12.1 lists the main companies identified by Cantrade Investments that could be excluded in this broadbrush approach and notes the proportion of the stockmarket as a whole which these companies represent.

Table 12.1 Large companies commonly avoided by ethical investors

Company	Stockmarket weighting %	Arms	Alcohol	Tobacco	Gambling
Allied Domecq	0.67		X		
Bass	1.02		X		X
BAT	2.12			X	
British Aerospace	0.78	X			
GEC	1.50	X			
GKN	0.50	X			
Grand Met	1.36		X		
Imperial Tobacco	0.28			X	
Ladbroke	0.38				X
Rank	0.51				X
Rolls Royce	0.54	X			
Scottish & Newc	0.60		X		
Smiths Industries	0.35	X			
TI	0.39	X			
Whitbread	0.54		X		
Total	**12.79**				

Source: Cantrade Investments

Even this very basic approach excludes about 13 per cent of the stockmarket by value and the figure grows if you add animal testing, nuclear power, environmental damage and so on.

SMALLER COMPANIES

In practice, if you want an ethical portfolio you will find it ends up weighted heavily towards medium-sized and smaller companies, which are easier to assess and less likely to fall foul of ethical criteria than a widely diversified blue chip company.

The full EIRIS screening disqualifies up to 60 per cent of the FTSE 100 companies. In October 1997, for example, the Credit Suisse Fellowship fund had 70 per cent in small companies, 10 per cent in medium-sized companies and only 15 per cent in FTSE 100 companies. Due to the policy of the fund and the high exposure to small companies, the fund tends to limit maximum holding in any one company to 2 per cent and the average holding is 1 per cent.

So how does the weighting towards smaller companies affect performance? Smaller companies have the ability to outperform their larger counterparts but they are inclined to be more volatile and must be selected with great care. When the FTSE SmallCap (the smallest 550 or so in the All-Share) does well it is often due to the stunning outperformance of a handful of companies rather than outperformance achieved equally by all.

In fact in 1997 most general ethical funds underperformed the market as a whole because they had limited exposure to the sectors that did well – in particular banks (excluded because most lend money indiscriminately to non-ethical companies and countries with poor human rights records), integrated oils (environmental damage) and pharmaceuticals (animal testing and, occasionally, exploitation in tests on humans in emerging countries).

ALTERNATIVE INVESTMENTS

EIRIS provides details of investments which it believes offer a distinct social value but which are not listed on the Stock Exchange. Examples include investment in a company that imports tropical hardwood from sustainable sources, or one involved in fair trade with developing economies.

The attraction here is that by investing in these companies you help them to grow. However, the downside is that the shares may not pay dividends and can be difficult to sell. Moreover, all the usual warnings about small companies outlined in the previous chapter apply with a vengeance.

Sources

Ethical investment: *Cantrade Compendium of Stockmarket Investment for the Private Investor* (Cantrade Investments, 4 Chiswell Street, Finsbury Square, London EC1Y 4UP); *EIRIS Money & Ethics*, a guide to collective funds is available from EIRIS, price £15. Also available free from EIRIS are a guide to financial advisers who offer advice on ethical investments and a guide to fund managers and stockbrokers who manage portfolios with ethical constraints. Contact EIRIS, 504 Bondway Business Centre, 71 Bondway, London SW8 1SQ; *Life and Pensions Moneyfacts* lists ethical and environmental life assurance and pension funds plus unit trusts. Contact Moneyfacts, North Walsham, Norfolk NR28 0BD. Tel: 01692 500765.

Summary

- Ethical views are very subjective so it is essential you give your stockbroker a clear mandate on exclusions.

- Decide if you want to screen in a positive manner or simply to eliminate the main culprits.

- Use the EIRIS screening service to draw up your list of acceptable companies.

- Be aware that an ethical portfolio usually will consist mainly of small to medium-sized companies.

13

Market cycles and how to beat the bears

- How bubbles burst and markets crash
- Your survival kit
- How to read economic information
- The market cycles
- How to deal with bears

At a glance

One of the most worrying aspects of stockmarket investment is the tendency of professional and private investor alike to behave like lemmings under certain economic conditions. Mass hysteria can trigger a dramatic fall in equity prices and even a full-scale crash.

In fact crashes are few and far between. Of more concern – and a much more likely contingency – is a slow slide into a long bear market. At the risk of over-simplification, a bear market is where share prices are falling, while a bull market is where shares are rising. If you are feeling bearish you believe share prices are due to take a tumble, while if you are bullish you believe the opposite.

Given the lengthy bull market we have experienced in recent years, this Chapter concentrates more on the bearish aspects.

HOW BUBBLES BURST AND MARKETS CRASH

To understand the lemming-like activity associated with a market crash (or 'burst bubble', as in South Sea and Mississippi) it is useful to consider the period leading up to these events to spot the common denominators. This is not a technical exercise. The most obvious features of the pre-crash market mentality are those well-known human characteristics, greed and fear.

In a wise little volume called *Bluff your way in Economics* Stuart Trow describes the bubble mentality and what happened when the Mississippi bubble burst:

> 'A speculative bubble occurs when people become obsessed with a particular investment. Fear plays a large part in the bubble's build-up, with investors desperate not to miss the boat and willing to buy at any price, completely disregarding logic.'

History provides some examples which are both illuminating and, due to the passage of time, quaintly amusing. Take the Mississippi Bubble. In the early 18th century, the Mississippi Company held a monopoly on all French territories in North America. The King of France and the French government were enthralled by the prospect of untold riches promised from the New World to the extent that they allowed the Royal Bank to issue bank notes backed, not by gold or silver as was common at the time, but by shares in the Mississippi company.

> The most obvious features of the pre-crash market mentality are those well-known human characteristics greed and fear.

Trow explained: 'When the company crashed in 1720, the entire French monetary system was wiped out. Even people who had not invested in the company lost out as the bank notes became worthless'.

Britain escaped a similar fate, but nevertheless thousands of investors suffered terribly when the South Sea Bubble burst after the collapse of the extraordinarily speculative South Sea Company in the 18th century. This followed a period of extreme stockmarket activity so the sudden loss of confidence in one company appeared to trigger a loss of confidence in the entire market.

So we can see that market crashes are devastatingly indiscriminate. For tumbling along with the bubble company's shares go the share prices of some of the most respected companies in the economy.

Nor do markets always recover quickly – hence the need to take a long-term view with equities. The Wall Street Crash of 1929, for example, saw US stocks lose almost 90 per cent of their value. They did not regain their pre-crash levels until the mid-1950s.

Turning to more recent history, in October 1987 the UK stockmarket crashed. Although pundits still argue about the precise cause, the essential point is that once again greed and an unbridled speculative frenzy had overtaken logic. Investors continued to buy shares because they failed to see that the prices could not go on rising indefinitely.

The bubble mentality does not just apply to shares. Other assets are equally vulnerable. A similar frenzy was characteristic of the UK housing boom in the late 1980s when people paid silly prices only to find themselves in the negative equity trap once the housing bubble had burst. Ten years on, many are still there.

> **Leveraged investors are more common than you might think.**

We are just as vulnerable today as we were in 1987. Some would argue, more so due to the increased number of leveraged investors, where people take out a loan in order to invest in the stockmarket. It sounds highly risky yet this is precisely what an increasing number of home owners do when they arrange an interest-only mortgage backed by an endowment, Pep or pension plan.

For this arrangement to succeed you need to achieve sufficient rates of return to service the loan and make a profit. Leveraged investors are more common than you might think.

YOUR SURVIVAL KIT

To survive, and indeed thrive, during bull and bear market cycles you need a clear strategy. Fortunately, this is one time when private investors can score over the professionals because there are no clients waiting for their next quarterly figures and there is no pressure on you to follow the market trend.

Think first why you are in the market at all. If you are typical of most private investors, you will purchase shares for the long-term income and gains and will recognise that it is inefficient, time-consuming and costly to change or churn your portfolio on a regular basis.

TIP So, in theory at least, if you invest in the right type of shares – even if it is at the wrong time – your portfolio should be able to ride market cycles. If, after careful research, you thought a company was worth investing in two weeks ago, its shares will still be worth holding today.

It will still pay out dividends, even if there has been a sudden switch from a bull to a bear market and capital growth has temporarily followed a few investment analysts out of the window. Provided you chose wisely in the first place, unlike the analysts, capital growth will return.

This logic is particularly sound when applied to blue chips because these businesses are themselves well diversified and represent a spread of risk across markets (and often continents too) within just one shareholding.

However, the logic does not necessarily extend to smaller, more speculative companies. In the run up to October 1987, for example, some companies came to the stockmarket which were very speculative and considerably overpriced. They did not recover. In this case you would have got the worst of all worlds. You paid dearly for your shares in the first place, their price fell and they never recovered capital value. Moreover, you did not even benefit from a decent run of dividends.

Remember also that certain market sectors are cyclical. Shares in engineering or construction companies, for example, usually do well when the general economy is flourishing, while shares in consumer goods companies and retailers will do well while consumer spending is expected to rise.

So, while the following explanation attempts to demystify some of the economic jargon, do bear in mind that these are generalisations only and that if you bought a tin pot company in the first place, no amount of economic alchemy is going to turn it into a crock of gold.

Tables 13.1 and 13.2 show the recent history of bull and bear markets in the UK.

Table 13.1 A recent history of UK bull markets

	Months	Change %
9th November 1966 – 31st January 1969	27	106
27th May 1970 – 1st May 1972	23	100
13th December 1974 – 30th January 1976	13	179
27th October 1976 – 4th May 1979	30	145
15th November 1979 – 17th August 1981	22	55
28th September 1981 – 16th July 1987	69	365
10th November 1987 – 3rd January 1990	26	56
24th September 1990 – 11th May 1992	19	38
25th August 1992 – 2nd February 1994	17	70
Average	**27**	**124**

Note: The latest bull market which started in June 1994 was still running at the time of writing.
Source: UBS. Published in Cantrade Investments Compendium

Table 13.2 A recent history of UK bear markets

	Months	Change %
31st January 1969 – 27th May 1970	16	−37
1st May 1972 – 13th December 1974	32	−73
30th January 1976 – 27th October 1976	9	−33
4th May 1979 – 15th November 1979	6	−23
17th August 1981 – 28th September 1981	1	−22
16th July 1987 – 19th November 1987	4	−37
3rd January 1990 – 24th September 1990	9	−22
14th May 1992 – 25th August 1992	3	−22
2nd February 1994 – 24th June 1994	5	−18
Average	**9**	**−32**

Source: UBS. Published in Cantrade Investments Compendium

HOW TO READ ECONOMIC INFORMATION

This is a *very* brief lesson in economic cycles and how they affect your shares. If it sounds theoretical, that's because it is. No sooner do we spot a clear trend for certain companies (categorised by size, sector, or some other characteristic) to behave in a certain way during a certain stage in the economic cycle than we are proved wrong. This is when we have to remember yet again that investment is an art not a science. So, while it is useful to know the theory, never expect reality to mirror it.

First, let's get to grips with some handy vocabulary. The economics reports in newspapers rely on just a few key phrases and with these manage to mystify most of the people most of the time. Regard the jargon as no more than a form of shorthand and remember that it is one thing to understand the theory, but entirely another to interpret economic events correctly. Economics is a very imprecise science (rather like investment) and the experts usually get it wrong, but nevertheless are paid a great deal for their views.

■ The essential jargon

Before you start you need to understand what is meant by 'the economy'. Think of it in terms of old-fashioned home economics – which was all about making the housekeeping last for the entire week and boiling the Sunday roast bones for soup on Thursdays. Nowadays of course we all have credit cards so we don't have to make income meet expenditure – or at least not very often.

The economy is the financial state of the nation. The state of the economy tells us how much housekeeping is coming in and whether we are being prudent and boiling bones for soup, or borrowing in order to spend what we do not have.

Certain statistics, known as economic indicators, show the state of the economy at a particular time.

The most important economic indicators to remember are interest rates and inflation because whatever happens to the UK economy or the world as a whole, it usually ends up affecting one or both of these rates and this in turn has an effect on Government lending policy and companies' performance, which in turn affect your investments.

■ Interest rates

Interest rates are important because they may directly affect the amount a company is charged for borrowing, although the extent will depend on the structure of the debt.

The Bank of England is responsible for setting short-term interest rates and uses them to curb or encourage spending. If we are all spending far too much ('we' being both individuals and companies) then the Bank will increase interest rates to stop us borrowing to spend.

Likewise, if we are saving too much and not spending enough, Bank might lower interest rates to encourage more borrowing and spending.

■ Retail Price Index

This is published by the Office for National Statistics every month and is the most common measure for inflation. It is calculated by constructing a so-called 'basket' of goods and services used by the typical household (based on a sample survey of about 7000 households throughout the country).

The basket includes housing and household expenditure, personal expenditure, travel and leisure, food and catering, alcohol and tobacco. The most recent base date was January 1987 which had a value of 100.

You may come across other types of inflation. For example, underlying inflation is the unofficial term given to the inflation rate in an economy measured by retail price index minus mortgage interest payments. Headline inflation is the full RPI including mortgage interest costs.

■ Impact on companies and their share prices

So how does all this come to affect your investments? Well, rising interest rates increase the cost of borrowing for the companies in which you invest. The profits of a company that is highly geared (that is, it has a high ratio of borrowing to assets) naturally will suffer if the cost of servicing its debts increases. This cost will be passed on to shareholders because it will lower the profits out of which it pays the dividends.

At the same time the dividends available from equities will start to look uncompetitive to income investors who will find better sources elsewhere if interest rates are high. Double digit rates of interest on deposits are very appealing no matter what the rate of inflation is.

Moreover, high interest rates may damage a company's growth prospects because they will encourage a company to keep its spare cash in deposits rather than to take a risk and invest it in expanding the business.

Low interest rates have the opposite effect and can be good for companies because the cost of borrowing comes down, and the share value rises. So, although a fall in interest rates sounds gloomy because it follows news of high unemployment or a slowdown in the economic growth (usually expressed as the gross domestic product or GDP), for equity investors it can be good news.

Gilts react to fluctuations in inflation. A rise in inflation usually forces gilt prices down and therefore yields go up. This is because there is less demand for fixed interest securities at these times. An improvement in gilt yields in turn can have a detrimental effect on the stockmarket because gilts become more attractive relative to equities.

The *public sector borrowing requirement* (PSBR) also has an impact on the gilt market. The PSBR is the public sector deficit – the amount by which Government spending (including local authorities and nationalised industries) exceeds the income from taxation, rates and other revenues. One of the main methods the Government uses to finance this debt is to sell gilts. If the PSBR is higher than expected, the price of gilts may fall as there will be a greater supply.

The budget deficit is similar to the PSBR but also includes income from occasional 'extraordinary revenue' – for example from privatisations of public sector companies. So, a cut in the budget deficit or PSBR will be good news for gilts because supply is more limited and so prices rise. However, if the Government has achieved the cut by increasing corporate taxation, this will be generally bad news for shares.

Other factors include the health or otherwise of retail sales, which obviously largely affects the retail stores and supermarkets, and housing starts (the number of new homes being built) which are generally viewed as a leading indicator of a future pick-up in the economy.

THE MARKET CYCLES

Everyone knows that the timing of investment decisions is critical. Getting it right is not easy though, even for the experts. As Mark Twain once said, 'October is one of the peculiarly dangerous months to speculate in stocks. The others are July, January, September, April, November, May …'.

What follows is again a very brief overview of the main features of market cycles and their impact on share prices. Please remember, this is the *theory* and should not unduly influence your decisions.

If you have a large lump sum to invest then almost certainly you would be wise to drip feed it into the market over a period of, say, six months to a year (see Chapters 10 and 11). In this case you would want to check how the economy is behaving at the particular times you invest in order to determine the effect on companies and sectors. But to switch from one sector to another, in the hope of cashing in on the market's weakness or, even more risky, to keep one step ahead, is almost certain to fail all but the most dedicated full-time investor. Moreover, it will prove very costly.

Bear in mind also that all the institutional investors will interpret economic trends and anticipated changes in market cycles ahead of you, so share prices will reflect both the current and expected future trends. Trying to spot the change in cycle well before the professional analysts is not a game for the novice or indeed for anyone who values their capital. Some regard this activity as very scientific – others reckon it has nothing to do with informed investment decisions and everything to do with gambling.

Finally, do remember that when it comes to shorter-term investment decisions all things are relative. Shares are only worth the additional risk if they offer returns well above what you can get from gilts, bonds and deposits, taking into account tax and the dealing costs. Always refer back to the common sense checklist on page 52 before investing your money.

■ Phase 1: early stage of a recovery

At this point interest rates are high and economic activity is at a low ebb. Inflation is falling and interest rates also begin to fall – perhaps anticipated by rises in the bond markets. Blue chip companies begin to improve but interest in smaller companies is non-existent.

The first shares to benefit are interest rate-sensitive shares such as banks, property, building and construction companies – some of which previously may have been very depressed. However, analysts view this as a dangerous phase, because banks may regard their problem clients as more valuable if they go into liquidation. More companies go bust in the early stages of a recovery than in the depths of a recession.

Which shares may do well? Banks and well-financed property companies.

■ Phase 2: well into recovery

This is when the recovery gathers pace and short-term interest rates continue to fall. As a rule, at this point the recovery ought to begin to feed through into consumer spending. Share prices rise.

Which shares may do well?: Retailers, car dealers, and manufacturers of durable goods, such as furniture, should begin to improve.

■ Phase 3: recovery

Interest rates have now reached the bottom and investors fear they may rise. At this point the market may see a major 'correction' to its generally upward trend.

Which shares may do well? Capital goods, engineering and other heavy industry.

■ Phase 4: heading for recession

The flow of money into the markets is rather like an oil tanker – it keeps going for quite a while after the signal to stop. So, the market makes sharp gains on heavy volume (in other words, there is a lot of money coming into the markets) despite rising interest rates. Smaller companies prove very popular. Conglomerates, 'people' businesses and 'concept stocks' are all the rage. Commodity prices are booming and stoking up inflation for the future. (Commodities are raw materials and foodstuffs, among other items.)

Which shares should do well? While there will be money to be made in the stockmarket at this phase of the market cycle, it is important to recognise that this period is the one which generally will precede a fall. You might consider taking steps to anticipate a fall by gradually but steadily shifting some of your assets out of shares and into cash or other more defensive investments. Avoid trendy companies like the plague.

■ Phase 5: into recession

The stockmarket falls, possibly in response to an external event but in any event interest in shares dries up. Commodity shares might do well at this point because the underlying economy still has to turn down.

Which shares do well? Defensive shares like food, manufacturers and brewers will tend to do better than the market as a whole but may still drop in price.

■ Achieving a balance of sectors

No combination of investments will be absolutely suited to a particular phase of the market and even if you plan ahead, you will find that each successive market cycle displays different characteristics. Nevertheless, a diversified portfolio is more likely to hold its value or at least limit the blows, compared with a portfolio that is weighted towards just one or two sectors.

HOW TO DEAL WITH BEARS

If you are confident that your portfolio contains good quality shares and are prepared to hold for the long term, you are probably as well placed as any to sit out a bear market. Even so, it is worth watching for opportunities to buy into quality companies at depressed levels.

If you want to take further action to prepare your portfolio for a bear market, then there are certain steps you might consider. At all times keep in mind the aims of your portfolio.

■ Change your asset allocation

Gilts and bonds may be more appealing if you are concerned about the equity markets. If you are already looking for income then you might consider moving more of your portfolio into conventional gilts. Gilts and bonds are discussed in Chapter 15.

There are alternatives. You can try to reduce risk by including overseas as well as UK equities in your portfolio. In addition you could build in a 'protection' by using more predictable investments (not all of which will be low risk), such as zero dividend preference shares, National Savings Certificates and gilt and corporate bond funds. Remember though, if you invest directly, gilts and bonds are only predictable if you hold them to maturity. If you need to sell before this date you will find these instruments can be almost as volatile as equities.

■ Derivatives

For a short-term bear market, derivatives can prove effective, if rather expensive.

There are three main methods. First, you can shield yourself from a fall in the market by buying a protected or guaranteed fund. Second, if you are a very active and confident investor you could consider using a bear fund to hedge your portfolio. Third, if you hold a large portfolio, you can buy derivatives direct.

> For a short-term bear market, derivatives can prove effective, if rather expensive.

The important point to note about these techniques is that the first is a comparatively safe, if expensive, bet for the medium to long term, provided you choose your fund carefully. The second and third alternatives – the bear fund and the directly purchased derivatives contracts – are tactical instruments which you can use to make short term gains or to hedge your portfolio against a short, sharp drop in the market.

■ Protected funds

These are collective funds which limit the downside of an index and so protect your capital from severe loss.

It is important not to regard the guarantee as the investment goal. Provided the guarantor is financially sound these products will protect your capital in the event of a stock market crash.

So, the main attraction of these funds should be their potential for capital growth. In particular you should check if your exposure to a rise in the market is limited to a certain percentage and whether the cost of the guarantee is likely to act as a significant drag on performance. Maximum growth is essential because these funds are mainly held in cash and so, unlike a true equity fund, the guaranteed fund does not benefit from reinvested dividends which, as mentioned before, on the FTSE 100 index typically account for half of the total return over ten years.

Moreover, many funds, particularly those offered by insurance companies, tie up your capital for five years. A better alternative is the type of protected unit trust fund which either has no specific term or has a quarterly lock-in.

The cost of the options purchased to protect your money is significant. Outside of the protected/guaranteed market you can find a unit trust tracker fund with no initial charge and an annual management charge of 0.5 per cent. Compare this with the popular guaranteed Peps which charge an additional 1.5 per cent plus VAT per annum for the guarantee in addition to the 1 per cent unit trust annual management charge. Instead of a higher annual charge, some plans have an extra initial charge, typically of about 4 per cent.

■ Bear funds

As mentioned at the outset, while protected funds can be a good idea for some investors, provided the cost is not too high, very few private investors should consider dabbling in bear funds (authorised option unit trusts). The choice is very limited, so clearly managers do not see this as a boom business.

So how do these work? Essentially these funds operate like an index tracker in reverse. If the market goes up, the value of the bear fund falls, whereas if the market falls, the value of the bear fund rises.

The fund itself would be largely held in cash with a small proportion, say 5–10 per cent, used to purchase the derivatives that are sold when the market falls in order to make a profit. It is rather an oversimplification but basically, if the market falls by 10 per cent you can expect your bear fund to rise by 10 per cent. Since derivatives usually are far more liquid than the underlying conventional securities, this makes buying and selling easier.

These are highly specialised funds aimed at investors or managers who think they can make a profit from a short-term fall in the market. In this case you would be using the fund for tactical rather than strategic purposes. Your aim is to make a quick profit and then return to a portfolio of direct equities or collective funds based on active management principles.

Other investors might use them to hedge part of their portfolio. For example, if you have a significant holding in US equities and you fear a US bear market, you could buy a US bear fund so that when the value of your equities falls this will be offset by the rise in the value of the bear fund.

This may be cheaper than selling your US shares and repurchasing them when the market looks set to rise again – and it avoids any potential capital gains tax implications.

■ Buying options direct

An alternative for the active and wealthy investor is to buy equity 'put' options which can be used either to profit from a fall in share prices or to protect the value of your equity portfolio against share price falls.

Put options give you the right to sell shares at a fixed price. So, if you buy a three-month individual put option at today's share price and in three months the underlying share price has fallen significantly, you stand to make a tidy profit. (There are also 'call' options which give you the right to buy shares at a predetermined price on a predetermined date in the future.)

If you want to hedge your portfolio, you can buy traded put options to match your individual equity holdings (options are available for about 70 leading UK companies) or, if you have a broad spread of blue chips, you can buy a FTSE 100 index put option. Again, if the shares or the index as a whole plummets, you can sell at the original higher price and make good your losses on your underlying shares.

The problem with buying equity options direct is that they are traded in whole contracts. which would normally represent 1000 shares of the underlying security. This can cost several hundred pounds per holding, while to cover against a fall in the entire FTSE 100 index might cost several thousand pounds.

In conclusion, a put option can represent good value if the share price or the whole index goes down but it could prove to be a pricey insurance policy if your predictions of a market fall do not materialise.

Sources

ProShare, *The Private Investor's Guide to the Stockmarket*, was the main source for the guide to economic cycles. If you want to buy put options contact your stockbroker or, for more information, contact the London International Financial Futures and Options Exchange (LIFFE) private investor helpline on 0171 379 2486.

Summary

- Many private investors select shares for the long term and so, provided you choose well, you should be able to sit out market cycles.

- When share prices are depressed this might be a good time to pick up quality shares at bargain prices.

- Understanding the economic theory and indicators is very helpful but always remember that what happens in practice may be very different.

- Rising interest rates affect a company's ability to borrow and increase the cost of servicing the debt. This is likely to reduce profits and hence dividends.

- Gilts react to fluctuations in inflation. If inflation rises, gilt prices go down and so their yields go up.

- Be wary of investing directly in derivatives or derivative-based funds. This can be a useful tactic against a short-term market fall but can prove to be an expensive insurance policy.

14

Buying and selling

- Administration
- Shares
- The mechanics of buying your shares
- New issues, privatisations and company share schemes
- Rolling settlement and nominee accounts
- Stock Exchange Electronics Trading Services (SETS)
- Collective funds
- Fund charges
- Investments held within a Pep or ISA
- Information and dealing services on the Internet

At a glance

This Chapter covers the mechanics of buying and selling some of the most popular types of investments ranging from direct equities and bonds to collective funds.

Experienced investors often are keen to arrange the best deals available and negotiation often pays off. For most people, however, it is important to keep a sense of perspective. Long-term investors may only deal a dozen times or less in any year so the choice of shares is far more important than the saving of a few pence on transaction charges.

ADMINISTRATION

For those DIY investors who have not yet devised a sensible computer- or paper-based administration system, it is worth starting off with either the *Investors' Chronicle* 'Private Investor's Ledger' or ProShare's 'Portfolio Management System', both of which will help you keep track of your transactions and to calculate your profits and losses.*

The ProShare system, for example, helps you to:

- record acquisitions and disposals of shares and fixed interest stocks through the transaction log and profit/loss calculation record pages
- account accurately to the Inland Revenue for the dividends and interest received
- account to the Revenue for Capital Gains Tax (CGT) on disposals
- keep track of your investments using charts provided.

SHARES

How you buy your shares (this includes investment trust shares) will depend on the nature of the agreement you have with your stockbroker. If you have a discretionary or advisory stockbroker, the firm will act on your behalf once you have completed a terms of business agreement and paid a cash and/or stock deposit. The firm automatically will provide a tariff of charges.

The choice of stockbroker services was discussed in Chapter 3. You may prefer, and need, a traditional discretionary or advisory service from a stockbroker but if you are looking for convenience and low cost and you have the expertise to make your own share selection, an execution-

> How you buy your shares will depend on the nature of the agreement you have with your stockbroker.

only firm will be adequate provided it offers a good combination of price and service. Some firms have had teething trouble as they have attempted to deal with a large volume of orders with insufficient phone lines.

Typical costs if you buy through a stockbroker are 1.75 per cent per deal, with charges reducing proportionately as the value of the deal increases. Some execution-only services have a fixed charge for certain deals – for example for FTSE 100 companies.

On top of this you will pay stamp duty at 0.5 per cent. This is collected by the stockbroker and passed on to the Treasury. Where applicable you must also pay for the advice. This may be calculated on a time basis, or it may be an annual fee for unlimited advice or for a certain amount of advice above which you would pay extra on an hourly basis. You may pay this advice fee separately or it may be included in the broker's commission charges.

THE MECHANICS OF BUYING YOUR SHARES

To get an idea of the current price of the shares you wish to purchase you can refer to the *Financial Times* 'Companies and Markets' pages (or the financial pages of your preferred newspaper) to find yesterday's closing price. (Online services will show more up to date information.) This will be the mid-market price – that is halfway between the bid and offer prices.

To remind you, the *bid price* is the price at which the market maker buys back from you shares or units in a collective fund. This is lower than the *offer price*, which is the price at which the market maker sells shares to you. The spread between the bid and offer price represents the market maker's fee or mark-up on the actual cost.

When reading the financial pages, remember the significance of the terms 'cum' (with) and 'ex' (without). In most cases the shares will be *cum dividend* or occasionally *cum rights*. This means that you have the right as a shareholder to certain features such as the interim or final dividend payments, or the rights issue currently on offer.

Usually, if you have full rights the published details will not include the term 'cum'. If, however, the dividend or rights issue has been declared, for example, then, as a prospective purchaser you will buy the shares *ex-dividend* or *ex-rights* – that is, without the entitlement to the dividends or rights issue, which instead will go to the previous owner.

The price of the shares will always reflect the status. (Chapter 17 explains how to read the financial pages, while Chapter 18 sets out your rights as a shareholder.)

To buy is quite simply a matter of picking up the phone and placing your order with your stockbroker. You must also state the price you wish to pay if you have a limit (this is usually a good idea for the smaller, more volatile shares) or you may ask the broker to buy 'at best' – in which case he or she will obtain the best possible price at that time. Remember that if you opt for a postal service you have less control over the price.

When the shares are purchased you will receive a *settlement* note with the details of the number of shares and price paid per share. The total or 'consideration' is the former multiplied by the latter. The note should also tell you the time the deal was struck, so that you can check the price was fair and accurate.

By the time you have taken into account the stockbroker's commission, stamp duty, plus the difference between the bid and offer price, your grand total is likely to be around 4-5 per cent more than the actual value of the shares purchased.

The stockmarket works on what is known as a five-day settlement basis which means your broker must pay for your shares five days after the purchase date, and as an investor you have to make sure your money is there to meet the bill on time.

Many brokers now hold cash and shares on behalf of clients so they can settle claims rapidly. If not, check how your broker prefers to be paid. For example, will a credit or debit card be acceptable?

NEW ISSUES, PRIVATISATIONS AND COMPANY SHARE SCHEMES

As explained in Chapter 10, a new issue is when a company sells its shares on the stockmarket for the first time. These days very few new issues are sold directly to the public and where they are you will probably see large advertisements in the press which provide all the information you need to make your application.

Several stockbrokers have developed a special service which attempts to secure allocations for their clients. For details, request the ProShare guide *Brokers' New Issue Services* (see Chapter 2).

Windfalls, as the name suggests, just drop into your lap. These are free shares from building societies and life offices which convert from mutual status – where they are owned by their members (the savers and borrowers) – to a public limited company. If you qualify for a windfall allocation when your building society or life assurance company joins the stockmarket you will be informed directly by the company of your allocation and the date you can expect to receive it.

You should also be told how to buy more shares, if you wish, and how to sell if you do not want direct shares in your portfolio of investments. To help with the latter process the converting institution usually makes available a cheap and easy share disposal service for its customers.

Privatisation issues are also relatively easy to understand. Usually, all you have to do is to fill out a form and send off a cheque.

Company share option schemes are fairly straightforward and do not involve transactions in the secondary market. Once you have signed up for the scheme (see Chapter 8), the shares automatically are offered to you on a predetermined date. In most cases it is worthwhile buying even if you sell again immediately to make a profit.

Most of the FTSE 100 companies offer cheap dealing facilities to employees, usually through one of the major stockbrokers or banks.

The above cases are the exception rather than the rule. Most of the time you will be buying and selling in the secondary market and you will need a stockbroker's services to do so.

ROLLING SETTLEMENT AND NOMINEE ACCOUNTS

In the past all deals completed over a two-week period had to be settled on just one day. The modern system, known as CREST (not an acronym), provides an electronic share dealing settlement and registration system which gives investors the choice to settle with or without the use of share certificates.

CREST works on a rolling settlement basis, whereby a transaction must be settled a certain number of days after dealing. This means that settlement is taking place every day.

Under five-day rolling settlement your stockbroker must pay for the shares you buy, or deliver the shares you sell five business days after the transaction was made. As an investor you must make sure that you supply your adviser with money or share certificates and signed transfers in good time to meet the deadline.

■ Nominee accounts

To help meet the deadlines you may be asked to use a *nominee account*. Under a nominee account you are still the *beneficial owner* of the shares but the share certificates are kept by the nominee company which is the registered shareholder.

This means that the nominee company's name appears on the share register for the companies in which you invest. The nominee company, which is legally separate from your stockbroker, can offer a range of services including administration and banking.

> To help meet the deadlines you may be asked to use a nominee account.

Nominee companies do not have to be authorised by one of the financial services regulators, so if you use a nominee account do check that your investment adviser accepts responsibility for any losses and has professional indemnity insurance to cover any claims of negligence.

If you would like to use a nominee account, ProShare suggests you ask your broker the following questions:

- What are the charges?
- Will I continue to get all information and other shareholder rights in those companies in which I hold shares?
- How often are dividends sent to me? Will they be sent immediately?
- If there are certain dates for dividend payments will I receive interest on the money while it is held in the nominee account?
- Do you offer alternative ways of dealing in shares other than through the nominee?
- What is the limit on the insurance used to guard against fraud and other contingencies, including assets held in nominees?
- What compensation arrangements are available if the service goes bust? (Don't just rely on the Investors' Compensation Scheme – this only covers you up to £48 000 and is a last resort. The firm should have its own professional indemnity insurance, preferably of up to £1 million per claim.)

You might also ask what happens to any perks offered by the companies in which you invest. Share perks are very rarely a good enough reason on their own for investing but some are very nice to have – for example substantial discounts on retailers' goods. If your shares are held in a nominee account, you may not be entitled to the perks. This may not be the fault of the nominee. Some companies will exclude investors who hold their shares in a nominee account from perks and other shareholder rights. So do check if there are any additional charges for the basic shareholder information such as the annual report and accounts, and attending the AGM.

Finally, if you have windfall shares think carefully before you accept the converting company's nominee arrangements. In some cases the nominee account may only allow you to hold that one parcel of shares so you would need a second nominee account to hold the rest of your portfolio of shares, which could make life unnecessarily complicated from the administration point of view.

■ The ProShare Nominee Code

To help investors who choose to hold their shares through a nominee account, ProShare has drawn up a code of practice for nominee operators to try to ensure that investors are clearly informed of the costs involved, the safety of their assets and the information they should receive from the companies in which they invest. (Not all stockbrokers subscribe to the code. If yours does not, ask why.)

The code requires nominee operators to:

- disclose fully the charges involved, including withdrawals of holdings from the nominee account
- provide a clear statement of how your investments are protected while they are in the nominee account
- make arrangements, if requested, for investors to receive copies of the annual reports and accounts of the relevant companies in which they invest.

The code is voluntary but those firms which adhere to it are allowed to use the symbol. ProShare maintains and publishes a list of companies which subscribe to the code (for details about ProShare, see Chapter 20).

STOCK EXCHANGE ELECTRONIC TRADING SERVICE (SETS)

SETS was introduced in October 1997 and offers automated buying and selling of the top 100 UK companies (i.e., the FTSE 100, including those that have been in since October 1997 but subsequently have been demoted). Until the introduction of SETS all share transactions took place under a quote-driven service. SETS makes this market order-driven.

The quote-driven trading system uses market makers as middle men to quote prices at which they will buy and sell shares. This information is displayed on screens around the City. Brokers and market makers then speak to each other by telephone and agree trades.

The order-driven market is fundamentally different. Buyers and sellers enter their orders for shares and these are displayed to other market participants and executed against matching sales. This technology makes the intermediary role of the market maker redundant.

The traditional quote-driven system still applies to non-FTSE 100 companies, although gradually the FTSE 250 (the next largest 250 companies in the All-Share) will be added to SETS. Deals of under 1000 shares (or 500 if the share price is over £5) are excluded from SETS.

■ Cost savings of SETS

In theory for the FTSE 100 companies SETS should result in better prices for investors because the middle man is cut out. As a rough estimate, the average spread between the buying and selling price should drop from 0.6 per cent to 0.2 per cent, representing a saving of £100 on a £25 000 deal.

> In theory for the FTSE 100 companies SETS should result in better prices for investors because the middle man is cut out.

There should be other savings in future as the new electronic system helps brokers to cut down their paperwork and therefore to reduce their costs. With luck these savings will be passed on to the customer through cheaper dealing commissions.

SETS has had its teething problems, particularly for execution-only stockbrokers who have not always been able to secure a good price because they trade right at the very beginning or end of the trading day.

These teething problems should be overcome quickly, but in the meantime you should ask your stockbroker how he or she copes with the system and secures the best possible prices for your deals.

COLLECTIVE FUNDS

Buying unit trusts and insurance company funds is quite straightforward. All you have to do is to contact your stockbroker, financial adviser or the financial institution directly and ask for an application form.

Most major investment trust houses have their own share dealing service, set up by the management company to help its shareholders buy and sell. Effectively this is just an intermediary service between shareholders and the market makers. Nominee companies may also be used.

If you have some shares already you might consider a share exchange scheme whereby you swap your direct holdings in return for the same or different shares or a collective fund held within a Pep (or, from April 1999, an individual savings account). This can be attractive if you have a few small holdings of shares – for example in the company where you work or from privatisation issues. It could be cheaper to swap these rather than for you to sell at private investor rates.

In the case of single-company Peps, if your shares have recently come from an Inland Revenue approved all-employee savings-related share option or profit-sharing scheme, from a privatisation issue or from a preferential offer you should not need to sell them if you wish to retain the same holdings within your Pep or ISA.

FUND CHARGES

TIP Most investment managers would argue, quite rightly, that good performance more than outweighs a high initial or annual management charge. However, since it is impossible to predict future performance it makes sense to ensure that returns are not undermined by excessive costs.

Be particularly careful when you are looking at the so-called 'tax-efficient' investments – the personal equity plans and, when they are launched in 1999, the individual savings accounts. Find out if the charges outweigh the tax advantages. This is particularly important for those investing smaller sums and for basic-rate and lower-rate taxpayers where the charges may be disproportionately high compared to the tax savings actually achieved.

Take Peps, for example. If the annual management charge is 1 per cent then the income tax savings for a basic-rate taxpayer investing in shares yielding less than 4 per cent is also about 1 per cent so the income tax saving is illusory, while in most cases any capital gains could be offset against the annual allowance (see page 263).

For all the major types of collective fund it is now a regulatory requirement for the company to provide investors with a pre-sale 'key features' document which sets out the charges and how they build up over different investment periods. This will help you make comparisons between different products.

■ Unit trust and unit linked charges

The 'initial' charge is deducted immediately from the original capital invested. It is calculated as a percentage of the lump sum – typically 5 per cent on a UK unit trust. The charge may include your adviser's sales commission, if applicable, which is likely to account for about 3 per cent. An increasing number of the low-cost index-tracking funds keep their charges to a minimum by eliminating the middle man and selling direct to the public. In this case there may not be an initial charge at all (but see The annual management charge below).

The initial charge does not reveal the full up-front costs, which instead are shown in the *bid/offer spread*. This is likely to be 0.5 per cent to 1 per cent higher than the initial charge and in some cases the increase may be as much as 3 per cent. The 'spread' includes *stamp duty*, among other items, and as such represents the true purchase cost of the investment.

■ The annual management charge

This represents the cost of the investment management and administration and is deducted as an annual percentage of the fund –

so its value grows along with your investment. The annual charge also includes the cost of any 'renewal' commission paid to financial advisers – that is, the annual commission that is paid from year 2 onwards – typically 0.5 per cent of your fund value. Although included in the annual charge, your key features document will separate out the cost of the advice – that is, the commission paid – if applicable.

Most managers deduct the annual charge from income but some deduct from capital. The latter practice has the effect of artificially inflating the yield and has proved contentious in the context of corporate bond funds where it is likely to lead to capital erosion.

Although the initial charge often appears the most significant deduction, advisers warn that it is the compound effect of high annual charges that most damage your prospects of a good return over the long term. For this reason you should watch out for unit trust Pep companies (and the future ISA companies) that have lowered or abolished altogether their initial charges (often compensated by equally high 'exit' charges if you pull out early) and raised their annual charge. A typical exit penalty might be 4.5 per cent of your fund in year 1, 4 per cent in year 2, 3 per cent in year 3, 2 per cent in year 4 and 1 per cent in year 5.

■ Pep/ISA charges

Unit trust managers may add an extra layer of cost on top of the charges for the underlying unit trust to cover Pep administration and may well do the same for ISAs. In practice, however, most managers charge the same whether or not the client invests through a Pep wrapper and several companies reduce the initial unit trust charge to encourage Pep investment. The effect of any additional costs or discounts for the Pep or ISA wrapper must be shown in the key features document.

■ How to get the best deal

Unless you are an experienced investor you probably should seek help from an independent financial adviser and accept you will have to pay for the advice. However, there are opportunities for investors who know what they want and are looking for the cheapest way to buy.

Several companies offer a discount by cutting the initial charge when they sell direct or if the adviser has given up some or all of the commission. Do remember, though, that unit trust managers have a degree of discretion over their initial charge and if you plan to make a substantial investment it is worth haggling. You should also adopt these tactics when you switch units within the same management group.

Assuming you are satisfied that the timing is appropriate, it is easy and quick to sell units in unit trusts and unit linked insurance funds. You can either sell your total holding or just some of your units, provided you leave sufficient to meet the manager's minimum investment requirements.

The documents you receive when you make your investment and the regular manager's reports should include an explanation of how to sell units. This may involve completing a special withdrawal form on the back of your unit trust certificate or it may be sufficient to send a written instruction. Alternatively you could ask your adviser to arrange a withdrawal for you.

Once the manager receives your instruction you should get your cheque, accompanied by a 'sell' contract note within a week.

■ Income payments

If you elect to receive income you will do so on fixed dates each year, half year or at whatever frequency you have agreed. Income is usually paid directly into your bank account unless you ask for it to be reinvested.

INVESTMENTS HELD WITHIN A PEP OR ISA

Buying and selling investments held within a Pep (and, from April 1999, an ISA) is quite different from the usual practice for shares and collective funds held outside the plan.

You can buy direct from the Pep/ISA manager or through your financial adviser. The adviser will handle all the paperwork for you and help you with any questions you may have. Some advisers are authorised to handle client money but many are not, in which case you must make all cheques out to the investment manager not the adviser's firm.

An increasing number of Peps and other collective funds are sold through advertisements in the press. Here the regulators insist the company provides a considerable amount of detail so that you can make an informed decision. If you decide to go ahead you will deal directly with the investment manager. Once again, the idea is to eliminate the middle man and so to cut costs. Given the Government's emphasis on low costs for ISAs, it seems likely that direct selling through advertisements or supermarket checkouts, for example, will be commonplace.

With a Pep (and the ISA), although the investor is the 'beneficial' owner, generally it is the Pep manager who is the title owner and who deals with all the paperwork. As a Pep investor you would not usually receive a copy of the reports and accounts of the companies in which you invest. You may not even receive the Pep manager's report unless you specifically request it. Some management groups make an additional charge for this information.

INFORMATION AND DEALING SERVICES ON THE INTERNET

There are many guides to the Internet itself and to the rapidly growing number of financial services now available. Investors keen to explore these information sources should equip themselves with *Investing Online** which takes you on a conducted tour of the most important web sites and includes a directory of the financial services on disk.

If information is essential to successful investing then the Internet is investors' heaven. As a method of communication, the Internet does not have an equal.

Today, most large companies, financial institutions, stock exchanges, Government departments, regulators and financial trade organisations have their own web site so you can read all the latest news and trawl through the offers in the comfort of your own home.

Whether you want to investigate a company's trading history or buy shares and collective funds at bargain rates, the Internet can help.

■ Wealth warning

What you must remember, though, is that the Internet is like a high street. Indeed it has even been referred to as a galactic car boot sale, a description which conveys very well the potential dangers for the unsuspecting investor.

Bear in mind that although many of the companies that sell services or goods are themselves regulated, the Internet itself is not. Like the car boot sale, all the vendors display their wares in the most attractive way possible but you are given no advice to help you spot the genuine bargains and pukka information. The web sites are totally indiscriminate. The financial companies that offer value for money, well-regulated services jostle for space with the rip-off merchants and plain fraudsters.

So, use the Internet with caution and check out any service very thoroughly before using it. Before you buy anything check the company's address and its regulatory status. The *Financial Services Authority* (FSA) has a register of all firms authorised by the Financial Services Act in the UK (see page 270). If a firm is not authorised in the UK and you lose your money there is virtually no hope of getting it back and if the company goes bust, you won't get a penny from the UK's Investors Compensation Scheme.

The FSA also runs a web site which includes details of the latest Internet scams.

Watch out in particular for the 'copycat' sites which fraudulent companies set up and incorporate legitimate companies' web pages. The FSA urges Internet users to take a close look at the web site address. It may be very similar to one used by a well-known company but, for example, it might have an unusual overseas location or contain additional, misleading letters.

The Internet makes it easy to buy goods and services from organisations in other countries without knowing that they are based abroad. A web site with an address which includes .co.uk or just .uk doesn't necessarily mean it is based in the UK.

If in doubt the FSA recommends that you look up the firm's number in the phone book and call in person to double-check their site address. Don't rely on any phone number given on the site – the chances are that this will be false too.

The Consumers Association also recommends that you print out relevant web pages, including terms and conditions, so that you have a permanent record in case of future disputes.

■ What's available?

Bloomberg, Dow Jones Telerate, FT Extel and Reuters all offer news services, market reports and price quotations to customer screens in financial institutions.

For the private investor, Stephen Eckett's *Investing Online* (see Sources on page 193) lists some of the highlights worth examining. Investors with an ordinary PC and local telephone call can:

- view closing market prices for most markets in the world
- for many markets, view real-time stock prices and chart price histories
- in the UK and US markets, give your orders via the computer
- monitor news stories on CNN and Bloomberg
- read online the daily financial papers, for example the *Financial Times* and the *Wall Street Journal*, and most other major newspapers worldwide
- monitor a portfolio's value and receive customised news stories relevant to the portfolio
- view real-time currency movements, with charts and technical analysis
- monitor the value and relative performance of collective funds
- read investment newsletters, which specialise in specific sectors
- consult online investment glossaries, read about futures and options, experiment with simulated trading programmes and receive buy/sell signals from online trading systems
- analyse company financial information and view corporate filings as quickly as the professional investors
- download economic data from government and bank databases and read regular economics reports and forecasts
- discuss all this with other investors online, and monitor what the market is talking about.

Many of these services are free.

Sources

The Stock Exchange publishes useful leaflets on buying and selling shares and on rolling settlement and nominee accounts. For copies telephone 0171 797 1000 or write to The Stock Exchange, London EC2N 1HP. For a copy of ProShare's guide *Brokers' New Issue Services*, send an A4 SAE with a 39p stamp to ProShare New Issues Guide, Library Chambers, 13 & 14 Basinghall Street, London EC2V 5BQ. Also available from ProShare is the Portfolio Management System. An alternative is the *Investors Chronicle's* Private Investor's Ledger. Details from the Investors Chronicle,Tel: 0171 896 2073.

The Internet: Probably the best guide to financial information and dealing on the Internet is Stephen Eckett's *Investing Online*, which was the main source of information for this Chapter. *Investing Online* is published by Pitman Publishing, price £39.99 (including a financial Internet directory).

Summary

■ How you buy shares will depend on the nature of the agreement with your stockbroker.

■ With the exception of shares from new issues, privatisations, windfalls and employee share option schemes, you will make your purchases in the secondary market.

■ Be prompt when your adviser asks for the money/shares and other paperwork necessary to settle a deal.

■ Under CREST your stockbroker must pay for shares five days after the purchase date.

■ Nominee accounts can help speed up settlement but do check that your adviser accepts responsibility for any losses made by the nominee company.

■ With collective funds, the annual charge is the one to watch on medium to long-term investments.

■ Under new rules, which came into force in 1997, your adviser or plan manager must disclose the full cost of your funds in a pre-sale 'key features' document.

■ If you plan to make a substantial investment try haggling over the charges.

■ For Pep and the new ISA investments, find out exactly what information you will receive – for example if you want to see the company or trust's annual report and accounts, do you have to pay extra?

■ The Internet provides a vast source of information but before you use a service, particularly a dealing service, check the firm is authorised with the Financial Services Authority (see page 270 for details of the FSA Central Register of authorised financial firms).

15

Selecting gilts and bonds

- How to assess the income from conventional gilts and bonds
- The safety of your investment
- Price fluctations
- Index-linked gilts
- Corporate bonds

At a glance

Gilts, corporate bonds and, to a much lesser extent, sterling foreign government bonds are popular with investors seeking income. In each case in return for the loan of your money the borrower, be it a company or a government, promises to repay the loan in full at a fixed date in the future.

With conventional gilts and bonds the borrower pays interest, known as the *coupon*, twice a year at a fixed rate. As a general rule, the longer the term the higher the income – but also the greater the drop in the real value of your capital at the maturity or *redemption* date.

From April 1998, most gilts pay interest gross. Previously it was only possible to secure gross payments if you bought through the National Savings Stock Register (NSSR). This still remains a very convenient way for non-taxpayers to make purchases and it is also the cheapest. The main drawback for active investors is that NSSR applications must be made by post, so you will not know in advance what the buying price will be.

Both gilts and qualifying bonds (not convertibles and preference shares) are free of capital gains tax on any profits because the 'return' is classed as income. However, this is not a win-win situation since you cannot offset a loss against capital gains in excess of the exemption.

The merits of gilts and bonds were discussed in some detail in Chapters 2 and 9. Here we take a closer look at how to assess the income and the place these products have in your portfolio.

HOW TO ASSESS THE INCOME FROM CONVENTIONAL GILTS AND BONDS

There are three important features of a bond or gilt to consider in this calculation:

- The nominal value represents the amount you receive at redemption, when the borrower repays the loan. This might be different from the original purchase price (if the gilts were sold at auction) and almost certainly will be different from the price at which you buy during the life span of the gilt (see market price below).

- The coupon tells you the interest rate that applies to the nominal value throughout the loan period.

- The market price is the current value if you buy or sell between the date of issue and the redemption date.

The coupon and nominal figures determine the level of interest, but the actual income return or yield will depend on the buying price. If the buying or market price of a gilt or bond goes up, the yield goes down because the coupon is a percentage of a higher price.

This see-saw effect is demonstrated in the following example. Suppose you buy a gilt which has a nominal price of 100 pence and the interest rate is 10 per cent. However, the price you pay is more than the nominal price at, say, 120 pence. Remember, the interest is still only 10 per cent of 100 – that is, 10 pence. This means the yield on your investment is 8.33 per cent (10 pence as a percentage of 120p).

> **The coupon and nominal figures determine the level of interest, but the actual income return or yield will depend on the buying price.**

Now consider the reverse situation. If the nominal is 100, the coupon 10 per cent and you buy at 80, you will still get 10 per cent of 100 pence, which is 10 pence – a yield of 12 per cent.

THE SAFETY OF YOUR INVESTMENT

The important difference between gilts and other bonds is the nature of the guarantee. If you buy gilts you are lending money to the UK Government, which is the safest borrower in terms of creditworthiness. Other bonds might be guaranteed by banks, companies and foreign governments, so there is an element of credit risk. This is reflected in the slightly higher yield – often about 0.3 per cent above gilt yields – offered to compensate you for the higher risk.

One other point on the security of corporate bonds. Issuers and advisers may make much of the fact that in the event of a company going bust, bonds rank before shares in the creditors' pecking order. Quite frankly, it is unlikely that a company in these circumstances could afford to repay bond holders but not shareholders. In most cases, therefore, it is wise to take this apparent additional security with a pinch of salt.

PRICE FLUCTUATIONS

Gilts and bonds are traded during the loan period, and there are no guarantees on the return of capital if you sell before the redemption date. Prices tend to reflect the market's view on future interest rates. This means that although in general gilts and bonds are less volatile than shares, there have been many exceptions which prove that this is a flimsy rule to rely upon. Over an exceptional period in 1994, for example, gilts fell by as much as 15–20 per cent.

Gilt interest is paid in arrears so the price will also take into account whether a recent interest payment has been made to the holder – in which case the price is *ex-dividend*. If the interest is still to be paid, the price is *cum-dividend*. The price quoted in the *Financial Times* is the mid-point between buying and selling prices.

INDEX-LINKED GILTS

Many investors, particularly if they are retired, need to squeeze as much income as possible out of their assets and are reluctant to take any risks with the capital. Advisers usually recommend that even an income-orientated portfolio should contain at least some equity-based investments. These, they argue, should provide some capital protection plus a rising income. (see Chapter 2 for the equity v bonds argument and Chapter 9 for an example of the asset allocation of an income portfolio.)

If you are not comfortable with ordinary shares it may be worth considering a half-way house, namely investments which offer a rising income plus some capital protection. The most common choice is index-linked gilts, which pay interest at a certain percentage above the rate of RPI. You might also consider index-linked corporate bonds (not many of these), *stepped preference shares* of *split capital investment trusts* (not many of these either), and escalator bonds, available from a few building societies, all of which were discussed briefly in Chapter 5. Here we just concentrate on index-linked gilts.

Index-linked gilts guarantee to increase both the six-monthly interest payments and the 'nominal' or original capital investment due at redemption in line with increases in the *retail prices index* (RPI).

> Many investors, particularly if they are retired, need to squeeze as much income as possible out of their assets and are reluctant to take any risks with the capital.

Since the starting RPI used is eight months before the date of issue, the final value of the investment can be calculated precisely seven months before redemption (RPI figures are published a month in arrears).

Like conventional gilts, the index-linked variety is traded actively so the price and real value of the yield can fluctuate significantly between the issue and redemption dates. However, there is no inflation (RPI) risk for the investor in index-linked gilts other than the eight-month period without indexation at the end of each stock's life.

■ Comparisons with alternative investments

So, how does this compare with the yields on *equities*? The income on index-linked gilts is guaranteed to grow in line with inflation over the years but cannot grow more quickly.

> **The income on index-linked gilts is guaranteed to grow in line with inflation over the years but cannot grow more quickly.**

Equities, however, offer no guarantees, but historically have grown more quickly than the rate of inflation. However, under certain economic conditions, equities can lag behind inflation for a considerable period.

A similar comparison can be made with conventional gilts, which have a fixed income throughout their term.

Index-linked gilts have not offered particularly competitive returns compared with equities, conventional gilts or cash since they were first issued in 1981. They have provided a real return of 3.2 per cent in a period when the other two investment categories have provided real returns way above their long-term trend.

Having said that, index-linked gilts have provided their return for a much lower level of risk than the other two categories, and if you make adjustments for tax, their net return is a little more competitive.

Investors seeking absolute guarantees from their income-yielding portfolio may be tempted to put all their money in gilts. If you are in this position do go for a balance between conventional gilts, which offer a comparatively high fixed income but no index-linking of the capital value, and index-linked gilts, which offer a low initial income but protect the income and capital from rising inflation.

Points to consider:

- *Name of gilt:* the title of the gilt tells you the gross percentage of interest payable per £100 'nominal' of a conventional stock. The nominal value is the expected original purchase price (although the actual purchase price might have been different if it was bought at auction) and redemption price. Since gilts are traded in the market, this might be quite different from the price at which you bought.

  The names 'Treasury' and 'Exchequer' have no particular significance. Treasury is the name given to the more recent issues, while Exchequer is just an historic term to denote the same source.

  You may also come across the terms 'convertible' and 'loan'. In the past the Treasury has issued convertible gilts which allow you to exchange the gilt for another issue at certain predetermined dates. At the time of writing there were no gilts outstanding with a conversion option still attached but the Government can choose to consolidate one issue with another.

The term 'loan' refers to a bearer instrument which, rather like a bank note, represents the actual gilt. This means that if you lose the bearer certificate, you have lost your investment.

■ *Dividend payment dates:* conventional gilts usually pay dividends twice a year (also known as the interest or coupon). The second payment date is determined by taking the redemption date and knocking off the year. The first payment date is determined by working back six months from that second date. For example, the 6% Treasury Stock 1999 has a redemption date of 10 August 1999 so its dividend payment dates in 1998 are 10 February and 10 August.

■ *Redemption date:* this is the date on which the nominal value of the gilt will be repaid.

■ *Amount of issue:* this is a good indication of the liquidity of the market. Where there is only a small amount of issue the gilt may be difficult to buy and to sell.

Information on prices and yields to maturity is published in the second section of the *Financial Times* on weekdays and in the first section on Saturdays.

CORPORATE BONDS

One of the most popular ways of holding corporate bonds is through a unit trust. Many corporate bond funds were launched for the Pep market but these will continue to be available after the demise of Peps in April 1999, when you can hold them in an individual savings account (ISA) if you wish (see Chapter 7).

There is no reason why confident and experienced investors should not choose their own individual bonds provided you can achieve a sensible spread of risk.

To date the corporate bond Peps which have proved most popular are the 'guaranteed' variety. For the bulk of bond funds which do not offer a guarantee it is important to view with caution the assumption made by some promoters that these funds offer investors absolute safety and security. With some funds your capital could be eroded to maintain high income payments.

Rather like index-tracking funds, charges are a more significant factor in the corporate bond fund selection process than is the case with equity funds. With a bond fund the gap in performance between the best and the worst is small, so differences in charges are highly significant.

■ Charges and yields

The *Association of Unit Trusts and Investment Funds* (Autif) has co-ordinated the way corporate bond fund yields are calculated by its members so that managers show yields on a consistent basis.

The yield figures should not be examined without reference to the way the annual management charge is deducted. If this is taken out of capital, as opposed to the usual practice of deducting it from income, then the yields will look artificially high. This may sound rather trivial but it is actually quite important. The argument goes something like this: it is not so unreasonable to deduct the annual charge from capital on an equity fund because the charge comes out of the capital growth (assuming there is some) rather than the original capital invested. However, for a bond fund there is usually no capital growth (unless it is partly invested in convertibles). This means that if the annual management charge is deducted from capital this will erode your initial lump sum investment. And if the manager wants to regain the capital base he or she has little choice but to take above-average risk even to achieve a reasonable return

When it comes to the yield, there are two figures to consider: the gross redemption yield and the running yield.

- The 'gross redemption yield' or 'projected total yield' takes into account both the income received and changes in the capital value of the bonds if they are held to maturity.

- *The running yield* or 'projected income yield' only takes into account the current rate of income received from the bonds. No allowance is made for any changes in the capital value so this could mask capital erosion, for example if the annual charge is deducted from capital.

As a general rule the gross redemption yield is the better measure of the total expected investment return. A high gross redemption yield might be accompanied by a higher credit risk and often greater volatility in the capital value of the fund.

The running yield is important for investors concerned about the income they will receive. A high running yield is often associated with capital erosion.

Summary

- To assess the income of a conventional gilt or bond you need to look at the nominal value, which represents the amount you will receive at redemption, the coupon, which tells you the interest rate that applies to the nominal value, and the market or current price.

- Consider the safety or creditworthiness of the borrower in order to assess the risk.

- Gilts are issued by the Government and so represent the safest type of bond.

- Index-linked gilts provide an income which rises each year by a fixed percentage (e.g. 2 or 3 per cent) above retail price inflation.

- If you are interested in corporate bonds, there is a good range of unit trusts which provide access to this market on a collective basis.

- If you buy a corporate bond unit trust find out whether the annual management charge is deducted from income or capital. Charges deducted from capital can lead to capital erosion.

KEEPING YOUR PORTFOLIO ON TRACK

Section 5

16

Company reports and accounts

- An accurate medical check
- The format
- Key ratios and statistics
- Key questions
- Balance sheet
- Group cash flow statement/profit and loss account
- Other financial information
- Any questions?

At a glance

Many new investors consider the annual report and accounts doubtless very worthy but nevertheless rather dull reading. In fact this can be one of the most important sources of information on a company's financial health. And in most cases it is free.

So, roll up your sleeves and have a go. Once you get a grip on the jargon, you will gain confidence in your abilities to interpret the key financial data.

Remember, though, by the time you see the annual report and accounts the information is already out of date. Regard it as a snapshot of the company's recent history. Clearly, you need to supplement it with more timely sources – for example from your stockbroker and from reports in the financial press (see 'Recommended reading' (page 277) and 'Newspapers and magazine' (page 278).

AN ACCURATE MEDICAL CHECK

Companies whose shares are traded on the Stock Exchange or the *Alternative Investment Market* must publish an annual report and accounts after the end of their financial year. (The financial year is not necessarily the same as the fiscal year, which runs from April 6 to April 5.)

The report is sent to shareholders, who, as the owners of the company, want to see how well it is doing and whether it is meeting its stated targets. As a prospective investor you can also get a copy of the report either directly from the company or via the *Financial Times* share information service (see page 239 for details).

To guide you through a typical report this Chapter uses examples from two well-known FTSE 100 companies – Boots and Marks & Spencer. The choice is not in any way a recommendation – it merely helps you to see how the report is laid out. Not all of the references will appear in every annual report.

Two very useful guides to this topic are the ProShare *Introduction to Annual Reports & Accounts*, and *The Financial Times Guide to Using the Financial Pages* (details in Sources section at the end of this Chapter).

THE FORMAT

Reports are divided into several sections.

- *Chairman's statement:* here the chairman draws attention to the positive achievements in the company's past year. This can be very helpful to the investor as it will highlight the major developments to date and opportunities which lie ahead. The chairman might comment on the dividend paid to shareholders and the company's strategic plans in terms of acquisitions.

  As a general rule the chairman's statement will help you to gain a brief but important overview of the company's progress. Once you get past the first few paragraphs you are likely to find the stuff the chairman is less than pleased with. Watch out for expressions like 'In the face of very difficult trading conditions' and 'The strong pound currently affects the translation into sterling of overseas profits'.

The chairman may also take this opportunity to thank various key members of the board of directors and to announce important changes in personnel. If there are changes in the board's composition, find out why. (You receive the *Financial Times'* important news stories for the past 12 months when you request a report on a company – see page 239 for details).

■ *A mission statement:* this is not compulsory but companies find it helpful to remind shareholders what they are trying to achieve over the longer term. Although this can be rather woolly, it may help you make comparisons between similar companies and to set benchmarks against which you can measure a company's progress.

■ *Chief executive's report:* this may not be written by the chief executive but there should always be a progress report on the company's or group's business operations and financial state of health.

■ *Directors' report:* this is the regulatory and legal bit. The Companies Act requires the company to disclose a heap of information including – and this is of interest – who the directors are and their total remuneration including salary, profit shares, benefits and bonuses. More detail is provided in particular on their shareholdings and on their pensions – their most valuable company benefit after salary.

> The two most important sections of the report are the balance sheet and the profit and loss account.

■ *Financial statements:* the two most important sections of the report are the balance sheet and the profit and loss account. For a snapshot view, focus on the following facts and figures:
  – size
  – profitability
  – ability to generate cash (this indicates how lenders and investors view the company's strength and long-term financial health)
  – financial summary – this shows whether the company is growing, treading water or shrinking.

KEY RATIOS AND STATISTICS

The ratios analysts use to assess a company's financial strength were discussed in Chapter 13.

Some companies show certain key statistics in their reports and accounts. Otherwise it is quite easy to calculate them for yourself. Do remember, though, these are only useful in identifying trends and must be seen in the right context – for example in a comparison with other similar companies in terms of size and sector. Key ratios are:

- *The current ratio:* this is the value of the current assets divided by current liabilities and is used as a measure of liquidity – in other words, to show to what extent the company is solvent or up to its neck in debt.

  A ratio of 1.0 simply shows that the company's books balance and that their assets are equal to their debts. If the ratio is less than 1.0 it shows that the company has more debts than it has assets to pay them. This is not always a bad thing, so do check the context. For example, a fast growing company may have borrowed heavily but wisely to finance its expansion.

- *The quick ratio:* this is the value of 'quick' assets (that is, easily converted to cash) divided by current liabilities and is similar to the current ratio but it takes a very short-term view. 'Quick' assets excludes comparatively illiquid assets such as stocks because they generally take time to turn into cash. Also excluded are trade debtors who are not expected to pay up within a month.

- *The gearing ratio:* this is net borrowings divided by shareholders' funds and minority interests. The ratio is designed to indicate the extent to which the company relies on borrowings. If the ratio is low then the company profits are not vulnerable if there is a sharp rise in interest rates. A high ratio means that profits are at risk if interest rates rise sharply.

- *Return on capital employed:* this is the profits before tax divided by the shareholders' funds and indicates the return the company is making on all the capital tied up in the business.

KEY QUESTIONS

The interpretation and importance of the above ratios will vary depending on the type of company and sector. As mentioned, in some cases it might be perfectly healthy for the company to have a high level of borrowing. So, check what is considered typical for the type of company and compare it with companies in the same sector.

> In some cases it might be perfectly healthy for the company to have a high level of borrowing.

You should also check past reports to identify important trends. For example, if the current ratio is falling this would indicate that the company's assets are falling in comparison with their liabilities and this should be investigated.

ProShare recommends that you consider the following five questions as you wade through company reports and accounts:

- *Cash flow:* the cash flow refers to the funds available within the company that are generated by its operation rather than borrowed. What you need to consider here is whether cash balances are rising or falling. This is very important because companies get into difficulties when they run out of cash and can even go bust, despite the fact they may appear to be making profits.

  Does the ability of the company to generate cash from trading activities (this is shown as a separate line in the statement) indicate it can convert profits into cash? If so, this indicates the company can fund expansion and pay dividends to shareholders.

- *Turnover and profit:* is turnover rising or falling? How much of the change in turnover (compared with recent years) is due to the company buying or selling businesses during the year in question? Are costs increasing or decreasing? If so, what particular overheads have changed? Are there any exceptional items in the sales or overheads this year which distort profit figures?

- *Interest and borrowings:* are interest charges up or down compared with last year? Is the change due to the size of the borrowings or to differences in interest rates? Are borrowings increasing or decreasing and what effect does this have on the company's gearing ratio?

- *Taxation:* is the tax charge rising or falling as a percentage of profits and why?

- *Accounting policies:* has the company changed its method of accounting and if so why? It is obliged to tell you and to show the effect of the change.

BALANCE SHEET

Companies whose shares are traded on the stockmarket often own or control a number of other, subsidiary companies. They prepare group accounts which include a consolidated balance sheet showing the assets and liabilities of all the businesses combined, as well as the balance sheet of the parent company.

The style of presentation in annual reports and accounts differs between companies but they will all include a balance sheet which looks similar to the example shown for Boots (see page 223).

This is a snapshot of Boots at the end of its trading year. It shows you what the company owns – its *assets* – and what it owes – its *liabilities*. The figures are in £ millions. Negative figures are usually shown in brackets. The previous year's figures are shown for comparison purposes, although clearly you should look back over more than one year to identify any important trends.

The notes indicate that the company provides further explanations and a more detailed breakdown of the figures later in the report. FRS indicates that the figures are provided in accordance with Financial Reporting Standards.

The balance sheet shows the following:

- *Assets:* divided into fixed or tangible assets (land and buildings, fixtures and fittings, equipment etc.) and current assets (money owed, investments and cash).

- *Current liabilities:* referring here to money the company owes and must repay within one year. It might also refer to bank overdrafts and any other debt – such as money owed to suppliers. A company's total assets should normally be greater than its liabilities – the surplus belongs to the shareholders, although part is also used to fund future expansion.

- *Net current assets:* this is the current assets minus the current liabilities.

- *Total assets less current liabilities:* this includes everything the company owns – not just the fixed assets.

- *Net assets:* several further items are deducted from the previous figures – in this case long-term borrowing and provision for any long-term liability. This calculation reveals the net assets figure – in other words, what the company is worth.

- *Capital and reserves:* this provides details about the shares allotted under the company's share schemes, and makes a reference to the profit and loss account.

- *Equity shareholders' funds:* this is the capital invested by shareholders, plus the profits built up over the years and not yet distributed as dividends.

- *Total capital employed:* this combines the shareholders' funds and equity minority interests.

GROUP CASH FLOW STATEMENT/PROFIT AND LOSS ACCOUNT

This page of the company report and accounts (see page 223 for Boots) shows how much profit the company or group made and is no different in principle from totting up the costs of cakes and drinks and deducting this figure from takings on the door at the local school summer fair. If income exceeds expenditure, the company has made a profit.

Profit includes turnover, which is the total amount of goods and/or services sold throughout the financial year.

Losses include all the company's costs – labour costs, purchases and other overheads incurred in running the business.

■ Where the profit goes

Of course, not all of the net profit can be used by the company. First the Inland Revenue takes its share by charging, among other items, corporation tax, which is the company's equivalent of income tax on profits. Then there is National Insurance, which is effectively a form of taxation levied on salaries paid to employees.

> As a rule the FTSE 100 companies in particular try to maintain a sustainable dividend year in year out.

Part of the remaining slice of profit is distributed to shareholders as *dividends* and the rest is ploughed back into the business. It is the directors of the company who decide how much of the profit should be paid out to shareholders, although their decision is subject to shareholder approval at the annual general meeting.

As a rule the FTSE 100 companies in particular try to maintain a sustainable dividend year in year out. This is good news for investors who are looking for a regular stream of income but the rule is not infallible.

■ Sources of turnover

Companies must also show how the turnover is divided between their different operations. To do this the group presents a consolidated profit and loss account which sets out the combined results of the parent company and all its subsidiaries.

Once again figures are in £millions and negative figures are shown in brackets. This section includes:

- turnover
- gross profit (turnover less costs)
- profit attributable to shareholders (the profit earned by and distributed to ordinary shares)
- undistributed surplus for the year (this is what the company intends to keep to build the business)
- earnings per share (the amount of dividend per share expressed as pence) and
- headline earnings per share.

The last entry is an additional measure of earnings per share recommended by the Institute of Investment Management and Research (IIMR). It adjusts standard earnings to eliminate certain capital items – for example, loss on disposal of discontinued operations, sale of property and other fixed assets.

OTHER FINANCIAL INFORMATION

■ Auditor's report

This is the independent auditor's statement that the report and accounts comply with regulatory and legal requirements, in other words that they are honest and accurate.

■ Notes to the accounts

As mentioned earlier, there is a detailed breakdown of figures and further explanations in the notes to the balance sheet and profit and loss accounts. This is particularly useful in assessing the company's international operations – an important factor in its diversification and stability.

The notes may also include any contingent liabilities – for example a pending lawsuit.

■ Consolidated statement of total recognised gains and losses

This shows the total of all gains and losses made by the company, including exchange differences on foreign currency and reevaluations of property.

■ Cash flow information

This shows how much cash has come into the business from customers, suppliers, among others, and how much has gone out in payments to suppliers and employees, among others. This statement will also show such items as returns on investments, taxation, and capital expenditure.

■ Group financial record

This provides a summary of the most important figures for the past five years.

■ Shareholder information

This sets out the dates for key events such as the AGM, and the dates for dividend payments, interim results, interim dividend payments, and preliminary announcement of results.

ANY QUESTIONS?

If you have an advisory service with your stockbroker you could discuss any concerns or aspects of the report which you do not fully understand. But there is nothing to stop you going to the horse's mouth. Most companies have a special department for dealing with shareholder enquiries – just as they do for press enquiries – and they will be only too pleased to answer your questions, although if you are concerned about something you may well need to seek an independent analyst's view via your broker.

Whenever possible, do take advantage of your right to go to the annual general meeting. This can be an excellent source of information – particularly listening to the informed questions from the institutional investors and other private shareholders.

Sources

ProShare's *Introduction to Annual Reports & Accounts* is available to private investors for £4.95 (for contact details see page 277); Details for *The Financial Times Guide to Using the Financial Pages* are also on page 277.

Summary

- The annual report and accounts provides a wealth of information but remember that by the time you see it this is already out of date.

- The chairman's statement provides a good summary of past achievements and future strategic plans.

- The two most important financial statements are the balance sheet and the profit and loss account.

- In particular check cash flow, turnover and profits, interest and borrowings.

- If you do not understand an entry ask the company directly (most large companies have a department for dealing with shareholders' queries) or ask your stockbroker.

THE BOOTS COMPANY PLC

Extract from the Annual Report and Accounts for the Year Ended 31st March 1997

Group Profit and Loss Account
For the year ended 31st March 1997

	Notes	Before exceptional items 1997 £m	Exceptional items (note 3) 1997 £m	Total 1997 £m	Before exceptional items 1996 £m	Exceptional items (note 3) 1996 £m	Total 1996 £m
Turnover							
Continuing operations							
– excluding acquisitions		4,291.8	–	4,291.8	4,010.4	–	4,010.4
– acquisitions		273.3	–	273.3			
Turnover from continuing operations		4,565.1	–	4,565.1	4,010.4	–	4,010.4
Discontinued operation		12.9	–	12.9	114.3	–	114.3
Total turnover	1	4,578.0	–	4.578.0	4,124.7	–	4,124.7
Operating profit							
Continuing operations							
– excluding acquisitions		496.4	8.6	505.0	444.0	12.8	456.8
– acquisitions		(4.7)	–	(4.7)			
Operating profit from continuing operations		491.7	8.6	500.3	444.0	12.8	456.8
Discontinued operation		0.1	–	0.1	(1.4)	–	(1.4)
Total operating profit	1,2	491.8	8.6	500.4	442.6	12.8	455.4
Profit/(loss) on disposal of fixed assets	3						
Continuing operations		–	11.3	11.3	–	1.2	1.2
Profit on disposal of businesses	4						
Continuing operations		–	–	–	–	0.2	0.2
Discontinued operation		–	15.0	15.0	–	–	–
Profit on ordinary activities before interest		491.8	34.9	526.7	442.6	14.2	456.8
Net interest	5	44.4	–	44.4	50.9	–	50.9
Profit on ordinary activities before taxation		536.2	34.9	571.1	493.5	14.2	507.7
Tax on profit on ordinary activities	6	(175.0)	(3.3)	(178.3)	(163.4)	(3.7)	(167.1)
Profit on ordinary activities after taxation		361.2	31.6	392.8	330.1	10.5	340.6
Equity minority interests		0.5	–	0.5			
Profit for the financial year attributable to shareholders	7	361.7	31.6	393.3	330.1	10.5	340.6
Dividends	8			(586.1)			(176.4)
(Loss)/profit retained				(192.8)			164.2
Earnings per share	9	39.5p	3.4p	42.9p	34.7p	1.1p	35.8p

Other Primary Statements of the Group
For the year ended 31st March 1997

Statement of Total Recognised Gains and Losses

	1997 £m	1996 £m
Profit for the financial year attributable to shareholders	**393.3**	340.6
Surplus on revaluation of investment properties	**27.1**	16.0
Currency translation differences on foreign currency net investments	**(10.4)**	3.3
Other gains and losses	**0.3**	
Total recognised gains and losses for the year	**410.3**	359.9

Note on Historical Cost Profits and Losses

	1997 £m	1996 £m
Reported profit on ordinary activities before taxation	**571.1**	507.7
Realisation of property revaluation (deficits)/surpluses	**(3.1)**	5.3
Difference between historical cost depreciation charge and actual charge for the year calculated on revalued amounts	**0.2**	0.2
Historical cost profit on ordinary activities before taxation	**568.2**	513.2
Historical cost (loss)/profit retained	**(195.7)**	169.7

Reconciliation of Movements in Shareholders' Funds

	1997 £m	1996 £m
Total recognised gains and losses for the year	**410.3**	359.9
Dividends	**(586.1)**	(176.4)
New share capital issued (net of expenses)	**7.7**	9.1
Repurchase of shares (note 21)	**(300.0)**	
Goodwill purchased	**(124.5)**	(8.7)
Goodwill released on disposal of businesses and intangible fixed assets	**4.4**	0.1
Scrip dividends	**8.3**	10.6
Net (decrease)/increase in shareholders' funds	**(579.9)**	194.6
Opening shareholders' funds	**2,201.5**	2,006.9
Closing shareholders' funds	**1,621.6**	2,201.5

Balance Sheets
31st March 1997

	Notes	Group 1997 £m	Group 1996 £m	Parent 1997 £m	Parent 1996 £m
Fixed assets					
Intangible assets	10	**33.8**	26.6	**3.2**	2.6
Tangible assets	11	**1,769.7**	1,624.4	**584.8**	205.2
Investments	12	**0.5**	46.4	**944.3**	962.2
		1,804.0	1,697.4	**1,532.3**	1,170.0
Current assets					
Stocks	13	**667.3**	522.1	**186.1**	168.4
Debtors falling due within one year	14	**347.2**	358.9	**545.7**	735 3
Debtors falling due after more than one year	14	**133.2**	2.2	**293.9**	186 0
Investments and deposits	15	**603.0**	893.9	**584.0**	868.6
Cash at bank and in hand		**30.9**	15.3	**119.0**	0.1
		1,781.6	1,792.4	**1,728.7**	1,958.4
Creditors: Amounts falling due within one year	16	**(1,597.2)**	(1,092.1)	**(1,075.8)**	(1,264.1)
Net current assets		**184.4**	700.3	**652.9**	694.3
Total assets less current liabilities		**1,988.4**	2,397.7	**2,185.2**	1,864.3
Creditors: Amounts falling due after more than one year	17	**(274.9)**	(150.5)	**(1,162.5)**	(562.5)
Provisions for liabilities and charges	19	**(92.0)**	(45.7)	**(12.8)**	(15.8)
Net assets		**1,621.5**	2,201.5	**1,009.9**	1,286.0
Capital and reserves					
Called up share capital	20,21	**226.5**	238.4	**226.5**	238.4
Share premium account	20	**233.7**	226.9	**233.7**	226.9
Revaluation reserve	20	**351.9**	321.4	**–**	–
Capital redemption reserve	20	**36.8**	24.0	**36.8**	24.0
Profit and loss account	20	**772.7**	1,390.8	**512.9**	796.7
Equity shareholders' funds		**1,621.6**	2,201.5	**1,009.9**	1,286.0
Equity minority interests		**(0.1)**	–	**–**	-
		1,621.5	2,201.5	**1,009.9**	1,286.0

The financial statements were approved by the board of directors on 4th June 1997 and are signed on its behalf by:

Sir Michael Angus
Chairman

Lord Blyth of Rowington
Deputy Chairman and Chief Executive

David Thompson
Joint Group Managing Director and Finance Director

Gain on share options

Details of executive and SAYE share options are shown on pages 44 and 45. Gains on share options represent the number of shares under option which have been exercised, valued at the difference between the market price at the date of exercise and the exercise price paid.

Details of gains on share options exercised during the year are as follows:

	Exercise price	Number of shares	Market price at date of exercise	Gain 1997 £000	Gain 1996 £000
	399p	167,500	631p	389	
	337p	2,225	653p	7	
Lord Blyth				396	–
	399p	65,000	615p	140	
	437p	22,500	615p	40	
	438p	52,500	615p	93	
	337p	2,017	648p	6	
	410p	634	647p	1	
A H Hawksworth				280	18
	399p	60,000	624p	135	
	337p	2,225	656p	7	
M F Ruddell				142	–
S G Russell	–	–	–	–	136
	399p	45,000	632p	105	
	437p	27,500	632p	54	
	337p	3,338	656p	11	
D A R Thompson				170	–
J J H Watson	–	–	–	–	–
B E Whalan	–	–	–	–	139
Total				988	293

Directors' shareholdings and share options

The beneficial interests of the directors and their families in the share capital of the company at 31st March 1997 are shown below. The company's register of directors' interests, which is open to inspection, contains full details of directors' shareholdings and options to subscribe.

Shareholdings

	Ordinary shares 1997	Ordinary shares 1996
Sir Michael Angus	3,348	3,348
Lord Blyth	214,269	41,562
Sir Peter Davis	3,194	3,098
F M Harrison	1,041	1,010
Sir Peter Reynolds	3,557	3,502
M F Ruddell	32,763	29,473
S G Russell	21,327	20,689
D A R Thompson	48,959	40,583
J J H Watson	22,371	22,150*
B E Whalan	6,775	6,569
Sir Clive Whitmore	1,562	1,515
R P Wilson	2,000	2,000

*at date of appointment

In addition, Sir Peter Reynolds has a non-beneficial interest in 1,300 (1996 1,300) ordinary shares. All directors are also deemed to have an interest in the 116,209 ordinary shares of the company held by the Boots ESOP Trust Ltd established to facilitate the operation of the company's executive bonus schemes. No director holds any loan capital. Directors' shareholdings on 4th June 1997 remain unchanged except that Mr M F Ruddell has acquired an additional nine shares.

Share Options

An analysis of the number of outstanding directors' share options at each exercise price is as follows:

Under SAYE scheme

	350p	352p	410p	415p	421p	485p	1997 Total	1996 Total
Lord Blyth	1,971	–	841	–	–	–	2,812	5,037
M F Ruddell	–	2,130	841	–	–	–	2,971	5,196
S G Russell	–	_	_	_	4,097	_	4,097	4,097
D A R Thompson	–	–	–	–	–	1,422	1,422	3,338
J J H Watson	–	–	–	–	–	3,556	3,556	3,556*
B E Whalan	2,957	–	–	1,662	–	–	4,619	4,619

*at date of appointment

SAYE options in respect of 1,422 shares were granted to Mr D A R Thompson during the year. Following the retirement of Mr A H Hawksworth, options in respect of 2,098 shares previously granted to him have lapsed.

Under executive scheme

	286p	399p	437p	438p	482p	531p	1997 Total	1996 Total
Lord Blyth	–	–	100,000	95,000	27,500	20,000	242,500	410,000
M F Ruddell	–	17,500	5,000	45,000	35,000	5,000	107,500	167,500
S G Russell	10,000	35,000	20,000	–	–	5,000	70,000	70,000
D A R Thompson	–	–	–	45,000	–	70,000	115,000	187,500
J J H Watson	–	17,500	22,500	5,000	12,500	5,000	62,500	62,500*
B E Whalan	–	–	–	32,500	–	7,500	40,000	40,000

*at date of appointment

Executive share options allow the holders to buy the company's shares at a future date at a price based on the market price prevailing a few days before the date of grant. As stated on page 40, the practice of granting executive share options has ceased.

No executive options lapsed during the year and no new ones were granted. The directors have agreed to exercise all outstanding executive share options by 31st March 1998.

Information on the company's share option schemes, including dates from when options are exercisable and expiry dates, is shown in note 21. The market price of the company's shares at 31st March 1997 was 675p and the range of market prices during the year was 555p to 701 p.
Directors' interests in share options on 4th June 1997 remain unchanged.

Pension entitlement
All executive directors receive pension entitlements from the company's principal UK defined benefit pension scheme, referred to in note 25, and supplementary pension arrangements which provide additional benefits aimed at producing a pension of two-thirds final base salary. Six executive directors are members of the pension scheme and non-executive directors do not participate. There are no money purchase schemes. Pension entitlement is calculated only on the salary element of remuneration. The chief executive is entitled to the same level of pension benefits enjoyed by other executive directors despite his shorter service but after adjusting for pensions arising from earlier employment.

The study group on directors' remuneration chaired by Sir Richard Greenbury recommended that the remuneration committee's report should include details of pension entitlements calculated on a basis to be recommended by the Faculty of Actuaries and the Institute of Actuaries. Definitive requirements have now been established by the London Stock Exchange and details of pensions earned by the executive directors are shown below.

	Age at 31st March 1997	Directors' contributions year £000	Increase in accrued pension entitlement during the year £000	Total accrued pension entitlement 1997 £000
Lord Blyth (highest paid director)	56	24	34	237
A H Hawksworth (to 31st July 1996)	61	3	3	150*
M F Ruddell	53	10	10	115
S G Russell	52	11	32	122
D A R Thompson	54	12	14	143
J J H Watson (from 26th September 1996)	55	4	19	81
B E Whalan	52	8	9	86

*at date of retirement

The pension entitlement shown is that which would be paid annually on retirement based on service to the end of the year and the increase in accrued pension during the year excludes any increase for inflation. Members of the scheme have the option to pay additional voluntary contributions; neither the contributions nor the resulting benefits are included in the above table.

The normal retirement age is 60. Early retirement is available subject to Trustee consent and a reduction in the accrued pension. Under the current early retirement terms the pension can be drawn from age 59 without reduction.

On death after retirement spouses' pensions of two-thirds of members' pensions and children's pensions of two-ninths of members' pensions for up to three dependant children are payable (subject to Inland Revenue limits).

Pensions in payment are guaranteed to be increased annually by 5% or the increase in the Index of Retail Prices (RPI) if less. Additional increases may be granted at the discretion of the Trustees and subject to the consent of the company.

Any transfer value calculations would make allowance for discretionary benefits including pension increases and early retirement.

Contracts of service

The chairman has a fixed term service contract with the company which has been extended by a year to expire in July 1998. None of the non-executive directors has a service contract, including Sir Peter Reynolds and Mr R P Wilson who are standing for re-appointment as directors at the annual general meeting.

Each executive director has a service contract which is terminable by the company on two years' notice including Mr J J H Watson who is standing for re-appointment at the annual general meeting. All such contracts terminate when the director in question reaches the age of 60. The remuneration committee considers that it is appropriate for executive directors to have a service contract on such terms having regard to their seniority and value to the company and the generally prevailing practice among comparable companies. If any service contract were to be terminated by the company giving less than the contractual period of notice, the requirement for the director to mitigate his loss would be taken into account in determining any resulting compensation.

It is recognised that directors may be invited to become non-executive directors of other companies and that the additional experience and knowledge that this brings will benefit the company. Accordingly, the policy is to allow executive directors to accept up to two such appointments where no conflict of interest arises and to retain the fees received.

Signed for the remuneration committee on behalf of the board:

Sir Michael Angus
Chairman

Directors' Responsibilities Statement

The directors are required by the Companies Act 1985 to prepare financial statements which give a true and fair view of the profit or loss for the financial year and of the state of affairs of the company and the group at the end of that period. The directors are of the opinion that suitable accounting policies have been used and applied consistently, applicable accounting standards have been followed, and reasonable and prudent judgements and estimates have been made. The financial statements have been prepared on a going concern basis. The directors have a responsibility to ensure that the company and its subsidiaries have suitable internal controls for maintaining adequate accounting records, for safeguarding the assets of the group, and for preventing and detecting fraud and other irregularities.

Fixed assets

The directors are of the opinion that the market value of the group's properties at 31st March 1997 was not materially different from that stated in the financial statements.

Payment of suppliers

It is the policy of the company to agree appropriate terms and conditions for its transactions with suppliers (by means ranging from standard written terms to individually negotiated contracts) and that payment should be made in accordance with those terms and conditions, provided that the supplier has also complied with them.

The number of days purchases outstanding at 31st March 1997 was 25.

Staff

The company continues to involve staff in the decision-making process and communicates regularly with them during the year. Their involvement in the company's performance is encouraged with employee bonus and share schemes. The involvement extends to the board of Boots Pensions Ltd, on which there are three employee representatives. The company's aim for all members of staff and applicants for employment is to fit the qualifications, aptitude and ability of each individual to the appropriate job, and to provide equal opportunity, regardless of sex, religion or ethnic origin. The company does all that is practicable to meet its responsibility towards the employment and training of disabled people. Where an employee becomes disabled, every effort is made to provide continuity of employment in the same job or a suitable alternative. Further information is shown on page 34.

Charitable donations

Donations for charitable and educational purposes in the UK for the year were £2,126,000 (1996 £2,060,000). There were no political payments. Further information on community relations is shown on pages 35 and 36.

Directors

Details of directors in office on 31st March 1997 are shown on pages 10 and 11. In addition, Sir Ian Prosser and Mr A H Hawksworth were directors until their retirement on 25th July 1996 and 31st July 1996 respectively.

Sir Michael Angus, Sir Peter Reynolds and Mr R P Wilson retire by rotation at the annual general meeting in accordance with Article 87 and offer themselves for re-appointment.

Mr J J H Watson, having been appointed on 26th September 1996, retires at the annual general meeting in accordance with Article 86 and offers himself for re-appointment.

Mr B E Whalan is retiring as a director of the company on 31st July 1997.

No director had any interest, either during or at the end of the financial year, in any contract which was significant in relation to the group's business, other than a service contract.

Information on service contracts and details of the interests of the directors and their families in the share capital of the company at 31st March 1997 are shown in the Board Remuneration Committee's Report on pages 44 and 45.

Auditors

A resolution to re-appoint KPMG Audit Plc and to authorise the directors to fix their remuneration will be proposed at the annual general meeting.

By order of the board
4th June 1997
I A Hawtin
Secretary

MARKS AND SPENCER PLC

Extract from the Annual Report and Accounts for the Year Ended 31st March 1997

Report of the directors

No director seeking re-election has a Service Contract with the Company or any of its subsidiaries.

The beneficial interests of the directors and their families in the shares of the Company and its subsidiaries, together with their interests as trustees of both charitable and other trusts, are given on page 44.

EMPLOYEE INVOLVEMENT
We have maintained our commitment to employee involvement throughout the business.

Staff are kept well informed of the performance and objectives of the Group through personal briefings and regular meetings. These are supplemented by our staff publications, *St Michael News* and *M&S World*, and video presentations. 'Focus teams' in stores, distribution centres and head office enable management to meet with staff representatives. These groups provide opportunities for staff to contribute to the everyday running of the business.

The second meeting of the European Council took place last July. This council provides an additional forum for informing and consulting employee representatives from the European countries in which we trade.

Directors and executives regularly visit stores and discuss, with members of staff, matters of current interest and concern to the business. Staff representatives attend the Annual General Meeting and all members of staff have the Group results explained in *St Michael News*.

We have long-established Employees' Profit Sharing and Savings-Related Share Option Schemes, membership of which is service-related .

EQUAL OPPORTUNITIES
The Group is committed to an active Equal Opportunities Policy from recruitment and selection, through training and development, appraisal and promotion to retirement.

It is our policy to promote an environment free from discrimination, harassment and victimisation where everyone will receive equal treatment regardless of gender, colour, ethnic or national origin, disability, age, marital status, sexual orientation or religion. All decisions relating to employment practices will be objective, free from bias and based solely upon work criteria and individual merit.

The Company is responsive to the needs of its employees, customers and the community at large and we are an organisation that uses everyone's talents and abilities to the full.

EMPLOYEES WITH DISABILITIES
It is our policy that people with disabilities should have full and fair consideration for all vacancies. During the year we earned the right to use the Government's 'two tick' disability symbol to demonstrate our commitment to interviewing those people with disabilities who fulfil the minimum criteria, and endeavouring to retain staff in the workforce if they become disabled during employment. We will actively retrain and adjust their environment where possible to allow them to maximise their potential.

CHARITABLE AND POLITICAL CONTRIBUTIONS
During the year, we spent £9.8m in the UK in support of the community. Within this, direct donations to charitable organisations amounted to £5.5m. A political contribution of £40,000 was made to the Conservative Party.

ANNUAL GENERAL MEETING
Special Business Resolutions

Explanations of these resolutions are as follows:

Resolution Number 12
The Companies Act 1985 prevents directors from allotting unissued shares without the authority of shareholders in general meeting. In certain circumstances this could be unduly restrictive.

The Company's Articles empower your directors to allot unissued shares but the power is subject to annual renewal. Renewal of the power is sought for the period specified in the resolution, subject to the limitations that your directors may only allot:

(a) Shares in total, up to a nominal value of £89,000,000 ('the Section 80 Amount') which represents 12.5% of the nominal value of the issued share capital of the Company as at 20 April 1997, being a date not more than one month prior to the date of this report.

(b) Shares for cash, other than to existing shareholders in proportion to their holdings, up to a nominal value of £35,463,548 ('the Section 89 Amount'), being 5% of the nominal value of the issued share capital of the Company as at 20 April 1997, being a date not more than one month prior to the date of this report.

If shareholders approve this resolution:

(i) The authority given to the directors will expire on the date of the Annual General Meeting in 1998 or, if earlier, on 16 October 1998.

(ii) Within that period shareholders' consent will not be required for each allotment of shares made for cash otherwise than to existing shareholders in proportion to their existing holdings provided that such allotments do not exceed £35,463,548 in total.

Your directors have no current intention to exercise the authority sought by this resolution.

Resolutions Number 13 to 16

These resolutions, which will be proposed as Ordinary Resolutions, are for the adoption, respectively of new Delayed Profit Sharing; Immediate Profit Sharing; Savings Related Share Option; and Executive Share Option: Schemes. Full details of the Schemes referred to in these resolutions are set out with the Chairman's letter to shareholders dated 18 June 1997 which accompanies this Annual Report and Financial Statements.

Resolution Number 17

This resolution, which will be proposed as an Ordinary Resolution, seeks authority for the directors to introduce local Share Schemes, similar to the UK Share Schemes dealt with by Resolutions 13 to 16, for the benefit of non-UK resident Group employees if the directors consider it appropriate to do so. Any such local Schemes could differ from their UK equivalent Schemes to take account of local laws. Any options granted and any shares issued under such local Scheme would be counted against the limits on shares which can be issued under the UK Scheme from which the local Scheme is derived.

AUDITORS

A resolution proposing the re-appointment of Coopers & Lybrand as auditors to the Company will be put to the Annual General Meeting.

By order of the Board
Sir Richard Greenbury, Chairman
London
19 May 1997

Consolidated profit and loss account
FOR THE YEAR ENDED 31 MARCH 1997

	Notes	1997 £m	1996 £m
TURNOVER			
Continuing operations		**7,841.9**	7,211.3
Discontinued operations		–	22.4
	2, 3	**7,841.9**	7,233.7
Cost of sales	3	**(5,103.8)**	(4,720.5)
GROSS PROFIT		**2,738.1**	2,513.2
Other expenses	3	**(1,700.2)**	(1,575.8)
OPERATING PROFIT	2, 3	**1,037.9**	937.4
analysed between:			
Continuing operations		**1,037.9**	939.6
Discontinued operations		–	(2.2)
Disposal of discontinued operations:			
Loss on disposal		–	(15.0)
Goodwill previously written off to reserves		–	(10.0)
	4	–	(25.0)
Loss on sale of property and other fixed assets		**(1.8)**	(4.2)
Net interest income	5	**65.9**	57.6
PROFIT ON ORDINARY ACTIVITIES BEFORE TAXATION	2	**1,102.0**	965.8
analysed between:			
Continuing operations		**1,102.0**	993.7
Discontinued operations		–	(27.9)
Taxation on ordinary activities	6	**(346.1)**	(312.0)
PROFIT ON ORDINARY ACTIVITIES AFTER TAXATION		**755.9**	653.8
Minority interests (all equity)		**(1.3)**	(1.2)
PROFIT ATTRIBUTABLE TO SHAREHOLDERS	7	**754.6**	652.6
Dividends	8	**(368.6)**	(320.9)
UNDISTRIBUTED SURPLUS FOR THE YEAR	22	**386.0**	331.7
EARNINGS PER SHARE (Defined by FRS3)	9	**26.7p**	23.3p
HEADLINE EARNINGS PER SHARE (Defined by IIMR)	9	**26.8p**	24.3p

Consolidated statement of total recognised gains and losses
FOR THE YEAR ENDED 31 MARCH 1997

	Notes	1997 £m	1996 £m
PROFIT ATTRIBUTABLE TO SHAREHOLDERS		**754.6**	652.6
Exchange differences on foreign currency translation	22	**(54.3)**	4.0
Unrealised surpluses on revaluation	22	**10.0**	
TOTAL RECOGNISED GAINS AND LOSSES RELATING TO THE YEAR		**710.3**	656.6

Balance sheets
AT 31 MARCH 1997

	Notes	THE GROUP 1997 £m	1996 £m	THE COMPANY 1997 £m	1996 £m
FIXED ASSETS					
Tangible assets:					
Land and buildings		**3,056.7**	2,846.2	**2,736.6**	2,540.3
Fixtures, fittings and equipment		**500.1**	531.8	**364.5**	386.0
Assets in the course of construction		**53.1**	50.4	**26.5**	26.4
	12	**3,609.9**	3,428.4	**3,127.6**	2,952.7
Investments	13	**36.6**	46.0	**371.6**	369.3
		3,646.5	3,474.4	**3,499.2**	3,322.0
CURRENT ASSETS					
Stocks		**445.1**	422.8	**310.6**	292.7
Debtors:					
Receivable within one year	14	**819.2**	687.3	**1,456.4**	1,392.5
Receivable after more than one year	14	**906.6**	682.9	**167.4**	131.7
Investments	15	**361.8**	300.0	**–**	-
Cash at bank and in hand	16	**671.5**	782.5	**87.8**	66.2
		3,204.2	2,875.5	**2,022.2**	1,883.1
CURRENT LIABILITIES					
Creditors: amounts falling due within one year	17	**1,775.1**	1,674.9	**1,124.0**	1,160.0
NET CURRENT ASSETS		**1,429.1**	1,200.6	**898.2**	723.1
TOTAL ASSETS LESS CURRENT LIABILITIES		**5,075.6**	4,675.0	**4,397.4**	4,045.1
Creditors: amounts falling due after more than one year	18	**495.8**	497.8	**150.0**	150.0
Provisions for liabilities and charges	19	**31.8**	35.0	**27.9**	27.9
NET ASSETS		**4,548.0**	4,142.2	**4,219.5**	3,867.2
CAPITAL AND RESERVES					
Called up share capital	21	**709.2**	703.9	**709.2**	703.9
Share premium account		**259.8**	221.4	**259.8**	221.4
Revaluation reserve		**456.3**	449.8	**461.9**	458.4
Profit and loss account		**3,104.0**	2,744.5	**2,788.6**	2,483.5
SHAREHOLDERS' FUNDS (all equity)	22	**4,529.3**	4,119.6	**4,219.5**	3,867.2
Minonty interests (all equity)		**18.7**	22.6	**–**	-
TOTAL CAPITAL EMPLOYED		**4,548.0**	4,142.2	**4,219.5**	3,867.2

Approved by the Board
19 May 1997

Sir Richard Greenbury, Chairman
J K Oates, Deputy Chairman and Joint Managing Director

Consolidated cash flow information
FOR THE YEAR ENDED 31 MARCH 1997

CASH FLOW STATEMENT

	Notes	1997 £m	1997 £m	1996 £m	1996 £m
OPERATING ACTIVITIES					
Received from customers		**7,509.5**		7,045.2	
Payments to suppliers		**(5,109.8)**		(4,737.5)	
Payments to and on behalf of employees		**(909.4)**		(929.0)	
Other payments		**(593.2)**		(580.3)	
CASH INFLOW FROM OPERATING ACTIVITIES	25		**897.1**		798.4
RETURNS ON INVESTMENTS AND SERVICING					
OF FINANCE	26A		**65.4**		55.7
TAXATION	26B		**(318.6)**		(296.8)
CAPITAL EXPENDITURE AND FINANCIAL					
INVESTMENT	26C		**(413.1)**		(319.4)
ACQUISITIONS AND DISPOSALS	26D		**(0.2)**		(4 9)
EQUITY DIVIDENDS PAID			**(305.6)**		(271.3)
Cash outflow before management of liquid resources and financing			**(75.0)**		(38.3)
MANAGEMENT OF LIQUID RESOURCES AND FINANCING					
Management of liquid resources	26E	**91.3**		(127.7)	
Financing	26F	**64.7**		113.5	
			156.0		(14.2)
INCREASE/(DECREASE) IN CASH			**81.0**		(52.5)

RECONCILIATION OF NET CASH FLOW TO MOVEMENT IN NET FUNDS (see note 27)

	1997 £m	1996 £m
INCREASE/(DECREASE) IN CASH	**81.0**	(52.5)
Cash (inflow)/outflow from (decrease)/ increase in liquid resources	**(91.3)**	127.7
Cash inflow from increase in debt financing	**(21.0)**	(77.3)
Exchange movements	**(4.2)**	(2.2)
MOVEMENT IN NET FUNDS	**(35.5)**	(4.3)
Net funds at 1 April	**97.0**	101.3
NET FUNDS AT 31 MARCH	**61.5**	97.0

The cash flow information shown above is presented in accordance with the revised version of FRS1 'Cash flow statements'.
The comparative figures have been restated (see note 24).

17

Performance monitoring

- Portfolio measurement
- Collective funds
- Performance measurement services
- Periods of measurement
- Guide to reading the financial pages

At a glance

To measure the progress of your portfolio and the individual shares and funds it contains, you need an appropriate benchmark or yardstick.

This Chapter explains how to judge the performance of your portfolio in a realistic manner by comparing it with a range of suitable benchmarks, including recently launched model portfolios devised by performance measurement services.

Equally important is to set your own performance targets. These should be realistic and refer specifically to the aims and objectives of your investment choice.

Don't feel daunted by the mass of detail in the *Financial Times* 'Company and Markets' section. This is the best starting point for any investor who wants to check the progress of a private portfolio of shares and provides a wealth of useful information once you learn to read the language. This Chapter provides a quick course in how to interpret the pink pages.

PORTFOLIO MEASUREMENT

■ Compare with 'safe' investments

Before you consider the performance of your choice of shares, it is always a good idea to check what returns you could achieve from comparatively 'safe' investments. For the purpose of comparisons with equities, a 'safe' benchmark would be one that offers a high degree of capital protection.

So, take a look at what the after-tax returns have been on 60 and 120 day building society postal deposit accounts and short-term and medium-term gilts. These benchmarks will reveal whether over these periods the returns from equities have been worth the additional risks to your capital.

■ Compare with inflation

There are several ways of evaluating the performance of your portfolio. The simplest measure also has the most serious drawbacks. This is an absolute benchmark. Let's say, for example, that retail price inflation is 3 per cent and your portfolio, which is designed to achieve a balance of income and growth, returns 6 per cent over the year. Considered in isolation you might be quite satisfied that your capital has grown by 3 per cent in real terms – that is, 3 per cent above the rate of inflation.

However, you might be less satisfied if you discovered that the FTSE All-Share (the main yardstick for the UK stockmarket as a whole) had risen by 12 per cent, or that many other investors with similar portfolio aims to your own had achieved 13 per cent.

The point to note here is that when markets are rising most professional investors and private amateurs can achieve what look like reasonable results. The real skill is in achieving above average returns.

■ Compare with an index or peer group

TIP To measure performance in this way you need a benchmark relative to an index or a peer group. As mentioned, the most relevant index for a portfolio of UK shares is the FTSE All-Share, which contains about 900 companies listed on the UK stockmarket.

If you specialise in medium-sized or smaller companies you might also measure against a more specific index such as the SmallCap (the companies in the All-Share which are outside the top 350) or the FTSE 250 (the largest 250 companies after the FTSE 100).

This is fine provided you keep the results in context. Whatever your specialisation, it is always worth checking your progress compared with a broad benchmark. If you are in smaller companies and the best performing shares are in the FTSE 100 you may decide that taking the extra risk associated with small companies isn't worth it.

For Internet fans, the FTSE International web site is packed with useful information about the FTSE indices (see page 247).

COLLECTIVE FUNDS

With collective funds it is easy to measure against a peer group because the funds are categorised according to investment aim. For example, managed (a combination of equities, bonds and, sometimes, property), UK equity income, international fixed interest and so on.

Having said that, within the managed fund sector for life assurance and pension funds there is a wide range of different risk levels, so do check the asset allocation and the types of shares selected by the manager.

> Within the managed fund sector for life assurance and pension funds there is a wide range of different risk levels.

You might find, for example, that the manager has achieved an outstanding performance only because he or she took bigger risks than is typical for the fund sector as a whole. A good example is a managed fund where the manager invests almost wholly in equities when most of the other funds are, say, 70 per cent in equities with the rest in bonds and gilts to reduce risk.

It is also important to check performance on a discrete basis. Discrete results show year on year rather than cumulative performance. This is important because a good cumulative result over five years might hide an outstanding (possibly lucky) short-term performance followed by several years of mediocrity.

Unfortunately most published results for collective funds are cumulative and discrete results are difficult to analyse without access to a major statistics database such as Micropal or HSW Hindsight. However, your stockbroker or financial adviser certainly should have access to these statistics.

PERFORMANCE MEASUREMENT SERVICES

In the past private investors did not have any recognised scientific and independent performance measurement service comparable to what is available in the institutional market.

Recently, two independent services for private investors have been launched which both aim to provide a benchmark against which you can measure your portfolio. The first is the Private Investor Indices from FTSE International and the stockbrokers association APCIMS , and the second is from WM, one of the leading performance measurers in the institutional market.

> Two independent services for private investors have been launched which both aim to provide a benchmark against which you can measure your portfolio.

The asset allocations for the FTSE International three indices (income, growth and balanced) were shown in Chapter 9. Two versions of each index are calculated. A capital only index shows the growth in the value of the portfolio excluding income received and a total return index which assumes that gross income is reinvested in the portfolio.

You can use these indices, which are published in the *Financial Times*, in several ways:

■ to make a direct comparison with your own portfolio

■ to use as the basis for a review of the asset allocation and structure of your portfolio with your investment adviser

■ as a benchmark against which you can compare and assess the performance of discretionary stockbrokers.

The FTSE/APCIMS indices show what happens to a portfolio which is run like a collection of index-tracking funds – each element representing the appropriate index for UK equities, various overseas equity indices, cash and so on. Clearly, the asset allocation of any 'model' portfolio is to some extent arbitrary, but given the expertise of the providers, this is as good a benchmark as any and will show whether you or your manager's deviations from the indices actually improved returns or undermined performance.

WM's service is slightly different. This shows whether you and/or your manager did better or worse than your peers, and is based on asset mix information from over 20 managers and brokers, combined with the returns on the appropriate investment indices over the quarter measured.

WM's choice of indices are as follows:

- *UK equities:* FTSE All-Share
- *North America:* FT/S&P North America
- *Continental Europe:* FT/S&P Europe ex UK
- *Japan:* FT/S&P Japan
- *Pacific Basin ex Japan:* FT/S&P Pacific ex Japan
- *Other international equities:* FT/S&P World ex UK
- *UK bonds:* FTSE UK Gilts – All Stocks
- *Overseas bonds:* JP Morgan Global (Non-UK) Traded Index (Unh'd)
- *UK index-linked:* FTSE Fixed Interest Index-linked All Stocks
- *Cash/Other:* LIBID 7-Day.

Both services are very useful, but remember that benchmarks are only intended to provide guidelines and should not be regarded as an absolute measure of performance. The FTSE indices, for example, are designed to relate to the average UK-based investor with a sterling denominated pool of savings.

FTSE International pointed out that investors may have potential capital gains tax liabilities which must be taken into account, as must any advisory fees. Also, investors may hold particular stocks for a variety of reasons.

Details of both services are provided in the Sources section at the end of the Chapter.

■ Collective funds

At the time of writing Peps were still available. Once the individual savings accounts take over in 1999, most providers of information on Peps will continue their service for the ISAs.

Chase de Vere publishes an annual guide to Peps and updates its performance supplement every six months (for details, see page 278). For the confident and experienced investor this represents a practical and authoritative DIY kit.

Another excellent source of informed commentary on Pep performance is BESt Investment's *Personal Equity Plan* publication. In addition to its recommendations, in a refreshingly brisk manner the company also publishes a *Spot the Dog* guide which lists all the funds you should consider avoiding or selling (see page 248).

For investment trusts probably the most useful source of performance data is the monthly information sheet (MIS) from the Association of Investment Trust Companies, which shows the results of £100 invested in each investment trust share and the performance of the underlying net assets. The latter is considered a far better measure of the company's investment expertise because it disregards the impact of market forces on the company's share price.

If you have the time you could build up a more detailed record of performance fluctuations by monitoring your fund's price changes, although this would not show the impact of dividend reinvestment. With unit trusts, for example, your unit trust manager should send you a quarterly or six-monthly valuation which will show the unit price. For more frequent updates you can check the price in the authorised unit trusts pages in the *Financial Times*. On Saturdays the information appears in the 'Weekend Money' section, while on weekdays you will find these figures in the 'Companies and Markets' section.

Compare percentage price changes with changes in an appropriate benchmark. Again, the FTSE All-Share is the best general index for UK equity-based unit trusts.

If you find reading the pink pages rather daunting, a basic description of the column headings is provided in the FT itself but a more detailed source is the *Financial Times Guide to Using the Financial Pages* (see the Sources section at the end of the Chapter and page 277).

Personal pension plan performance is covered by surveys in *Money Management*, among other specialist publications. Your adviser will probably also subscribe to one of the top consultants' annual surveys which provide detailed analysis of performance, how that performance was achieved and whether the team responsible is still in place. The surveys also consider the strength of the company and the flexibility of the contract. The Bacon & Woodrow methodology was discussed in Chapter 6.

PERIODS OF MEASUREMENT

The costs of buying shares, whether direct or through a unit or investment trust, combined with the short-term volatility of markets, has meant that performance tends to be measured over the medium to long term – typically over a minimum period of five years.

While this is a sensible approach for private investors it should be backed up by more regular monitoring which will pick up on changes in fund management style or personnel.

With equity investments clearly past performance is an imperfect guide to the future – whether you hold them directly or through collective funds. However, performance can give a good indication of a share's prospects where it is examined in conjunction with other essential data about the company and its investment processes.

Once you have identified the funds that are appropriate in terms of asset class and allocation it is important to assess different managers' investment style. For example, was the performance achieved through a consistent ability to pick the right stocks or did the total returns rely on occasional periods of outperformance based on a high-risk strategy?

It is also important that you or your adviser keep track of the actual management team responsible for the performance. Investment teams have a nasty habit of defecting to rival companies and if this happens in an investment house where star managers rule the roost, you might consider a similar move. Very sensibly, some investment houses keep a tight lid on individual managers and insist on a team mentality which provides a more stable environment.

GUIDE TO READING THE FINANCIAL PAGES

The sections below on 'How to read the figures' were drawn from the guides mentioned in the source material at the end of this chapter plus details provided in the *Financial Times* 'Guide to The London Share Service' which is published at the end of the share prices in the *Companies and Markets* section. For investment trust performance data, the AITC was the main source.

Financial Times services

The *Financial Times* London Share Service includes various investor services indicated by a symbol after the company name. A club symbol indicates you can obtain the current annual or interim report free of charge. All you have to do is phone a 24-hour number quoting the reference number provided in that edition of the *Financial Times*.

A character symbol indicates you can obtain a comprehensive 10–14 page report on the company including key FT stories from the past 12 months, the latest survey of City profit forecasts and investment recommendations, five-year financial and share price performance review, balance sheet and profit and loss data, plus recent Stock Exchange announcements. The price at the time of writing was a modest £8.45.

Up-to-the-second share prices are available by telephone from the *Financial Times* Cityline service.

Share prices information

Share prices, including investment trusts, are quoted each day in the *Financial Times* 'Companies and Markets' section. This includes companies in the All-Share, the Alternative Investment Market (the market for new smaller companies) and the foreign companies.

How to read the figures

The column headings used in the *Financial Times* are shown in brackets.

- *Name and notes (Notes):* the first column lists the company name or its abbreviation. The various symbols represent particular features of its shares. For example, if the company has several types of share in issue, a square will indicate which is the most actively traded, including those UK stocks where transactions and prices are published continuously through the Stock Exchange

Automated Quotation (SEAQ) system and non-UK stocks through the SEAQ International system. A club symbol indicates that there is a free annual or interim report available. A heart symbol indicates a stock not officially listed in the UK. Many shares of overseas mining companies fall into this category. A spade symbol indicates an unregulated collective investment scheme.

These are some of the main symbols used but for a comprehensive list refer to the 'Guide to London Share Service' in the 'Companies and Markets' section of the *Financial Times*.

■ *Market price (Price):* the second column shows the average (or mid-price) of the best buying and selling prices in pence quoted by market makers (the financial institutions that actually buy and sell shares) at the 4.30pm close of the market on the previous trading day. If trading in a share has been suspended, perhaps because the company in question is involved in a takeover, the figure shown is the price at suspension and this is indicated by a hash symbol (#). The letters 'xd' following a price mean ex-dividend and indicate that a dividend has been announced recently but buyers of the shares will not be entitled to receive it.

■ *Price change (+ or –):* the third column gives the change in the closing price compared with the end of the previous trading day.

■ *Previous price movements (52 week high/low):* columns four and five show the highest and lowest prices recorded for the stock over the past year.

■ *Trading volume (Volume '000s):* this shows the trading volume at the end of each day and is a good indication of a share's liquidity. Both buying and selling figures are counted, so divide by 2 to get the number of shares which changed hands.

■ *Gross dividend yield (Yld Gr's):* column seven shows the percentage return on the share before income tax is deducted at the rate of 20 per cent. It is calculated by dividing the gross dividend by the current share price.

■ *Price/earnings ratio (P/E):* the final column is the market price of the share divided by the company's earnings (profits) per share in its latest 12-month trading period. In effect this is a measure of investor confidence since it compares the price of a stock with the amount the company is earning in profits. Generally the higher

Table 17.1 Example share price

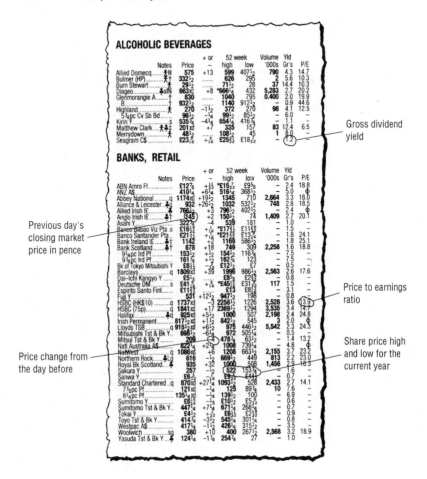

Gross dividend yield

Previous day's closing market price in pence

Price to earnings ratio

Share price high and low for the current year

Price change from the day before

Source: Financial Times, 10 March 1998

the figure the higher the confidence but you should only measure against companies in the same sector.

Yields and p/e ratios move in opposite directions. If the share price rises, since the gross dividend remains the same, the dividend yield falls. Also, if the share price rises, since the earnings per share are constant, the p/e ratio increases. Expect a big change in these figures when important company announcements are made on earnings and dividends.

Weekly summary

Table 17.2 Éxample Monday share prices

ALCOHOLIC BEVERAGES

	Notes	Price	W'k% ch'nge	Div net	Div cov.	Mkt cap£m	Last xd	City line
Allied Domecq	♣N	562	–4.0	Q24.44	1.6	5,856	24.11	1550
Bulmer (HP)	♙†	$332\frac{1}{2}$	–1.9	14.82	2.2	175.6	12.1	2005
Burn Stewart	♙	$29\frac{1}{2}$	5.4	3.4	0.8	17.5	27.10	1518
Diageo	♣stN	655xc	5.4	Q18.0	1.8	23,324	29.9	2791
Glenmorangie A	†	830	–.9	13.42	3.1	112.9	22.12	3257
B	†	$932\frac{1}{2}$	–.5	6.71	3.1	37.3	22.12	3258
Highland	♙	$271\frac{1}{2}$	–.4	8.9	2.4	362.5	1.12	2890
$5\frac{3}{4}$pc Cv Sb Bd		$96\frac{3}{4}$	0.5	Q$5\frac{3}{4}$%	–	47.4	5.1	2823
Kirin Y	s	540	1.6	Q24%	–	5,682	25.6	1119
Matthew Clark	♙♣‡	194xd	......	20.0	1.5	171.7	29.12	2153
Merrydown	♙	$48\frac{1}{2}$	–2.0	3.1	–	5.29	21.7	3352
Seagram C$		£23	–.6	Q66c	–	8,209	27.11	–

BANKS, RETAIL

	Notes	Price	W'k% ch'nge	Div net	Div cov.	Mkt cap£m	Last xd	City line
ABN Amro Fl		£$12\frac{17}{32}$	–2.6	Q84%	2.2	17,436	9.5	1010
ANZ A$		404	–3.3	Q48c	Φ	6,024	12'96	–
Abbey National	q	1175	–5.8	30.7	2.1	16,602	11.8	5411
Alliance & Leicester	♣q	$905\frac{1}{2}$	–6.1	20.8	2.4	5,270	8.9	5600
Allied Irish I£	♣	$763\frac{1}{2}$	–3.0	Q$88\frac{1}{2}$%	Φ	6,458	2'97	1354
Anglo Irish I£	♣†	143	–4.0	Q20%	2.4	492.1	1.12	–
Asahi Y		$326\frac{3}{4}$	1.7	Q14%	–	7,592	25.9	–
Banco Bilbao Viz Pta	s	£$16\frac{17}{32}$	–.1	Q10.4%	–	11,155	10.10	–
Banco Santander Pta		£$21\frac{15}{32}$	–.1	Q39.1%	2.3	10,287	31.10	–
Bank Ireland I£	♣†	1140	–2.1	Q23.4%	2.8	5,570	24.11	1360
Bank Scotland	♣†	660	–4.7	8.77	4.1	8,065	13.10	1742
$9\frac{1}{4}$pc Ird Pf		153	0.2	$9\frac{1}{4}$%	–	459.0	3.11	1462
$9\frac{3}{4}$pc Ird Pf		$161\frac{1}{4}$	......	$9\frac{3}{4}$%	–	161.2	3.11	1685
Bk of Tokyo Mitsubishi Y.		£$8\frac{7}{16}$	–1.9	Q17%	1.4	38,810	25.9	–
Barclays	q	1770xd	–1.9	37.0	2.8	27,045	23.2	1754
Dai-Ichi Kangyo Y		£$5\frac{1}{8}$	0.1	Q17%	1.2	16,028	25.9	–
Deutsche DM	s	£41	–.4	Q36%	–	20,510	5'96	1057
Espirito Santo Finl		£$11\frac{29}{32}$	0.6	Q60c	–	471.5	16.6	5187
Fuji Y		$518\frac{1}{2}$	10.0	Q17%	1.3	15,021	17.11	–
HSBC (HK$10)	q	1770	1.1	50.0	2.5	31,895	18.8	2796
HSBC (75p)	q	1854	–.6	50.0	2.5	16,204	18.8	2776
Halifax	♣q	937	–1.0	17.5	2.1	23,565	–	5601
Irish Permanent		816xd	–2.6	Q$77\frac{1}{2}$%	Φ	701.7	23.2	4709
Lloyds TSB	q	909xd	–.5	17.2	2.2	49,058	23.2	4320
Mitsubishi Tst & Bk Y		$704\frac{3}{4}$	–1.3	Q16%	–	9,177	25.9	5389
Mitsui Tst & Bk Y		213	4.7	Q12%	5.5	2,553	25.9	–
Natl Australia A$		820	–2.4	Q94c	Φ	12,266	12'96	–
NatWest	q	1080xd	–1.6	32.2	1.4	18,705	2.3	3463
Northern Rock	♣Lq	$616\frac{1}{2}$	–6.5	10.5	2.2	2,737	–	5604
Royal Bk Scotland	♣	903	–3.9	21.4	2.4	7,838	8.12	3874
Sakura Y		$257\frac{1}{2}$	1.4	Q17%	–	8,818	25.9	–
Sanwa Y		£$6\frac{5}{32}$	0.7	Q17%	–	17,849	25.9	–
Standard Chartered	q	856	–2.4	18.5	3.3	8,500	18.8	4094
$7\frac{3}{8}$pc Pf		125	1.4	7.37	–	125.0	8.9	1719
$8\frac{1}{4}$pc Pf		$139\frac{1}{2}$	1.3	7.42	–	139.5	8.9	1428
Sumitomo Y		£$7\frac{1}{16}$	–2.3	Q17%	–	22,210	25.9	–
Sumitomo Tst & Bk Y		440	1.7	Q14%	–	5,475	25.9	–
Tokai Y		£$4\frac{15}{32}$	4.2	Q17%	–	9,093	25.9	–
Toyo Tst & Bk Y		$418\frac{1}{4}$	–3.2	Q14%	–	3,290	25.9	–
Westpac A$		$418\frac{3}{4}$	–.6	Q36c	–	7,453	3.6	–
Woolwich	sq	370	–3.0	9.5	1.2	5,923	1.9	5603
Yasuda Tst & Bk Y	♣	126	1.9	Q5%	–	1,389	26.3	–

Dividend net of income tax

Ratio of profits to gross dividends

Last date the share went ex-dividend

Source: Financial Times, 10 March 1998

On Mondays the FT provides information on the following:

- *Price change:* the weekly percentage change.
- *Net dividend:* the after-tax dividends paid in the company's last full financial year. A double dagger symbol indicates that the interim dividend has been cut in the current financial year, while a single dagger indicates an increase.
- *Dividend cover:* this shows the number of times the dividend could have been paid out of net profits. The figure is a ratio of profits to

dividends, calculated by dividing the earnings per share by the gross dividend per share. Analysts regard this as a key figure in assessing the security of the company and its ability to maintain the level of future dividend payments.

- *Market capitalisation:* this is an indication of the stockmarket value of the company in millions of pounds sterling. It is calculated by multiplying the number of shares in issue by their market price. In order to calculate the number of shares in issue from the figures listed you can divide the market capitalisation figure by the market price. However, if there are other classes of share capital in issue, their value would also need to be added in order to calculate the company's total market capitalisation.

- *Ex-dividend date:* the last date the share went ex-dividend.

- *Cityline:* for up-to-the-second share prices call FT Cityline on 0336 43 or 0891 43 followed by the four digit code in this column.

■ Unit trust and open-ended investment company (OEIC) prices

Unit trust and OEIC prices appear under the 'Authorised investment funds' section. These are funds authorised by the Financial Services Authority and can be marketed direct to the public. Unauthorised funds are not sold to the public but are used as internal funds by the financial institutions.

Unit trust and OEIC management groups are obliged to provide certain information to unit holders and the accepted practice is to publish unit prices, together with other important information in the *Financial Times* and other national newspapers.

How to read the figures

- *Name of the investment group, its pricing system and trust names:* this is shown as, for example, 'AIB Unit Trust Managers Limited (1000)F' followed by the company's address and telephone number for dealing or enquiries. (Use this number if you want to get a free copy of the management group's most recent report and scheme particulars.) Under each company heading are listed its authorised unit trusts.

The figure in brackets in the heading is the basis of the company's pricing system. The figure refers to the time at which the price was

Table 17.3 Example unit trust and OEIC prices

Management company/investment group

Pricing system

Trust name

Initial charge

Bid/offer spread

Price change

Gross yield

Unit Trusts and OEICs
(Open-ended investment companies).

	Init Chrge	Notes	Selling Price	Buying Price	+ or −	Yield Gr's
ABN AMRO Fund Managers Ltd (0800)F					0171–678	4500
82 Bishopsgate, London EC2N 4BN						
UK Growth	5		327.94	348.87	+3.46	0.97
World	6		101.18	107.64	+0.94	0.54
Balanced	5	C	245.28	260.94	+2.53	3.08
Equity Income	5	C	161.77	171.19	+0.33	4.45
High Income	5	C	58.43	62.16	+0.09	7.25

AIB Govett Unit Trusts Limited (1000)F
Shackleton House, 4 Battlebridge Lane, London SE1 2HR
0171–378 7979   Dealing: 0171–407 7888

	Init Chrge		Selling Price	Buying Price	+ or −	Yield Gr's
Protected Funds						
UK Safeguard	5½		142.220	151.560	+0.38	0.00
Do (fixed minimum NAV to Mar 20)			134.56	134.56	.....	–
UK Equity Safeguard Acc	5½		112.45	120.25	+0.03	2.47
Do (Fixed Minimum NAV to Mar 20)	5½		105.85	105.85	.....	–
Cash ♦	½		£9.5543	9.6021	.....	5.75
UK Growth Funds						
UK Equity General	5		412.50	438.80	+7.00	1.65
UK Small Co's	5½		87.87	93.97	−0.05	0.49
FTSE 250 Index	5½		108.56	116.10	+0.44	2.11
Geared UK Index	5½		£27.4798	29.0094	+0.57	5.75
Income Funds						
Corporate Bond	3¼		83.84	86.91	+0.22	0.00
Monthly Income	5½		44.24xd	47.29	+0.17	8.72
International Funds						
American General	5		323.90	343.70	+6.30	0.00
American Strategy	5½		244.91	261.93	+3.13	0.00
European General	5		377.40	399.80	+6.90	0.68
European Strategy	5½		158.48	169.49	+2.43	0.00
Japan General	5		103.70	109.90	−1.60	0.00
Asia Pacific	5		65.07	69.38	+0.22	1.08
Pacific Strategy	5½		105.81xd	113.16	+0.59	0.00
Greater China	5½		199.34	213.18	−0.06	0.00
Latin America	5½		105.33xd	112.65	+1.46	0.00
Intl Growth	5½		176.97	189.26	+2.10	0.00
Balanced Exempt	3		174.40	181.40	.....	2.29
Global Strategy	5½		48.39	51.74	−0.69	0.00
Index & Bear Funds (Dealing: 0171–865 0033)						
UK Bear ♦	5½		£4.2939	4.5328	−0.02	5.25
US Bear ♦	5½		£4.1124	4.3429	−0.03	3.50
UK Index ♦	5½		£19.1451	20.2106	+0.09	5.25
JG US Index ♦	5¼		£25.4064	26.7692	+0.18	4.00

AXA Equity & Law Unit Tst Mngrs (1200)F
Equity & Law Hse, Corpn St, Coventry   01203 553231

	Init Chrge		Selling Price	Buying Price	+ or −	Yield Gr's
General Inc	5		759.40	807.80	+0.10	2.29
General Acc	5		937.10	996.90	+5.70	2.29
UK Growth Acc	6		644.80	685.90	+3.30	2.26
UK Growth Inc	6		407.50	433.50	+2.00	2.26
Higher Inc Acc	6	C	1194.00	1270.00	+9.00	4.30
Higher Inc Inc	6	C	613.10	652.20	+4.50	4.30
Gilts/Fxd Int Acc	5½		237.60	250.80	+1.00	5.63
Gilts/Fxd Int Inc	5½		96.53	101.90	+0.50	5.63
Nth America	6		466.30	496.00	+9.80	0.00
Europe	6		522.30	555.60	+5.90	0.51
Brit Excell	6		128.20	136.30	+0.90	2.12
Brit Fndmtls Acc	6		159.10	169.20	+0.90	4.17
Brit Fndmtls Inc	6		100.60	107.00	−1.00	4.17
Global Opps	6		126.10	134.10	+2.10	0.23
Balanced Acc	6		79.36	84.42	+0.46	2.18
Balanced Inc	6		72.61	77.24	+0.43	2.18
Japan Tst Acc	6		34.69	36.90	−0.47	0.00
Pacific Basin Tst Acc	6		294.10	312.80	+1.60	2.14

Source: Financial Times, 10 March 1998

measured (using a 24-hour clock) and the basis of calculation. 'F' refers to forward pricing, which means orders are taken from investors and the price of units is determined by the next valuation. All larger groups have a valuation point each day, often at noon. So, if an investor phones through their order at 10am, the price will be struck at noon that same day. An investor who phones at 1pm will have to wait for a price until the following midday valuation.

Some groups still deal on an historic price basis, indicated by 'H'. This means they buy and sell using the price agreed at the last valuation point.

- *Initial charge (Init chrge):* column two indicates the percentage charge deducted from your investment to cover certain costs – for example administration and the sales commission paid to advisers, if applicable. If the charge is 5 per cent then £95 out of every £100 will actually be available to be invested in your chosen fund.

- *Notes:* the symbols and letters in column three indicate particular features of a unit trust. For example, 'E' indicates there is an exit charge when you sell your units, 'C' indicates that the manager's annual charge is deducted from capital, not income. A full list of notes, some of which may appear against figures in other columns, can be found at the end of the FT Managed Funds section.

- *Selling price:* given in column four, this is also called the bid price. This is the price at which investors sell units back to the manager.

- *Buying price:* given in column five, this is also called the offer price. This is the price at which investors buy units.

- *Price change (+ or –):* the sixth column compares the mid-point between the bid and offer prices with the previous day's quotation.

- *Gross yield (Yield Gr's):* the last column shows the gross income paid by the unit trust as a percentage of the offer price. The quoted yield reflects income earned by the fund during the previous 12 months and therefore relates only to past performance.

■ Investment trust prices

As quoted companies, investment trusts are quoted in the London Share Service section. Most of the information is the same as for other companies, with the exception of the last two columns.

- *Net asset value (NAV):* this is the approximate value of the underlying assets owned by the company. As with the share price, the NAV is shown in pence.

Table 17.4 Investment trust prices

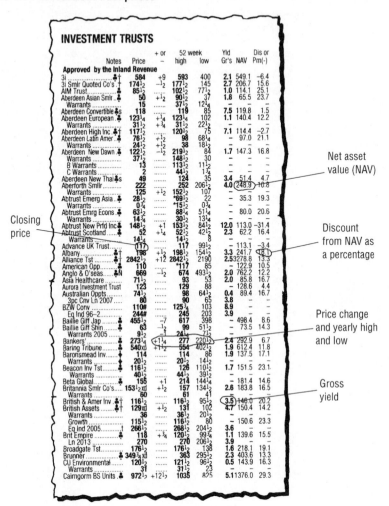

INVESTMENT TRUSTS

	Notes	Price	+ or –	52 week high	52 week low	Yld Gr's	NAV	Dis or Pm(-)
Approved by the Inland Revenue								
3i	♣†	**584**	+9	**593**	400	**2.1**	549.1	–6.4
3i Smlr Quoted Co's	†	**174½**	–½	**177½**	145	**2.7**	206.7	15.6
AIM Trust	♣	**85½**	......	**102½**	77½	**1.0**	114.1	25.1
Aberdeen Asian Smlr	♣	**50**	+½	**90½**	37	**1.8**	65.5	23.7
Warrants		**15**	......	**37½**	12¼	–	–	–
Aberdeen Convertible	♣s	**118**	......	**119**	85	**7.5**	119.8	1.5
Aberdeen European	♣	**123¼**	+¼	**123¼**	102	**1.1**	140.4	12.2
Warrants		**31½**	+¾	**31½**	22½	–	–	–
Aberdeen High Inc	♣†	**117½**	......	**120½**	75	**7.1**	114.4	–2.7
Aberdeen Latin Amer	♣	**76½**	+½	**98**	68¼	–	97.0	21.1
Warrants		**24½**	+½	**38**	18½	–	–	–
Aberdeen New Dawn	♣	**122½**	–½	**219½**	84	**1.7**	147.3	16.8
Warrants		**37½**	......	**148½**	30	–	–	–
B Warrants		**13**	......	**113½**	11½	–	–	–
C Warrants		**2**	......	**44½**	1¾	–	–	–
Aberdeen New Thai	♣s	**49**	......	**124**	35	**3.4**	51.4	4.7
Aberforth Smllr		**222**	......	**252**	206½	**4.0**	248.9	10.8
Warrants		**125**	+½	**152½**	107	–	–	–
Abtrust Emerg Asia	♣	**28½**	......	***69½**	22	–	35.3	19.3
Warrants		**0¾**	......	***15½**	0¾	–	–	–
Abtrust Emrg Econs	♣	**63½**	......	**88¼**	51¼	–	80.0	20.6
Warrants		**14¾**	......	**30½**	13¼	–	–	–
Abtrust New Prfd Inc	♣	**148½**	+1	**153½**	84½	**12.0**	113.0	–31.4
Abtrust Scotland	♣	**52**	+¼	**52½**	42½	**2.3**	62.2	16.4
Warrants		**14¼**	......	**14½**	8	–	–	–
Advance UK Trust		**117**	......	**117**	99½	–	113.1	–3.4
Albany	♣†	**198**	+½	**198½**	154½	**3.3**	241.7	18.1
Alliance Tst	♣†	**2842½**	+12	**2842½**	2190	**2.5**	3278.8	13.3
American Opp	♣	**110**	......	***117**	85	–	122.9	10.5
Anglo & O'seas	♣N	**669**	–½	**674**	493½	**2.0**	762.2	12.2
Asia Healthcare		**71½**	......	**93**	53	**2.0**	85.8	16.7
Aurora Investment Trust		**123**	......	**129**	88	–	128.6	4.4
Australian Oppts		**74½**	......	**98**	64½	**0.4**	89.4	16.7
3pc Cnv Ln 2007		**80**	......	**90**	65	**3.8**	–	–
BZW Conv		**110#**	......	**125¾**	103	**8.9**	–	–
Eq Ind 96–2		**244#**	......	**245**	203	**3.9**	–	–
Baillie Giff Jap	♣	**455½**	–7	**617**	398	–	498.4	8.6
Baillie Giff Shin	♣	**63**	–½	**99**	51½	–	73.5	14.3
Warrants 2005		**9½**	–1	**24¼**	7½	–	–	–
Bankers'	♣	**273¼**	+1¼	**277**	220½	**2.4**	292.9	6.7
Baring Tribune	♣	**540**xd	+1½	**554**	402½	**1.9**	612.4	11.8
Baronsmead Inv	♦	**114**	......	**114**	86	**1.9**	137.5	17.1
Warrants	♦	**20½**	......	**20½**	14½	–	–	–
Beacon Inv Tst	♣	**116½**	......	**126**	110½	**1.7**	151.5	23.1
Warrants		**40½**	......	**44½**	39½	–	–	–
Beta Global	♣	**155**	+1	**214**	144¼	–	181.4	14.6
Britannia Smlr Co's		**153½**xd	+½	**157**	134½	**2.6**	183.8	16.5
Warrants		**60**	......	**61**	41	–	–	–
British & Amer Inv	♣†	**116½**	......	**116½**	95½	**3.5**	146.0	20.2
British Assets	♣†	**129**xd	+½	**131**	102	**4.7**	150.4	14.2
Warrants		**36**	......	**36½**	20½	–	–	–
Growth		**115½**	......	**116½**	80	–	150.6	23.3
Eq Ind 2005	†	**266½**	......	**268½**	204½	**3.6**	–	–
Brit Empire	♣	**118**	+¾	**120½**	99¾	**1.1**	139.6	15.5
Ln 2013		**270**	......	**270**	206½	**3.9**	–	–
Broadgate Tst		**176½**	......	**176½**	138	**1.6**	218.1	19.1
Brunner	♣	**349¾**xd	......	**363**	295½	**2.3**	403.6	13.3
CU Environmental		**120½**	......	**121½**	96½	**0.5**	143.9	16.3
Warrants		**31**	......	**31½**	23	–	–	–
Cairngorm BS Units	♣	**972½**	+12½	**1035**	825	**5.1**	1376.0	29.3

Closing price

Net asset value (NAV)

Discount from NAV as a percentage

Price change and yearly high and low

Gross yield

Source: Financial Times, 10 March 1998

- *Discount or premium (Dis or PM(–):* the premium is shown as a minus sign. If the value of the underlying assets is higher than the share price, then the trust is said to be at a discount. In other words, assuming there is nothing untoward about the trust, the shares are likely to be good value because their underlying value is worth more than the price you pay. If the NAV is lower than the share price the shares are at a premium and generally should be avoided.

AITC Monthly Information Service

For a more detailed guide to investment trust performance, use the AITC's Monthly Information Service (see the Useful Publications Section on page 248). If you are new to the service you will find it helpful first to read the user's guide which explains how the MIS is organised and what the various figures represent.

The monthly service shows the performance of all the trusts over several time periods and includes a comparison of trust performance measured against various indices and other important benchmark figures such as unit trusts, building societies and the retail prices index.

Bear in mind that with the AITC it is the trust itself, not the management group, that is the member. The AITC covers most of the investment trust market by volume but there are several important omissions. In particular, four trusts run by M&G are not members, nor is the British Investment Trust, which is run by Edinburgh Fund Managers.

Sources

For shares, the *Financial Times* and *Investors Chronicle* are the best sources of information. The FT also covers collective funds but there are several additional sources of reference, for example the useful articles, surveys and statistics which appear in specialist publications such as *Money Management, Planned Savings* and *Moneywise* – all of which are available from newsagents. The Consumers Association publishes best buys for personal pensions, among other savings and investment plans, in its *Which?* magazine.

Details about the Private Investor Indices, including their construction and management and back histories are available free of charge from FTSE International's Internet site at http://www.ftse.com Details about WM's Private Client Indicators are available from WM, World Markets House, Crewe Toll, Edinburgh EH4 2PY. Tel: 0131 315 2000. Fax: 0131 315 2999.

Useful publications

Romesh Vaitilingam, *The Financial Times Guide to Using the Financial Pages*, published by the Financial Times and Pitman Publishing. For further details contact The Professional Marketing Department, Financial Times Pitman Publishing, 128 Long Acre, London WC2E 9AN.

BESt Investments *Personal Equity Plan Recommendations*, is available from BESt Investment, 20 Masons Yard, Duke Street, St James, London SW1Y 6BU. The *Spot the Dog* guide is available free by phoning 0990 112255.

Chase de Vere Pep Guide. Contact Chase de Vere Investments plc, 63 Lincoln's Inn Fields, London WC2A 3BR.

The London Stock Exchange, *How to Buy and Sell Shares*, contact The Stock Exchange, London EC2N 1HP.

For a free sample copy of the AITC Monthly Information Service write to the Association of Investment Trust Companies, Durrant House, 8-13 Chiswell Street, London EC1Y 4YY.

Summary

- In order to measure anything you need an appropriate benchmark with which to make comparisons.

- An absolute benchmark is useful and tells you the real growth achieved by your fund after taking into account the effects of inflation.

- A better benchmark, however, is to measure against an appropriate index or, in the case of collective funds, a peer group (for example UK equity income).

- A third benchmark is to measure against a similar portfolio to your own. There are two such services from the FTSE International/APCIMS, and from WM.

- Share prices, including investment trusts, and most collective funds are quoted daily in the *Financial Times*.

18

Shareholders' rights

- Your rights as a part owner of a company
- Dividends
- Rights issues
- Scrip issues
- Company literature
- The annual general meeting
- Voting rights
- Good corporate governance
- A change in management
- What if the company goes bust?

At a glance

This Chapter explains the significance of major events throughout the company's financial year, such as results and dividend announcements. We also examine important but ad hoc events such as a rights or scrip issue, a merger, takeover or acquisition.

Fortunately, even a seemingly hostile takeover bid has to conform to the equivalent of the Queensberry rules for corporations. Boxing gloves are mandatory, foul holds and blows are not permitted and the whole match must be over within a sensible period. If you know what to expect you can consider your options in principle long before it gets to voting time.

> Even a seemingly hostile takeover bid has to conform to the equivalent of the Queensberry rules. Boxing gloves are mandatory.

Of course if you have a discretionary manager he or she will be responsible for taking any necessary action. But if you want to check your investments yourself, and particularly if you are using an execution-only stockbroker, then you need to know your rights.

With modern technology and the Internet for communications, you would imagine that private investors are snowed under with information. Unfortunately you would be wrong. To speed up settlement of sales and purchases, increasingly, private investors are being asked to hold shares in a nominee account. This can have a devastating effect on the information you receive – either because the nominee does not offer the facility to distribute reports and accounts, among other items, or the company itself refuses to treat shareholders in nominees as real people. (See Chapter 14 for details of nominees.)

This Chapter will help you identify the information you need to monitor the progress of the companies in which you invest.

YOUR RIGHTS AS A PART OWNER OF A COMPANY

When you buy shares in a company you become a part owner of the business and under company law this confers, for example, the right to be told certain information about the company and to communicate your views to the board.

The most important shareholders' rights are explained in a useful guide from ProShare (details on page 277).

■ How you hold your shares

As a shareholder you can opt to hold your shares in one of three ways:

- *Nominee account:* this method enables fast and efficient settlement through CREST (see page 182). However, in a nominee account you lose certain automatic rights of ownership such as access to annual reports and accounts and voting rights. You may also lose any shareholder perks. Some nominees do make special provision to allow you to maintain these rights so, if you value them, it is worth shopping around.

- *Sponsored membership of CREST:* if you want to continue to get the advantages of speedy settlement and to continue to receive all information from the companies whose shares you own, you can choose sponsored membership of CREST.

- *Share certificates:* you are entitled to have your name added to the register of members of the company which will show how many shares you own. You are also entitled to a share certificate.

> **TIP** If you choose to retain your share certificate, you keep your automatic rights of ownership, but you may experience delays or possibly extra costs when you trade your shares.

DIVIDENDS

As a shareholder you have a right to a share of the company's earnings, known as dividends. These are generally paid twice a year. The first payment in a company's financial year is known as the 'interim' dividend and the second payment is known as the 'final' dividend. Along with the dividend payment you should receive a note setting out the number of shares you hold and the dividend rate payable per share.

If you hold preference shares you will usually receive a fixed dividend which will take priority over payments to ordinary shareholders if a company has any difficulty paying out the full range of dividends.

RIGHTS ISSUES

From time to time a company may wish to raise more money. As a shareholder you may be offered the chance to participate in a rights issue. This is where the company asks existing shareholders if they want to buy new shares in the company, usually at a discount to the current market price. However, the issue of new shares may cause the price of your existing shares to fall because an increase in the total number in circulation dilutes the per share value .

SCRIP ISSUES

Quoted companies in the UK do not like the price per share to get too large as this can affect liquidity and hence slow dealing activity. To dilute the share price a company will sometimes offer you 'free' shares. This increases the number of shares in circulation but the price per share falls in proportion to the total amount in issue so the value of your holding remains the same.

■ Scrip dividend

Occasionally a company may ask you to take your dividends in the form of shares. This is an easy way of saving and adding to your portfolio but it can complicate the administration in terms of the number of shares you own, the price at which you purchased them and the calculation of the capital gains tax liability when you eventually come to sell.

COMPANY LITERATURE

All shareholders who have their name on the register of shareholders are entitled to certain documents that the company issues from time to time. These include the annual report and accounts (see Chapter 16) and other notices about important events, such as major acquisitions, disposals, or very significant changes in the structure of the company – a demerger, for example.

It is important to remember that if you hold shares through a nominee account, it will not be your name but the nominee's name which appears on the register of the company shareholders. If you want company literature check whether your nominee will send it to you.

THE ANNUAL GENERAL MEETING

Every company must hold an annual general meeting (AGM) once a year. Shareholders whose names are on the register have the right to attend and speak at the meeting and they must be given at least 21 days' notice of the time and the venue. Clearly, the same point applies here as for the company literature. If you want to attend AGMs, check this point with your nominee.

VOTING RIGHTS

Companies must ask shareholders to vote on important matters that affect its future. You can either vote in person at the AGM or use a proxy card sent by the company, which allows you to vote by post.

By law the company must ask the shareholders their view on the following:

> Companies must ask shareholders to vote on important matters that affect its future.

- A decision which would dilute shareholdings such as the issue of more company shares – for example a rights issue or the establishment of an employee share option scheme.

- The appointment or dismissal of the auditors. Auditors are external accountants used by the company to check their financial statements. Their role is important because they protect the shareholders from the actions of irresponsible directors.

- The appointment and dismissal of directors. Shareholders must approve any such change because, as owners of the company, they have the right to elect the directors to run the business on their behalf and hold them accountable for its progress.

■ Proposed resolutions at the AGM

Under company law, shareholders can only put forward motions if they can muster 5 per cent of the company's total voting rights or 100 shareholders with at least £100 worth of shares. The company must submit resolutions no later than six weeks before the meeting and send a copy to all shareholders.

■ Extraordinary general meetings

These are company meetings other than the AGM. Directors often have to call an extraordinary general meeting to transact special business which cannot wait for the next AGM.

Shareholders concerned about a company's progress also have the right to force the board to call a meeting. To do this they must have the support of 10 per cent of the company's overall share capital, so this would involve rallying a large number of individual shareholders and almost certainly some of the big financial institutions such as life assurance and pension funds.

GOOD CORPORATE GOVERNANCE

Several important committees – Cadbury, Greenbury and Hampel – have established what is accepted as good corporate governance and in due course the London Stock Exchange is expected to take charge of a new 'supercode' on corporate governance which will set out to directors and shareholders how companies should be run.

This topic covers several important issues, including the following points which were provided in the Gartmore guide (see Sources):

- The chairman and chief executive should be separate roles in most cases.

- Non-executive directors should bring outside experience and independent judgement to the company's strategy.

- There should be appropriate remuneration and incentive schemes, with the chairman of the remuneration committee answerable to shareholders at the AGM.

- Service contracts for members of the board should be of two years or less.

- Directors normally stand for re-election after three years, though in some companies executives have been insulated from this requirement, which prevents shareholders from passing judgement on a director,

- Raising new capital should be supported where it is in the long-term interests of the shareholders. Existing shareholders should be given a right of first refusal to subscribe for such new shares.

- A proposed takeover should only go ahead if it is in the interests of shareholder.

A CHANGE IN MANAGEMENT

One of the most worrying times for private investors (apart from when their shares are plummeting) is when a company in which they invest is the target of a takeover or a partner to a merger.

This is the type of action that makes newspaper headlines and raises the profile of institutional investors, who carry a lot of clout in these battles. (Remember, pension funds and life assurance funds between them own about two-thirds of the UK stockmarket.)

But these events can be far from thrilling for the individual investor who may feel rather powerless.

It is possible for private investors to do well out of a takeover because the acquiring company is usually so keen to build up a controlling stake that it will pay over the odds for your shares.

If you own shares in the target company, you have two basic choices. You can grab the money and run (but only after checking your capital gains position first – see page 263). Alternatively, you can hang on and see if a white knight (a supporter of the takeover target company) or the aggressor will turn what might have been hitherto a rather stagnant investment into a growth stock.

If you hold shares in the acquiring company, the takeover could be a good boost to the business but if the management team are forced to pay dearly for their acquisition it will absorb any spare cash sloshing around in the company's coffers which otherwise might have been distributed to shareholders as dividends. Even if the acquired company is a good fit, it could take some time for the new structure to work well and to put profits and dividends back on track.

Clearly there are no easy answers in these situations. As always, information is your best friend and as a shareholder you are entitled to receive details of the proposed deal. In addition you should trawl the financial press for useful facts and opinions.

WHAT IF THE COMPANY GOES BUST?

This is the worst possible scenario because ordinary shareholders are just about last in the queue of unsecured creditors so unless it is an unusual situation – for example the winding up of an investment trust – there is rarely anything left after the taxman and Government have taken their share and the secured creditors (mortgage lenders, for example, who have a claim on the property) and banks have had theirs.

Remember, in the pecking order, bond holders come before shareholders, although stockbrokers suggest this is no great deal and that in the majority of cases bond holders will not get anything either.

In practice very few quoted companies go bust in the UK. If you are unfortunate enough to be left holding dud shares, there is a procedure for claiming the losses under the Capital Gains Tax rules (see page 264).

Sources

ProShare *Shareholders' rights* information sheet (see page 277 for details); The information on corporate governance was reproduced from a guide published by Gartmore. *Guide to corporate governance.*

Summary

- As a shareholder you are a part owner of the company and under company law this confers certain rights.

- Your rights are affected by the way you hold your shares – if you use a nominee account you may not be sent the annual report and accounts or any perks, for example.

- Dividends usually are paid twice a year. The first payment is the interim dividend and the second is the final dividend.

- Companies can raise extra money through a rights issue. Usually, as an existing shareholder you would be offered the shares at a discount to market price.

- A scrip issue simply increases the number of shares in circulation and reduces the per share price proportionately. This is to aid liquidity by keeping the share price within acceptable limits.

- The annual general meeting is an informative event and as a shareholder you have the right to attend or vote by proxy on any important issues.

19

Tax and your investments

- Keep it legal
- Your tax allowances and exemptions
- Income tax
- Capital gains tax
- Reduce your inheritance tax bill

At a glance

Smart tax saving begins at home. Here you can redistribute income and assets to make best use of each family member's annual personal allowances and exemptions. You might also consider making appropriate inheritance tax arrangements to help retain your wealth within the family when you die.

KEEP IT LEGAL

The hallmark of good tax planning is that it will pass the Inland Revenue's scrutiny with flying colours, even where complicated family trust arrangements and considerable wealth are involved.

> The hallmark of good tax planning is that it will pass the Inland Revenue's scrutiny with flying colours.

Before you read this Chapter, do keep in mind the way the Inland Revenue distinguishes between our various attempts to minimise our tax liability.

In particular you need to understand the terms 'evasion', 'avoidance' and 'mitigation'. Although these tend to be used indiscriminately, their meanings are very different.

TIP If you deliberately omit something from your tax return, or give a false description, that's evasion. You have not just been dishonest – you have acted criminally and could be fined or imprisoned.

Avoidance and mitigation are on the right side of the law but again, there is an important distinction. If your tax saving has been encouraged by the Government – for example you put your investments in a personal equity plan (Pep) or, in due course, in an individual savings account (ISA), that is mitigation. This is definitely on the right side of the Revenue.

Among other services, your accountants will help you to mitigate and avoid tax.

YOUR TAX ALLOWANCES AND EXEMPTIONS

Successful tax planning requires common sense and expert advice, in equal measures. So, before you change anything, check that the particular use of an allowance or exemption has a genuine benefit.

Unless you are very experienced, do consult a qualified accountant. All transactions must comply with current tax law and be carefully documented.

TIP In some cases the cost of setting up and maintaining the arrangement can outweigh any tax savings.

Table 19.1 Your main tax allowances and exemptions for 1998/99

Income tax allowances	£
Personal allowance under 65	4195
Married couples under 65*	1900
Personal allowance 65–74**	5410
Married couples 65–74*	3305
Income tax rates	
Lower rate 20%	1–4300
Basic rate 23%***	4301–27 100
Higher rate 40%	over 27 100
Annual CGT exemption	
Inheritance tax 40%	over 223 000

* The age allowance is reduced by £1 for every £2 you earn until you reach the basic personal allowance rate.
** Relief restricted to 15%.
*** 20% on interest and dividends.

There are three main personal allowances and exemptions. A full set of figures is provided in Table 19.1, but briefly, for the 1998/99 tax year, each member of your family has:

- the income tax annual personal allowance of £4195 (more if you qualify for the married couple's and/or the age allowances)

- the *capital gains tax* annual exemption of £6800

- the *inheritance tax* annual exemption for gifts of £3 000. The main exemption on death is £223 000.

INCOME TAX

Most families are not tax-efficient because their combined wealth – both in terms of earned income and assets – tends to be concentrated in the hands of the main breadwinner. He or she, therefore, is also responsible for paying most of the tax, often at the top rate.

One of the best ways to save on income tax is to share income between spouses, whether the source is earnings, investments or a combination of the two.

This makes use of the non-working or lower-earning spouse's allowance and, where the income exceeds the personal allowance, the lower and basic tax rates. The two most common redistribution techniques are to give income-generating assets to your spouse and, where you run your own business, to pay your spouse a salary.

It is also possible to give income-producing assets to children who can make use of their own allowances and, where necessary, their lower and basic rates of taxation.

However, this requires great care. If you give this type of asset to your children and the income exceeds £100 per annum, you, as the parents, will be taxed on the entire amount. For this reason usually it is necessary to hold the assets in a 'bare trust' under which the parents are the registered owners but hold them as nominees for the children and the income is accumulated until they are 18. This would not be necessary in the case of gifts from other family members – grandparents, for example.

Finally on this point, do remember that if you give a gift of assets this has to be unconditional otherwise the Revenue will see through the arrangement and continue to tax you on the asset's value. Think carefully before you give your favourite shares to your spouse or children!

CAPITAL GAINS TAX

The annual exemption of £6800 for the1998/99 tax year is the amount of capital gains you can make before you pay capital gains tax (CGT) at your top rate of income tax. As gifts between spouses are exempt from CGT the tax-efficient couple should consider sharing assets in order to make use of both exemptions.

■ CGT and your shares

In practice most investors manage to avoid CGT without making any special arrangements, simply because their liability regularly falls within the annual CGT exemption. Even if you have a very large portfolio and you are an active investor, you may still be able to avoid or reduce your liability but this will require some careful planning.

CGT is payable when you sell an asset and make a 'chargeable gain', that is, where the value of an asset you sell has increased since you acquired it, after taking into account the effect of inflation (see below – this figure is frozen). Remember, CGT is not charged on the asset itself but on its gain in value.

Investors who have received free *windfall* shares from demutualised building societies and life assurance companies should bear in mind that the proceeds of any sales will be classed as a pure capital gain unless they are held in a tax exempt investment such as a Pep or the new individual savings plan when they are launched in April 1999.

■ CGT 'tapering' relief

In the March 1998 budget, the chancellor revamped capital gains tax to reward long-term investors and small business owners. He also scrapped 'bed and breakfasting' of shares so you can no longer sell and repurchase the following day to crystallise a gain or loss.

Under the new rules, gains on assets held for three years or more will be taxed at a lower rate according to how long you have held them. The rate falls from the top level of 40 per cent on gains realised before year three to the lowest rate of 24 per cent on assets held for 10 years.

Small business owners who sell up will also be taxed at a lower rate, again depending on how long they owned the business, with a minimum rate of 10 per cent. However, retirement relief, which allowed small business owners over age 50 to reduce tax on up to £1 million of gains, will be phased out.

Finally, although the budget increased the CGT annual exemption (see page 263) the Treasury will freeze the 'indexation allowance', which reduced the taxable gain on an asset by taking account of inflation between the date of purchase and the date of sale.

■ Shares in companies which go bust

Once a company officially ceases to exist the tax rules automatically treat this as the date you disposed of your shares (for nothing).

However, fortunately you don't have to wait for this official extinction date to make a claim on dud shares and to use the loss to offset gains during that tax year. Instead, the purchase cost (or the 31 March 1982 value if appropriate) of shares declared by the Inland Revenue to be of 'negligible value' is regarded as an allowable capital loss. This loss is treated as taking place on the date you enter in your claim (within certain limits).

It is also possible to check if a company in which you hold shares is in receivership or liquidation. It may help you decide what to do if your shares clearly are worthless but have not yet been declared of 'negligible value' by the Inland Revenue.

A comprehensive list is published in Extel's *CGT Capital Losses* (see the Sources section at the end of the Chapter; your accountant or investment adviser should have a copy). Most of these shares eventually will end up on the 'negligible value' list but if the Inland Revenue appears to be taking its time in listing your dud shares, do seek advice. If you put in a claim on your tax return as soon as you believe the company faces ruin, the timing of your claim may not be appropriate from a tax planning point of view. First check your chargeable gains and other allowable losses to make sure you can fully utilise the loss.

Finally, bear in mind that not all of the shares listed are duds. Some belong to companies such as *investment trusts*, which are being reorganised or voluntarily wound up.

REDUCE YOUR INHERITANCE TAX BILL

Inheritance tax (IHT) is a tax on your wealth at death and the exemption (£223,000 in 1998/99) is deducted from your estate before it can be passed on to your heirs. There is no IHT liability on the assets you leave to your spouse, but once he or she dies, then the value of the estate in excess of the exemption is taxable.

There are several ways to mitigate your inheritance tax bill. Each year you can give away up to £3 000 free of CGT. If you didn't use last year's exemption you can add it to this year's giving a total gift of £12 000 per couple.

It is possible to give away any amount in excess of this but at present, if you die within seven years, you pay tax on a sliding scale based on when you made the gift and when you die. This arrangement, known as a 'potentially exempt transfer' (PET), may be abolished in a future budget along with other IHT-avoidance measures.

One option worth considering, if you anticipate a large IHT liability, is to take out a life assurance policy which will cover the costs when you die. This should be written in trust for the successors (the children, for example) to make sure the policy does not form part of your taxable estate on death.

Sources

Readers interested in doing their own CGT calculations will find more detailed information in a recently updated Inland Revenue booklet, CGT 14 *Capital Gains Tax: an introduction* available from tax offices. DIY enthusiasts may like to consult Extel's *CGT Capital Losses*. For information about any of Extel's publications, or to receive a catalogue, contact Extel, Business Information Products Sales Department, Financial Times Information, Fitzroy House, 13-17 Epworth Street, London EC2A 4DL. Tel: 0171 825 8000. Fax: 0171 608 2032.

Summary

- Make sure your tax arrangements are not so complicated that they eliminate any tax savings in administration costs.

- Where possible, married couples should share assets to make use of both partners' personal income tax allowance and capital gains tax exemption. This is particularly tax efficient if one partner is a non-taxpayer or pays tax at the lower or basic rate.

- A capital loss can be offset against any capital gains in excess of the exemption.

20

Getting help

- Investment clubs
- Financial advice
- Your guide to complaints
- Recommended reading

At a glance

In this Chapter we cover a variety of information which private investors will find useful. This includes:

■ *Investment clubs:* these are an excellent way to build up experience and share ideas with other private investors.

■ *Your guide to financial advisers and stockbrokers:* if you want to delegate the task of running your portfolio, clearly your choice of adviser is critical. Use our guide in conjunction with Chapter 3.

■ *How to complain:* if you are lucky you may never need this section but keep it handy, just in case.

■ *The good book guide:* this is not a comprehensive reading list but is unashamedly selective and represents the author's choice of the most helpful books and journals available.

INVESTMENT CLUBS

Investment clubs are beginning to take off in a big way and can be an ideal environment in which new investors – as well as the more experienced – can learn the art of investing successfully without having to risk a large amount of capital.

Many of these clubs belong to ProShare, the organisation dedicated to increasing the public's knowledge of the benefits of equity investment. There are about 1 800 clubs in the UK and ProShare already has over 1 500 of these affiliated to its services.

Not surprisingly, the best source of information on this topic is the *ProShare Investment Club Manual* (see Recommended reading on page 277 for contact details), which gives detailed information on setting up and running a club, explains how to use a stockbroker and how to register investments, and covers all the necessary accounting, tax and other administration.

■ How it works

The principle of an investment club is simple. A group of friends, family or work colleagues pool a regular amount of money each month to invest in equities. The group meets monthly to discuss its portfolio and its decisions to buy or sell are made democratically.

Inexperienced investors learn from fellow members who already own shares but everyone benefits from the general pooling of knowledge and experience.

By far the best way to get involved is to start up a new club. Rather like running a private business, it is much more fun and reassuring if you can invest with people you know and trust, whose company you enjoy and whose opinions you respect.

The maximum number of members for a ProShare club is 20 – otherwise it can become unwieldy. You and your fellow members decide how much the monthly subscription should be. Some clubs start off with as little as £10 per member but more typically the subscription is around £25–£30. According to ProShare, there are clubs in the UK with stocks and shares valued at £500 000.

Experienced investors can and do mirror the decisions taken by the club in their private investment portfolio. However, ProShare warns that substantial investors should not use the club for anything other than a small portion of their total portfolio.

■ Contacts

For further information write to ProShare Investment Clubs, Library Chambers, 13 & 14 Basinghall Street, London EC2V 5BQ, or phone 0171 394 5200.

The Daily Telegraph Investment Club Service is operated by Barclays Stockbrokers. For further details contact Barclays Stockbrokers Marketing Support Helpline on 0345 777 400 between 8.30am and 6.00pm, Monday to Friday.

FINANCIAL ADVICE

Finding the right adviser can take the pain out of investing if you do not have the time or inclination to tackle everything yourself. Here we provide some useful contact details to get you started. Read this section in conjunction with Chapter 3.

If you are both careful and lucky you should enjoy many trouble-free years of investing. Unfortunately, though, there are a few advisers and financial companies around that will beg, steal or borrow your money if they can. And then disappear.

■ Stockbrokers and financial planners/advisers

Where we do not provide a telephone number the organisations below prefer you to contact them by post. Before you contact a firm you can check with the chief regulator, the Financial Services Authority (FSA) that it is authorised and registered with the appropriate regulator. The FSA central register is on 0171 929 3652.

Fees vary considerably from firm to firm so if you have a tight budget ask about the hourly rate and get a rough idea of the total bill in advance. Financial advisers vary considerably in their qualifications, areas of expertise and fee rates so do check these points before signing up.

The Association of Private Client Investment Managers and Stockbrokers publishes a free directory of member firms, many of which provide a full financial planning service. Contact APCIMS, 112 Middlesex Street, London E1 7HY.

The Institute of Financial Planning (IFP) is multi-disciplinary and its members are well qualified in giving independent planning advice. Contact the IFP at Whitefriars Centre, Lewins Mead, Bristol BS1 2NT. For the register of fellows of the institute, Tel: 0117 930 4434.

The Society of Financial Advisers (SOFA) is part of the Chartered Insurance Institute and is a major examiner of independent advisers and life assurance company sales staff. Contact SOFA at 20 Aldermanbury, EC2V 7HY. Tel: 0171 417 4419.

Independent advisers

For a list of three local independent advisers, contact IFA Promotion on 0117 971 1177.

For fee-based independent advisers contact the Money Management Register on 0117 976 9444.

■ Accountants

Chartered Accountants

Seven hundred members of the Institute of Chartered Accountants are qualified to offer a full advisory service.

The Institute of Chartered Accountants in England & Wales, Moorgate Place, London EC2P 2BJ. Tel: 0171 920 8100/8711.

The Institute of Chartered Accountants in Scotland, 27 Queen Street, Edinburgh EH2 1LA. Tel: 0131 225 5673.

Association of Chartered Certified Accountants (ACCA), 29 Lincoln's Inn Fields, London WC2A 3EE. Tel: 0171 242 6855.

■ Tax advisers

The Chartered Institute of Taxation and Association of Tax Technicians, 12 Upper Belgrave Street, London SW1X 8BB. Chartered tax advisers and members of this institute specialise purely in tax work for companies and for individuals. Tel: 0171 235 9381.

■ Solicitors

The Law Society of England & Wales, 113 Chancery Lane, London WC2A 1PL. Tel: 0171 242 1222.

The Law Society of Scotland, 26 Drumsheugh Gardens, Edinburgh EH3 7YR. Tel: 0131 226 7411.

The Law Society of Northern Ireland, Law Society House, 98 Victoria Street, Belfast BT1 3JZ. Tel: 01232 231 614.

Solicitors are also strongly represented in the financial services market. For independent advice on general financial issues, contact the **Solicitors for Independent Financial Advice** (SIFA) helpline on 01372 721172.

For independent investment advice contact the **Association of Solicitor Investment Managers** (ASIM), Chiddingstone Causeway, Tonbridge, Kent TN11 8JX. Tel: 01892 870065.

■ Mortgage advisers

Your mortgage package is likely to consist of three main elements – the loan, an investment to repay the loan, and general insurance policies to cover mortgage protection, buildings and contents insurance. Mortgage loans are not covered by the Financial Services Act but you should make sure your lender subscribes to the new **Council of Mortgage Lenders Code**. General insurance also is not covered by the Financial Services Act. To get the best advice, be sure to shop around using an independent adviser.

Investment is regulated by the FSA and you should seek good quality independent investment advice. Don't assume that your lender necessarily has the right product range for your investment needs.

For free guides on how to buy a home, and on taxation and the homebuyer, contact the **Council of Mortgage Lenders**, BSA/CML Bookshop, 3 Savile Row, London W1X 1AF.

The National Association of Estate Agents is the main trade body for estate agency and has a code of conduct for members. For a copy of *Homelink* – the organisation's directory of members, phone 01926 410785.

■ Pension specialists

Actuaries

Membership of the Association of Consulting Actuaries (ACA) includes most firms of consulting actuaries and individuals engaged in private practice. Only qualified actuaries with a minimum of three years' experience are entitled to become full members. Contact **The Association of Consulting Actuaries**, Number 1 Wardrobe Place, London EC4V 5AH. Tel: 0171 248 3163.

Association of Pension Lawyers (APL). The APL membership includes solicitors and other firms with a special interest in legal aspects associated with pension schemes. Contact APL c/o Paul Stannard, Travers Smith Braithwaite, 10 Snow Hill, London EC1A 2AL. Tel: 0171 248 9133.

The Pensions Registry and Tracing Service helps investors trace their pension benefits if they have lost touch with a former employer. Complete form PR4 which can be obtained from a pensions consultant or from the office of the **Occupational Pensions Regulatory Authority** (OPRA), Occupational Pensions Board, Pension Schemes Registry, PO Box 1NN, Newcastle upon Tyne, NE99 1NN. Tel: 0191 225 6393/94.

■ Other useful organisations

The Association of Investment Trust Companies (AITC) is the trade body for investment trusts. It publishes a range of free information sheets on investment trusts which explain how they can be used for general and specific investment purposes. It also publishes performance details in its Monthly Information Service (MIS – a free sample copy is available to investors). Its directory, *The Complete Guide to Investment Trusts*, price £16.94 is available from PBI Publishing, Tel: 0171 638 1916. Contact AITC, Durrant House, 8-13 Chiswell Street, London EC1Y 4YY. Tel: 0171 431 5222.

The Association of Unit Trusts and Investment Companies (AUTIF) is the trade body for unit trusts and the new open-ended investment companies. It publishes a range of free fact sheets which explain how unit trusts can be used for general and specific investment purposes. Contact AUTIF, 65 Kingsway, London WC2B 6TD. Tel: 0171 831 0898.

The Stock Exchange publishes useful leaflets on buying and selling shares and on rolling settlement and nominee accounts. For copies telephone 0171 797 1000 or write to The Stock Exchange, London EC2N 1HP.

YOUR GUIDE TO COMPLAINTS

From the moral point of view there is a big difference between deliberate fraud and plain incompetence, but frankly, the effect on your investments can be pretty much the same.

If you think you have a complaint, your first task is to find out to whom you should complain. This might not be immediately obvious because different types of financial institutions and advisers are authorised by different regulatory bodies.

Details of the relevant regulatory service should included in the letter head of the company which sold you the investment. If you are in any doubt, contact the Financial Services Authority central register (see page 270).

■ What to say

Different regulators have different rules but in most cases they will insist that you tackle the company which sold you the plan or gave the advice, before taking your complaint further.

Clearly, your complaint stands a much greater chance of being taken seriously if you prepare your case well. The regulators and ombudsmen recommend the following procedure:

1 Write first to the compliance officer at the company which sold you or advised you on the investment.
2 State clearly the nature of the complaint.
3 Give contact details, including your daytime telephone number.
4 Provide the name of the plan (if relevant), the date you invested, and the name of your contact – for example, the adviser who dealt with your case.
5 Quote all relevant plan details and reference numbers.
6 Photocopy letters and supporting material.

7   Set a sensible deadline for the reply. Your letter should be acknowledged within seven days but allow two months for the actual investigation before taking the case to the ombudsman or regulator.

■ Which regulator?

The chief regulator under the Financial Services Act is the Financial Services Authority (FSA), which took over from the Securities and Investments Board in 1997. In due course the FSA is expected to absorb the other regulators so that there will be in effect just one super regulator.

At the time of writing, the main regulator for sales of retail investment products was the Personal Investment Authority (PIA), which has its own ombudsman (see page 276). Investment advisers and managers are likely to be regulated by the Securities and Futures Authority (SFA) and the Investment Management Regulatory Organisation (IMRO).

Most independent financial advisers are authorised by the PIA but if you were advised by a professional firm then you will deal with the appropriate 'recognised professional body' (RPB), for example the Institute of Chartered Accountants or the Law Society. Due to their complexity and number, company pension schemes have their own advisory service and ombudsman.

■ What's covered under the Act?

Not everything that looks like an investment or financial product is regulated under the FSA. For example, most protection insurances are classed as general insurance business and do not come under the aegis of the investment regulators. In these cases, if you have a problem you should contact the Insurance Ombudsman or possibly the Department of Trade and Industry (DTI). Again, the company which sold you the policy is obliged to tell you which is the correct complaints channel if you are dissatisfied with the company's own response.

Most of the regulators and ombudsmen publish a consumer guide to complaints which will help you prepare your case. For the professional bodies approach the institutes and societies listed under accountants and solicitors in the contacts list for advisers above.

■ The regulators and ombudsmen

The Financial Services Authority (FSA) is the chief regulator under the Financial Services Act. Contact The Financial Services Authority, Gavrelle House, 2-4 Bunhill Row, London EC1Y 8RA. Tel: 0171 929 3652.

The Investment Management Regulatory Organisation (IMRO) is responsible for authorising and monitoring the activities of many investment managers, including unit trust management companies. However, all complaints about IMRO firms must be directed to **The Investment Ombudsman**. Contact The Investment Ombudsman, 6 Frederick's Place, London EC2R 8BT. Tel: 0171 796 3065.

The Securities and Futures Authority (SFA) regulates stockbrokers. The SFA asks investors to write to their usual contact at the firm before writing to the compliance officer. If the complaint is not properly remedied the firm is obliged to inform you of your rights and to send you a copy of a complaints guide. Contact The Complaints Bureau, The Securities and Futures Authority, Cottons Centre, Cottons Lane, London SE1 2QB. Tel: 0171 378 9000.

If you are dissatisfied with the SFA's response, you can take the case to arbitration. Contact The Complaints Commissioner, c/o SFA Tribunal Secretariat, Cottons Centre, Cottons Lane, London SE1 2QB. Tel: 0171 378 9000.

The Personal Investments Authority (PIA) is responsible for regulating the sales and marketing operations of companies in the unit and investment trust market. Complaints regarding PIA members are dealt with by the PIA Ombudsman. Contact The PIA Ombudsman, Hertsmere House, Hertsmere Road, London E14 4AB. Tel: 0171 216 0016.

The PIA Pensions Unit helpline will help you if you are a victim of the personal pension mis-selling scandal. For any queries contact on 0171 417 7001.

The Insurance Brokers' Registration Council (IBRC) authorises some advisers.

Contact 15 St Helens Place, London EC3A 6DS. Tel: 0171 588 4387.

The Occupational Pensions Advisory Service (OPAS). The new Pensions Act requires scheme trustees to establish a two-stage internal dispute resolution process for members who have a complaint. This system will be the first port of call for any scheme member who has a problem or feels the scheme has in some way failed to provide the promised benefits.

If this fails to resolve your dispute you can go to OPAS, preferably via your local Citizens Advice Bureau. Contact OPAS at 11 Belgrave Road, London SW1V 1RB. Tel: 0171 233 8080.

The Pensions Ombudsman can be contacted at the OPAS address. Tel: 0171 834 9144. However, normally you would not approach him directly but ask OPAS to mediate in your case first. Only if this fails would the matter be referred to the Ombudsman.

The Banking Ombudsman 70 Gray's Inn Road, London WC1X 8NB. Tel: 0345 660902.

The Building Societies Ombudsman Millbank Tower, Millbank, London SW1P 4XF. Tel: 0171 931 0044.

The Council of Mortgage Lenders Mortgage Code Arbitration Scheme (for mortgage lenders not covered by the Building Society or Banking Ombudsman schemes) Tel: 0171 837 4483.

The Insurance Ombudsman Bureau 135 Park Street, London SE1 9EA. Tel: 0171 928 7600.

Registry of Friendly Societies 15–17 Great Marlborough Street, London W1V 2LL. Tel: 0171 437 9992.

RECOMMENDED READING

This is only a short list of publications selected by the author. For a wider range, buy the ProShare guide listed first below.

The Investor's Guide to Information Sources, a ProShare publication, price £5.95. This is the best summary of books, magazines, newspapers, TV, radio and Internet sites. ProShare also publishes a range of information sheets and books, for example: *Introduction to Annual Reports and Accounts*, price £4.95 and *The ProShare Guide to You and Your Stockbroker*, price £9.95. For details contact ProShare, Library Chambers, 13 & 14 Basinghall Street, London EC2V 5BQ. Tel: 0171 394 5200. Web site: http://www.proshare.org.uk

Beginners' Guide to Investment, by Bernard Gray, is one of the best guides for investors who want to increase their knowledge of investment and the stockmarkets. Published by Century Business Press, price £12.99.

A Guide to Stockpicking, by Gillian O'Connor, is the sequel to the *Beginners' Guide to Investment* and describes the tools and techniques used by professional investors. An excellent source of information for the experienced investor. Published by Century Business Press, price £14.99.

The Financial Times Guide to Using the Financial Pages, by Romesh Vaitilingam, published by the Financial Times and Pitman Publishing, price £15.99. Contact The Professional Marketing Department, Financial Times Pitman Publishing, 128 Long Acre, London WC2E 9AN. Tel: 0171 379 7383.

How to Buy and Sell Shares is published by The London Stock Exchange, London EC2N 1HP. Tel: 0171 797 1372. Fax: 0171 410 6861. Web site: http://www.londonstockex.co.uk

Investing Online, by Stephen Eckett, is a very useful guide to financial websites. Published by Financial Times Pitman Publishing, price £39.99.

Company REFS is designed for the very experienced active investor and contains a range of useful information and statistics on all UK quoted companies listed on the London Stock Exchange (including AIM). It includes five-year history, detailed broker forecasts, key investment ratios and details of the main shareholders and directors. For subscription rates for the book and CD version, telephone 0171 278 7769, fax 0171 278 9809.

Lamonts Glossary is probably the most comprehensive glossary of financial terms. Published by AMG, price £37.75 (CD-ROM version). Tel: 0171 287 6771. Web site address: http://www.lamonts-glossary.co.uk

The AITC Monthly Information Service. For a sample copy write to the Association of Investment Trust Companies, Durrant House, 8-13 Chiswell Street, London EC1Y 4YY. If you want to receive the MIS each month the subscription price is £35 a year. For a quarterly service the price is £20 a year.

Chase de Vere Pep Guide, price £12.95. A good reference book for the DIY enthusiast. Contact Chase de Vere Investments plc, 63 Lincoln's Inn Fields, London WC2A 3BR. Tel: 0800 526 092.

Barclays Stockbrokers Investment Study is an excellent guide to the chief asset classes and how their performance compares over the long term. Available from Barclays Stockbrokers, Ebbgate House, 2 Swan Lane, London EC4R 3TS. Tel: 0171 956 3511.

Other books by the same author

Personal Financial Planner and *The Good PEPs Guide* are both published by Pitman Publishing, price £15.99.

Pension Power is published by John Wiley & Sons, price £13.99.

■ Newspapers and magazines

For a full breakdown on the financial press, use the ProShare guide. Most newspapers have a business section but clearly the most relevant for the private investor is the *Financial Times*.

There are several valuable investor magazines. In particular, don't forget to order your weekly copy of *The Investors Chronicle*.

Also worth checking out is *The Investor*, published by PBIP in association with ProShare. Tel: 0171 338 1751.

For collective investments, try *Money Management*, published by FT Magazines, price £4.50. Subscriptions, back issues and enquiries: PO Box 461, Bromley, Kent BR2 9WP. Tel: 0181 402 8485.

Personal Equity Plan Recommendations, published by BESt Investments provides an excellent guide to the best (and worst) funds. For a complimentary copy and details of the free review of your portfolio, contact BESt Investment, 20 Masons Yard, Duke Street St. James's, London SW1Y 6BU. Tel: 0171 321 0100.

Glossary

Accumulation unit – Units in a *unit trust* where the income is reinvested automatically, increasing the unit price. The alternative is *income units* where the income is distributed to the unitholders.

Acid test – The ratio of a company's current assets (excluding stock) to its current liabilities.

Active management – Unlike passive investment management or *index tracking*, the active manager selects sectors in the light of expected economic conditions and individual stocks on the basis of research into a company's prospects.

Advisory management – An advisory stockbroker service allows you to discuss investment opportunities with your broker and receive tips but no action can be taken without your prior approval. Under a *discretionary management* arrangement the broker makes all the decisions for you. An *execution-only* service is where your broker acts on your instructions but gives no advice or opinion.

Alternative Investment Market – (AIM) is for small, fast growing companies. Can be a spring board to the *Official List* (main stockmarket).

Annual charge – The annual management charge made by your stockbroker or collective fund manager. For collective funds, this can be anything from 0.5 per cent for the low-cost tracker unit trusts and investment trusts, to 1.5 per cent (higher for the more specialist funds). This covers the cost of investment management, administration and any ongoing sales *commission* to your adviser.

Annual report and accounts – Companies that trade on the Stock Exchange or Alternative Investment Market must provide shareholders and the Exchange with an annual report and accounts which includes financial details of the past trading year.

Arithmetic average – This is a simple arithmetic calculation – the sum of the total returns for a given category of shares, divided by the number of companies within the category. (*See size-weighted average.*)

Assets – A catch-all phrase which refers to the fundamentally different type of investments, for example, UK *equities*, overseas equities, property, fixed interest securities (*gilts* and *bonds*), and *cash*.

Association of Investment Trust Companies (AITC) – The main trade body for *investment trusts*.

Association of Unit Trust and Investment Companies (AUTIF) – The main trade body for *unit trusts* and *open-ended investment companies*.

Authorised unit trust – Unit trusts sold to the public must be authorised by the *Financial Services Authority* (FSA), the chief regulator for financial services in the UK.

Balance sheet – Produced with the *annual report and accounts*. Shows what the company owns and owes.

Bargain – The term used when a purchase or sale agreement is struck.

Bear market – This is where share prices are falling over a prolonged period.

Bed and breakfast – At the end of the tax year it was common practice to sell shares and repurchase them (usually the following day) in order to crystallise a capital gain, which you could write off against your annual capital gains tax exemption, or a capital loss which you can offset against a CGT liability in excess of the exemption. B & B was banned in the March 1998 Budget.

Bed and Pep – As for *bed and breakfast*, but this time the shares are repurchased within the *Pep*. Pep rules require most Pep investments to be bought with cash so this transaction is usually necessary if you want to transfer existing shares or units in a unit trust into your plan. The only exception is where you transfer shares to a single company plan, for example from an employee share option scheme.

Beneficial owner – The real owner of shares held in a *nominee account*.

Beneficiaries – Those who benefit from a trust. With a unit trust, the trustees run the fund on behalf of the beneficiaries – in this case, the unit holders. With a pension fund the beneficiaries are the scheme members and their dependents.

Bid/offer spread – The full initial cost of your investment in a fund. This includes administration, sales commission if applicable, dealing costs and *stamp duty* among other items. Typically the spread is about 6 per cent but where the initial charge is reduced or abolished it could be as low as 0.5 per cent.

Bid price – The price at which you sell units in a unit trust back to the manager. You purchase at the *offer price*.

Big Bang – Major changes which opened up the Stock Exchange to greater competition, including foreign ownership of member firms and the abolition of minimum commissions.

Blue chip – Large, well-established company e.g. a *FTSE 100* company.

Bonds – UK bonds are issued by borrowers – for example the Government and companies – which undertake to repay the principal sum on a specified date, rather like an IOU. During the time the bond is outstanding a fixed rate of interest is paid to the lender, which might be an individual or a financial institution. Not to be confused with insurance company bonds which are collective investments sold by insurance companies.

Brokers – Shortened term for *stockbrokers*. Also, the original traders who bought and sold shares on behalf of clients. (*See jobbers.*)

Bull market – A market where share prices are rising over a prolonged period.

Cancellation price – The lowest possible valuation in any one day of your unit trust units. The actual selling or bid price usually is higher.

Capital gains tax – The tax on the increase in the value of an asset when it is sold, compared with its value at the time of purchase. (*See bed and breakfast.*)

Capital growth – An increase in the value of shares or assets in a fund.

Cash – As an asset class, cash usually refers to deposit accounts.

Chartist – An investor who uses charts of company price movements to determine investment decisions.

Commission – 1. The fee that a stockbroker charges clients for dealing on their behalf. 2. The remuneration an adviser receives from a financial institution for selling you one of its products. (*See fee-based adviser.*)

Company share option scheme – Run by an employer to allow employees (usually only executives and directors) to buy shares in the company at a discount. (*See Save as you earn.*)

Contract note – Confirmation of your share purchase.

Convertibles – Fixed interest securities which may be converted to equities on a predetermined future date.

Corporate bond – An IOU issued by a public company. In return for borrowing your money, the company pays a fixed income (*coupon*) for a specified period and guarantees to return the original capital (nominal) on a predetermined future date.

Corporate bond Pep – A general Pep which can invest in *corporate bonds, convertibles, preference shares* and *Eurosterling bonds*.

Corporate Pep – A general Pep which invests in the shares of just one company.

Coupon – The rate of interest as a percentage of the nominal price which is paid by a bond or gilt. The purchase price may be different from the nominal price.

Creation price – The highest possible purchase price for your units in a unit trust. The actual buying or offer price usually is lower.

CREST – An electronic service that handles the mechanics of settling share transactions.

Cum dividend – The purchase price includes the value of the dividend. *Ex-dividend* means the dividend will be paid to the previous owner.

Current ratio – The value of a company's current assets divided by current liabilities. Used as a measure of liquidity.

Custodian – Usually a bank whose primary function is to look after the assets of a trust (e.g. unit trust or pension fund), among other functions.

Debentures – Bonds issued by UK companies which are secured on the company's underlying assets – for example property. Unsecured bonds are known as loan stocks.

Demutualisation – The process by which a mutually owned building society or life office becomes a public limited company. Members of the former mutual usually receive *windfall* or free shares.

Derivatives – Financial instruments are referred to as derivative securities when their value is dependent upon the value of some other underlying asset. (*See futures, options* and *warrants.*)

Designated account – An account held in one name (often a child's) with a second name as additional identification.

Discount – If the share price of an *investment trust* is lower than the value per share of the underlying assets (net asset value) the difference is known as the discount. If it is higher the difference is known as the *premium*. As a general rule a share trading at a discount often represents good value.

Discretionary management – This is where your stockbroker makes all the investment service decisions for you. (*See advisory management* and *execution-only.*)

Distributions – Income paid out from an equity or bond fund.

Dividend – The owner of shares is entitled to dividends – usually a six-monthly distribution to shareholders of part of the company's profits.

Dividend cover – The number of times a company could pay its annual dividend out of earnings.

Dividend yield – *See gross yield*.

Earnings per share – The amount of profit earned for each ordinary share of the company.

Endowment – Combines life assurance and investment. Sold by life offices, usually to build up a fund to repay an interest-only mortgage.

Equities – The ordinary share capital of a company.

Equity risk premium – The higher risk/reward characteristic of equities when compared with, for example, *cash* and *bonds*.

Eurosterling bond – A *corporate bond* issued in pounds Sterling by a company which wants to borrow money on the international markets rather than just in the UK.

Ex-dividend – The period of about six weeks before a fund or equity pays out its dividend/income. If you buy during this period you are not entitled to that dividend. (*See cum dividend*.)

Execution-only – The investment manager/stockbroker simply buys and sells at your request without offering any advice. (*See advisory* and *discretionary*.)

Exit charges – A charge deducted from some collective funds if you pull out early – usually within the first five years.

Fee-based adviser – Professional advisers do not accept sales *commission*. Instead they usually charge a fee calculated on an hourly basis and/or an annual percentage of your fund.

Final dividend – Paid at the end of a company's financial year when the final report is made which sets out its financial position. (*See interim*.)

Financial gearing – The ratio between a company's borrowings and its capitalisation – i.e. a ratio between what it owes and what it owns.

Financial Services Act 1986 – The Act which established the system of self regulation for financial services and a series of self-regulatory organisations (SROs) which regulate different types of financial institutions and the advisers and representatives who sell their products.

Financial Services Authority (FSA) – The chief regulator for financial services in the UK (which replaced the Securities and Investments Board in 1997). (*See Financial Services Act 1986*.)

Fixed interest securities – Another term for bonds. (*See bonds, corporate bond*.)

Floatation – The initial offering in the *primary market* of a company coming to the Stock Exchange for the first time.

Free-standing additional voluntary contribution – You can top up your company pension either by paying into your employer's additional voluntary contribution scheme or an individual contract with a financial institution, known as a free-standing AVC (FSAVC.)

FTSE 100 Index – The index which covers the top 100 companies on the UK Stock Exchange measured by market capitalisation (the number of shares times the share value.)

FTSE All-Share Index – The yardstick for professional investors. The All-Share contains about 900 companies listed on the UK Stock Exchange.

FTSE Mid 250 Index – The index which measures the 250 companies below (by market capitalisation) the FTSE 100.

FTSE SmallCap – The All-Share minus the top 350 companies.

Fund of funds – Unit trusts which can only invest in other authorised unit trusts.

Future – A type of *derivative*. A futures contract is a legally binding agreement to buy or sell an amount of shares (or other instruments) at a fixed date in the future at a fixed price.

Gearing – In company terms, the ratio of long-term borrowing to assets. High gearing means that there is a large proportion of debt in relation to the assets held.

General Pep – Until April 1999, up to £6000 a year can be invested in a general Pep which can hold a variety of 'qualifying' and 'non-qualifying' assets including equities, fixed interest, unit and investment trusts.

Gilts – The most secure type of bonds because they are issued by the UK government. Conventional gilts pay a fixed percentage of the nominal price. *Index-linked* gilts rise each year by a fixed percentage above the rate of inflation.

Gross yield – A method of assessing the income from an investment. It is the annual gross dividends (as currently declared or forecast by the directors of the investment trust) as a percentage of current market price. This shows the rate of gross income return a shareholder would receive on an investment at the share price on the date specified – much as one might describe the interest received on a deposit account.

Income unit – If you buy income units in a unit trust you receive automatically your share of the income generated by the fund. However, you can opt to have the income reinvested within the fund. (*See accumulation unit.*)

Index-linked – An investment (e.g. a *gilt*) whose value increases each year in line with retail price inflation or by a fixed percentage above RPI.

Index tracking – With a tracker fund, the investment manager uses a computer model to select stocks to simulate the performance of a specific stockmarket index. In some cases all the shares in an index will be held. Index tracking is also known as passive management.

Individual Savings Account (ISA) – New tax-exempt investment accounts to be launched in April 1999, replacing *Personal Equity Plans* (Peps) and Tessas. (*See tax-efficient investments.*)

Inflation – An increase in the general level of prices over a prolonged period, which forces down the real value or purchasing power of money. There are various measures of inflation, the most common being the *Retail Prices Index* (*RPI*).

Inheritance tax (IHT) – A tax on the value of your estate above a certain limit when you die.

Initial charge – A charge, typically 5 per cent, levied by a fund manager to cover administration and sales commission. However, the full up-front cost of your investment is shown in the *bid/offer spread* which includes additional charges such as stamp duty.

Interest cover – The number of times profits can cover the interest payments on a company's debts.

Interest rates – The Bank of England is responsible for setting short-term interest rates – the premium borrowers charge for lending their money.

Interim – Statement by a company which sets out its financial position half way through its financial year. An interim dividend is also paid. (*See final dividend.*)

Investment club – A group of private investors who pay a small subscription which is collectively invested in shares.

Investment trust – A UK company, listed on the Stock Exchange, which invests in the shares of other companies in the UK and overseas. (See *discount* and *premium*.)

Jobbers – The original traders through whom *brokers* made their sales and purchases. Replaced by *market makers* in 1986.

Joint stock companies – The forerunner of today's public limited company.

Liabilities – What a company owes to suppliers and lenders.

Liquidation – When a company is wound up and its assets, if any, are distributed to its creditors.

Loan stocks – Unsecured *bonds* issued by UK companies. Bonds secured on a company's underlying assets (property, for example) are known as *debentures*.

Long-dated bond – A bond or gilt with 15 years or more to go to *redemption*, when the nominal capital is repaid to the holder.

Market maker – A dealer who can buy and sell shares. Replaced earlier system of *brokers* and *jobbers*.

Medium-dated bond – A bond or gilt with 5–15 years to go to *redemption*, when the nominal capital is repaid to the holder.

Maturity – Another word for *redemption*, when the investment period ends and, in the case of a *bond*, the nominal capital is repaid.

National Savings Certificates – Tax-free investments from the Government.

National Savings Stock Register (NSSR) – Postal facility for the public to buy *gilts*.

Negligible value – Shares in companies which have gone bust and which the Inland Revenue recognises as a capital loss.

Net asset value (NAV) – The market value of an *investment trust's* underlying assets. This may be different from the share price since the latter is subject to market forces and supply and demand. (*See discount* and *premium*.)

Net yield – The return on an investment after tax has been deducted. (*See gross yield*.)

Nominee account – To speed up transactions a stockbroker might recommend you hold your shares in its nominee account. You remain the beneficial owner but the nominee company is the registered shareholder.

Offer price – The price at which you buy units from the unit trust or Pep manager. You sell back to the manager at the 'bid' price. (*See bid/offer spread.*)

Official List – The daily report of all the transactions in the main 'secondary' market.

Offshore funds – For UK investors this usually refers to funds in the Dublin International Financial Centre, the Isle of Man, the Channel Islands and Luxembourg. Offshore locations are not subject to UK tax law, although usually if you are UK resident, when you repatriate money to the UK you must pay the appropriate income and capital gains tax.

Open-ended investment companies (OEICS) – These are a new type of investment fund first launched in 1996. They are similar to unit trusts but have a corporate structure and a single price rather than a *bid/offer spread*, so in some respects also resemble *investment trusts*.

Options – A type of *derivative*. A call option gives the buyer the right (but not the obligation – hence *option*) to buy a commodity, stock, bond or currency in the future at a mutually agreed price struck on the date of the contract. 'Put' options give you the right, but not the obligation, to sell.

Passive investment management – *See index tracking.*

Personal equity plan (Pep) – A Pep is a wrapper or basket which shelters Inland Revenue approved stockmarket investments from the taxman. Both income and capital gains are tax free for the lifetime of the investor. The current maximum allowable tax-free investment into a general Pep is £6000 in any one tax year from 6 April to 5 April of the following year. A further £3000 may be invested in a single company Pep. Peps will be replaced by ISAs in April 1999.

Personal Investment Authority (PIA) – Under the *Financial Services Act 1986*, the PIA is the regulator for companies which market and sell retail investments such as Peps, pensions and life assurance savings plans. To be merged with the *Financial Services Authority (FSA)* in due course.

Placing – A new issue of shares sold privately through a group of financial institutions.

Pooled funds – Another term for collective or mutual funds which invest in a range of different shares and other instruments to achieve diversification for the smaller investor who buys units in these funds.

Portfolio – A collection of assets.

Preference shares ('prefs') – These are similar to bonds in that they pay a fixed rate of interest, although its payment depends on company profits. Preference shares are first in the pecking order of payouts when an investment trust is wound up. (*See stepped preference shares* and *zero dividend preference shares.*)

Preliminary results – A report to the Stock Exchange on the company's annual results. This is issued about six weeks before the annual report and accounts are published.

Premium – If the share price of an investment trust is higher than the value of the underlying assets the difference is known as the premium. Normally investors are advised not to buy under these circumstances. If the price is lower than the net asset value the difference is known as the discount.

Pre-tax profit margin – A company's trading profit (before the deduction of depreciation, interest and tax) as a percentage of turnover.

Price/earnings ratio (PE) – The market price of a share divided by the company's earnings (profits) per share in its latest 12-month trading period.

Primary market – Used for floatations of new companies and for further raising of capital under a *rights issue*.

Profit and loss account – This is contained within a company's annual report and accounts, together with the *balance sheet*. It sets out what the company has sold (turnover) during the past 12 months and its expenses in terms of salaries, raw materials etc.

Protected funds – These funds limit your exposure to the downside of an index and so protect your capital from severe loss. However, as largely cash funds which use a *derivative* to provide the capital protection, they do not benefit from reinvestment of dividends.

Public sector borrowing requirement (PSBR) – The amount by which Government spending exceeds the income from taxation and other revenues.

Purchased life annuity – PLAs offer a guaranteed regular income in return for a lump sum investment. Sold by insurance companies.

Redemption – The date at which a bond becomes repayable. Also known as the maturity date.

Redemption yield – The current dividend or interest rate increased or decreased to take into account the capital value if the bond is held to maturity.

Retail Prices Index (RPI) – The main measure of consumer inflation.

Return – The amount by which your investment increases as a result of interest or dividend income and capital growth.

Rights issue – An issue of shares to raise additional capital. Usually offered to existing shareholders at a discount.

Risk – A measure of the probability that the value of your savings and the income they generate will fall as well as rise.

Running yield – The current dividend or interest payments on a fund.

Save as you earn (SAYE) – Schemes run by employers to allow employees to buy shares in the company, usually at a discount.

Scrip dividend – Dividends paid in the form of shares.

Scrip issue – 'Free' shares given to shareholders to dilute the share price to aid liquidity.

Secondary market – Where shares are bought and sold on the Stock Exchange after the initial *floatation* in the primary market.

Securities – The general name for all stocks and shares. Broadly speaking stocks are fixed interest securities and shares are the rest. The four main types of securities listed and traded on the UK Stock Exchange are UK *equities*, overseas equities (i.e. issued by non-UK companies), UK *gilts* (bonds issued by the UK Government) and *corporate bonds/fixed interest securities* (issued by companies and local authorities.)

Self-regulatory organisation (SRO) – One of the bodies established by the *Financial Services Act 1986* to authorise sales and marketing of financial services and products.

Self-select Pep – A plan that does not restrict you to the funds of one Pep manager but instead allows you to hold the entire range of pepable assets, including individual shares and bonds as well as unit and investment trusts.

Settlement – The transfer of shares from the existing owner to the new owner and the corresponding transfer of money.

Share exchange – A facility offered by plan managers whereby they take your shares, sell them and invest the cash in a Pep. In some cases they may be able to absorb the shares into their funds and reduce dealing costs.

Short-dated bond – A *gilt* or *bond* with up to five years to go to *redemption*. See *long-dated bond* and *medium-dated bond*.

Size-weighted average – The average return after weighting each company in the category or index by size of market capitalisation at the start of the period. This means that the performance of really small shares or trusts does not have a disproportionate impact on an index. Size-weighted average is the preferred method used by the independent measurers of the big institutional pension funds. (*See arithmetic average.*)

Split capital trust – An investment trust which has different types of shares – for example, some offer a high income but no capital growth and some offer pure capital growth but no income.

Stamp duty – A tax on the purchase (but not the sale) of shares, currently 0.5 per cent.

Stepped preference shares – Shares in a *split capital trust* which pay dividends which rise at a predetermined rate and have a fixed redemption value which is paid when the trust is wound up.

Stock Exchange Automated Quotations (SEAQ) – A computer-based system which allows stockbrokers to see share price information anywhere in the UK. The Stock Exchange Alternative Trading System (SEATS) was introduced in 1993 for less liquid securities.

Stock Exchange Trading Services (SETS) – Introduced in October 1997 to speed up order driven trading, initially in the FTSE 100 companies. Allows sales and purchases to be matched electronically.

Stockbroker – A member of the London Stock Exchange who buys and sells shares on behalf of clients.

Stockmarket – The place where shares, bonds and other assets change hands.

Stockmarket indices – An index is a specified basket or portfolio of shares and shows how these share prices are moving in order to give an indication of market trends. Every major world stockmarket is represented by at least one index. The FTSE 100 index, for example, reflects the movements of the share prices of the UK's largest 100 quoted companies by market capitalisation.

Tax avoidance – Saving tax by using loopholes in the law. This is legal but may be frowned upon by the Inland Revenue.

Tax evasion – A deliberate attempt to reduce your tax bill by withholding information or lying. This is illegal.

Tax-efficient investments – Investments which offer an element of tax exemption, reduction or deferral. The main UK investments that fall into this category are:

- *Pensions:* available from a range of financial institutions and also provided by many employers in the form of an occupational pension scheme. Pension schemes and plans approved by the Inland Revenue offer tax relief on contributions, virtually tax-free growth of the fund and, in some cases, a tax-free lump sum at retirement. The pension income is taxed.

- *Tax exempt special savings accounts (Tessas):* available from building societies and banks. Tessas are deposit accounts which offer secure five-year tax-free growth for capital that might otherwise sit in an ordinary deposit account. (To be replaced by ISAs in 1999.)

- *Personal equity plans (Peps):* available from a wide range of financial institutions. Peps offer full tax-free roll up for investments in UK equities either direct or through unit and investment trusts. Also available: EU shares, corporate bonds, preference shares and convertibles. (To be replaced by ISAs in 1999.)

- *Individual Savings Accounts:* ISAs replace Peps and Tessas and are available from April 1999. The annual maximum is £5000. The investment range is similar to Peps but also includes up to £1000 per annum in deposits and £1000 per annum in life assurance funds.

- *National Savings Certificates:* available direct from National Savings or via the Post office. NS certificates offer a tax-free return.

- *Enterprise zone trusts (EZTs):* available by direct subscription. EZTs are designated areas where tax reliefs and reduced administrative controls are used to attract new business, providing investment in property with income tax relief on most of the cost.

- *Enterprise investment schemes (EIS):* available by direct subscription. EISs offer a range of tax reliefs if you invest in the shares of mainly unquoted trading companies.

- *Venture capital trusts (VCTs):* available from a range of financial institutions and by direct subscription. VCTs allow you to participate in EIS-type investments on a collective basis.

- *Timber:* available by direct subscription. Timber offers an eight to ten-year investment for tax-free income through felling or a very long-term investment for the next generation.

Tax exempt special savings account (Tessa) – A deposit account where the fund accumulates tax free provided the capital is not withdrawn for a minimum of five years. To be replaced by ISA in April 1999.

Tax mitigation – Tax saving encouraged by the law, for example by investing in a pension plan.

Tax year – Tax and investment allowances apply to the 12 months from 6 April to the following 5 April.

Tracker funds – *See index tracking.*

Trust deed – The legal document on which a unit trust or pension is based, for example. The use of a trust separates the fund from the management or sponsoring company's assets.

Trustee – You can't have a trust without a trustee who, as legal owner of the fund, looks after the assets on behalf of the beneficiaries. UK pension funds are established under trust as are unit trusts.

UCITS (Undertaking for Collective Investments in Transferable Securities) – A European Union term for a collective fund, such as a *unit trust* or *OEIC* which can be marketed in all the Union's markets.

Unit trust – A collective investment. Your money purchases units, the value of which rises and falls in line with the value of the underlying assets.

Warrants – Risky and volatile investments which give the holder the right but not the obligation to buy investment trust shares at a predetermined price within a specified period. This type of share has no voting rights and holders do not normally receive dividends.

Windfalls – Free shares given to members of a building society or mutual life office when it demutualises to become a public limited company.

Yield – The annual dividend or income on an investment expressed as a percentage of the purchase price. (*See gross yield*.)

Zero dividend preference shares ('zeroes') – A lower risk and predetermined investment. They offer a fixed capital return in the form of a redemption value which is paid when the trust is wound up. These shares are not entitled to income and therefore there is no income tax liability.

Sources

Some of these definitions were drawn from the *Investors Chronicle Personal Financial Planner*, published by Pitman Publishing; the AUTIF *Unit Trust User's Handbook*; London International Financial Futures and Options Exchange, *LIFFE Futures and Options: A Guide for UK Fund Managers*; *Pension Power*, by Debbie Harrison, published by John Wiley & Sons, *The Good Peps Guide*, also by Debbie Harrison, published by Pitman Publishing.

Index